ORPHEUS

Landscape in Ovid's Metamorphoses:
A Study in the Transformation of a Literary Symbol

The Theme of the Mutilation of the Corpse in the Iliad

Tragedy and Civilization: An Interpretation of Sophocles

Poetry and Myth in Ancient Pastoral: Essays on Theocritus and Virgil

Dionysiac Poetics and Euripides' "Bacchae"

La musique du Sphinx: Mythe, langage et structure dans la tragédie grecque

Pindar's Mythmaking: The Fourth Pythian Ode

Language and Desire in Seneca's "Phaedra"

Interpreting Greek Tragedy: Myth, Poetry, Text

Lucretius on Death and Anxiety

Oedipus Tyrannus: Tragic Heroism and the Limits of Knowledge

ORPHEUS

The Myth of the Poet

Charles Segal

The Johns Hopkins University Press
BALTIMORE AND LONDON

This book has been brought to publication with the generous
assistance of the David M. Robinson Publication Fund.

Softshell Books edition, 1993

The Johns Hopkins University Press
2715 North Charles Street
Baltimore, Maryland 21218-4319
The Johns Hopkins Press Ltd., London

Library of Congress Cataloging-in-Publication Data

Segal, Charles, 1936–
    Orpheus : the myth of the poet.

.   Bibliography: p.
    Includes index.
    1. Classical literature—History and criticism.   2. Orpheus
(Greek mythology) in literature.   3. Poets in literature.
4. Classicism.   5. Literature, Modern—Classical influences.
I. Title.
PA3015.R50827 1989   880'.9'351   88-45411
ISBN 0-8018-3708-1 (alk. paper)
ISBN 0-8018-4720-6 (pbk.)

A catalog record for this book is available from the British
Library.

Frontispiece: Orpheus, Eurydice, and Hermes;
relief, Museo Nazionale, Naples.
(Photograph: Alinari, number 11171)

For Nancy

Il chante, assis au bord du ciel splendide, Orphée!
Le roc marche, et trébuche; et chaque pierre fée
Se sent un poids nouveau qui vers l'azur délire!

He sings, seated at the edge of the splendid heavens, Orpheus!
The rock steps forth and stumbles, and each fairy stone
feels a new weight that becomes delirious toward the azure sky.

—Paul Valéry, ''Orphée''

Contents

Preface

Inhabiting what the ancients considered the fringes of the civilized world, associated with the barbarian Thracians as much as with the Greeks, Orpheus embodies something of the strangeness of poetry in the world, the mystery of its power over us, and the troubling intrusiveness of its sympathy for the emotions that we cannot always afford. Orpheus sings the world's sorrow and the world's beauty with an intensity that compels the forests and the beasts to follow. His most famous song in the literary tradition is of love and death, of love-in-death, of death invading the happiness of love. For these reasons, perhaps, the Greeks were ambivalent about both his Hellenism and his divine parentage, treating him sometimes as the son of Apollo, sometimes as the son of the Thracian Oeagrus.

If Orpheus' magic recreates the sad music of lamentation with too irresistible a power, he also, as a recent commentator on Rilke suggests, turns "the hut of our emptiness into something positive, into a temple"; and so, for Rilke, as for many poets before and after him, Orpheus also embodies the essence of poetry, its ability "to find, in art, a way to transform the emptiness, the radical deficiency, of human longing into something else."[1] He is most familiar as the poet who can make the world respond to him; but he has another gift, an ability to hear the music of the world, to know its sights and sounds that others cannot perceive. His mythical cousin in this regard is the seer Melampus, who possessed the power to understand the language of birds, insects, and animals. This Orpheus too is the mythical forbear of Rilkean poetics, the poet's claim to know the hidden roots of things; but he has earlier incarnations in Heraclitus' knowledge of the paradoxes of existence or in Lucretius' conviction of the invisible realm of the atoms whose movements hold the secrets to all of life and death.

Although the ancient legend receives barely a page in H. J. Rose's *Handbook of Greek Mythology,* a full study of its myriad transformations over the centuries would require many volumes. This volume more modestly offers a reading of only a few of the major literary texts in the classical tradition. This is not a book about Orphic religion, Orphism, the Orphics, or the so-called Orphic poems, but about the myth of Orpheus as it appears in literature.[2]

My leitmotif is Orpheus' place in the triangular relation of art to life, and especially to love, death, and grief. I try to show how the various versions of the myth oscillate between a poetry of transcendence that asserts the power of poetry, song, and imagination over the necessities of nature, including the ultimate necessity, death, and a poetry that celebrates its full, vulnerable immersion in the stream of life. These two strands are already present in the fluctuation of the earlier Greek tradition between a successful and a mournful Orpheus and in Euripides' allusive use of the myth in his *Alcestis;* but they receive their sharpest delineation in the contrast between Aristaeus and Orpheus in Virgil's Fourth *Georgic* and in the two accounts of Orpheus in Ovid's *Metamorphoses* 10 and 11, the one showing the defeat of the poet, the other a kind of victory. Seneca's use of the myth, in his *Tragedies,* is less familiar and deserves more attention than it has received, particularly for the way in which Orpheus helps focus the wish for a relation of harmonious accord with nature and its impossibility in this discordant world.

In modern literature, Rilke's poems about Orpheus are arguably the richest poetical recasting of the myth since classical antiquity. Rilke draws on the ancient ambivalences between triumph and failure in the myth when he uses Orpheus in the *Sonnets to Orpheus* as an embodiment of poetry as monument and poetry as metamorphosis. In this work, Orpheus highlights the paradoxical relation between art and life. Poetry transcends time and change, expressing the invisible life of the spirit; and poetry necessarily exhausts itself as it accepts its physical impulse toward the momentary beauty that is its origin and inspiration and accepts also its own materiality in a world that flowers and dies. For other modern interpreters of the myth, Orpheus is important not so much because he is a poet as because he is a lover. But here too he is a privileged, alien figure, isolated by the fact that he feels and suffers with the totality of his being. If, as John Friedman remarks, "the key to a myth's vigor is its adaptability," then the Orpheus myth is indeed one of the most vigorous of the classical corpus.[3]

My first chapter provides a general overview of the myth and sets forth some of the main concerns of this study. I then turn in chapter 2 to Virgil, whose rendering in the fourth book of the *Georgics* has been decisive for almost all subsequent interpreters, both in poetry and prose. Chapters 3–5 follow the development of Orpheus into Virgil's immediate successors, Ovid and Seneca. Chapter 6 studies Rilke's two versions of the myth, his narrative poem *Orpheus. Eurydike. Hermes* and his *Sonnets to Orpheus.* In the last chapter I have attempted to fill in some of the gaps between the ancient and modern Orpheus, concentrating on the continuities with and divergences from the classical tradition. Here, perforce, I have had to be selective. My intention was not to survey the material but to take a few representative examples. I have also taken this opportunity to utilize many of the recent studies of the Orpheus myth; but I have not attempted a full bibliography. That task is well performed in the recent studies by John Friedman, Fritz Graf, and John Warden.

Chapters 1, 2, 3, 5, and parts of chapter 6 have been published before (see Acknowledgments), and I am grateful to the journals and editors for permission to reprint them. Chapter 4, which is new, reexamines the Virgilian and Ovidian versions of the Orpheus myth in the light of recent criticism and from a fresh perspective. The discussion of *Orpheus. Eurydike. Hermes.* in chapter 6 incorporates a few pages from my 1973 study in the *Bucknell Review,* but on the whole it takes a rather different perspective and is largely new. To the study of the *Sonnets* in this chapter I have added some comments on Rilke's notion of "figure" and developed some points that are not in the originally published version. In addition to the modifications noted above, I have deleted two pages about the *Troades* from the Seneca chapter (5) that were not directly related to Orpheus, made a few stylistic changes here and there, abbreviated or deleted a few notes, and eliminated anachronisms where possible. The reprinting of earlier work inevitably leaves the author with hard choices and mixed feelings. Aside from chapter 6, where I have made considerable additions to the original publication, I have changed relatively little in these pieces and instead have presented my current views in the new chapters 4 and 7. I have also translated whatever Greek, Latin, or German was untranslated in the original publications.

Acknowledgments

Material previously published appeared in the following journals. Permission of the editors and publishers is gratefully acknowledged.

Chapter 1: "The Magic of Orpheus and the Ambiguities of Language," *Ramus* 7 (1978): 106–42. Reprinted by permission of Aureal Publications and *Ramus*.

Chapter 2: "Orpheus and the Fourth *Georgic:* Vergil on Nature and Civilization," *American Journal of Philology* 87 (1966): 307–25. Reprinted by permission of the *American Journal of Philology* and the Johns Hopkins University Press.

Chapter 3: "Ovid's Orpheus and Augustan Ideology," *Transactions of the American Philological Association* 103 (1972): 473–94.

Chapter 5: "Dissonant Sympathy: Song, Orpheus, and the Golden Age in Seneca's Tragedies," in A. J. Boyle, ed., *Seneca Tragicus. Ramus Essays on Senecan Drama* (Berwick, Australia, 1983): 229–51. (= *Ramus* 12 [1983]: 229–51). Reprinted by permission of Aureal Publications and *Ramus*.

Chapter 6: "Rilke's Sonnets to Orpheus and the Orphic Tradition," *Literatur in Wissenschaft und Unterricht* 15 (1982): 367–80. I have also incorporated into this chapter three paragraphs from pages 139–41 of my essay, "Eurydice: Rilke's Transformations of a Classical Myth," *Bucknell Review* 21 (1973): 137–44.

Citations of ancient authors follow the conventions of classical scholarship. Translations are my own unless otherwise noted.

I would like to thank the Johns Hopkins University Press for its initiative in gathering these essays and suggesting their continuation. I am indebted to the anonymous readers of the Press for helpful comments.

I thank Eric Halpern of the Press for his interest and patience. I am also grateful to Irma Garlick for intelligent and incisive copy-editing and to Stephen Hall for help with indexing. The composition of chapters 1 and 5 was aided by research fellowships from the National Endowment for the Humanities and from the John Simon Guggenheim Memorial Foundation respectively, and I warmly renew my thanks to both institutions. For various forms of aid and hospitality I am grateful to the Fulbright Exchange Program, the Australian-American Educational Exchange Foundation, the departments of classical studies at the University of Melbourne and Monash University respectively, the American Academy in Rome, the American School of Classical Studies in Athens, and the Seeger Foundation and the Hellenic Studies Committee of Princeton University. Professor William Childs of Princeton generously provided a print of the Orpheus relief in Naples. Mrs. Ronnie Hanley patiently helped with the final preparation of the typescript. I thank again the many friends and colleagues who have helped with counsel and criticism over the many years spanned by these essays. Last but far from least are the deep thanks I owe to my wife, Nancy Jones, for support, understanding, and advice.

ORPHEUS

1

The Magic of Orpheus and
The Ambiguities of Language

Language is among the most mysterious of man's attributes. Its power not only to communicate truths about reality, but also to compel assent in the face of reality has often appeared miraculous, magical, and also dangerous. The marvel that mere words can impel us to the most momentous actions, and the admiration or fear that this fact inspires, are recurrent themes in classical literature. To express and understand this power, Greek myth early framed the figure of Orpheus, a magical singer, half-man, half-god, able to move all of nature by his song. How that myth shifts in meaning and emphasis in representing that power is the subject of this chapter. Though primarily concerned with classical writers, I shall also consider how a few modern poets used and transmuted this mythic material. My reading of the myth is both diachronic and synchronic. I attempt to study some aspects of its historical development and also to interpret it (especially in section I) as if all of its versions, taken together, form a contemporary statement about the relation of art and life.

Orpheus is a complex, multifaceted figure. For the ancients he is not only the archetypal poet but also the founder of a mystical religion known as Orphism, with a well-developed theology, cosmogony, and eschatology of which much survives in hymns and short epics, mostly of late date.[1] The ''poetic'' Orpheus inevitably overlaps with the founder of Orphism, but it is the Orpheus of the poetic tradition that this chapter discusses.

I ·

In Orpheus music, poetry, and rhetoric are composite, virtually indistinguishable parts of the power of art. "Rhetoric and music" are his pursuits in the fourteenth-century Catalan humanist, Bernat Metge (ca. 1340–1413), who has Orpheus begin his tale thus:

> Apolló fo pare meu, e Callíope ma mare, e nasquí en lo regne de Tràcia. La major temps de ma vida despenguí en Retòrica e Música.

> Apollo was my father and Calliope my mother, and I was born in the realm of Thrace. The larger part of my life I spent in rhetoric and music.[2]

The most familiar version of the myth is that of Virgil and Ovid. Eurydice, the bride of Orpheus, is fatally bitten by a snake; the singer, relying on the power of his art, descends to Hades to win her back, persuades the gods of the underworld to relinquish her, but loses her again when he disobeys their command not to look back. Renouncing women (and in one version turning to homosexual love), he is torn apart by a band of angry Maenads. The head and lyre, still singing, float down the Hebrus river to the island of Lesbos, where Apollo protects the head from a snake and endows it with prophetic power.

The fundamental elements in the myth form a triangle, thus:

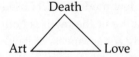

The meaning of the myth shifts as different points form the base: love-death, love-art, art-death. On the one hand, Orpheus embodies the ability of art, poetry, language—"rhetoric and music"—to triumph over death; the creative power of art allies itself with the creative power of love. On the other hand, the myth can symbolize the failure of art before the ultimate necessity, death. In the former case the myth celebrates the poetic inspiration and the power of persuasive language. It is this aspect of the myth that Ovid dramatizes when, even at the poet's death, he represents the spears and stones cast by the Maenads as charmed by the song and reluctant to wound the singer until the women's raucous shouting drowns out the music (*Met.* 11.9–14). Two thousand years later, Rilke has his Orpheus "outsound [the Maenads'] cry with order," and his "upbuilding play arises from among the destroyers."

Du aber, Göttlicher, du, bis zuletzt noch Ertöner,
da ihn der Schwarm der verschmähten Mänaden befiel,
hast ihr Geschrei übertönt mit Ordnung, du Schöner,
aus den Zerstörenden stieg dein erbauendes Spiel.

But you, divine one, you, till the end still sounding,
when beset by the swarm of disdained maenads,
you outsounded their cries with order, beautiful one,
from among the destroyers arose your upbuilding music.
(Sonnets to Orpheus 1.26.1–4)[3]

If, on the other hand, stress falls on the failure of the poet, the myth expresses the intransigence of reality before the plasticity of language. "Rhetoric and music" then appear as symbols of the creations of human culture in general. Death sets art and culture back into the perspective of nature.

It is this tragic aspect of Orpheus that Milton draws upon in the Orphic imagery of Lycidas.

Where were ye, Nymphs, when the remorseless deep
Closed o'er the head of your loved Lycidas? . . .
Ay me, I fondly dream!
Had ye been there—for what could that have done?
What could the Muse herself that Orpheus bore,
The Muse herself, for her enchanting son
Whom universal nature did lament,
When, by the rout that made the hideous roar,
His gory visage down the stream was sent,
Down the swift Hebrus to the Lesbian shore.
(50–59)

Even Milton's elegiac Orpheus, however, though subject to the inexorable power of death and the violence of nature, has his double and opposite in the shepherd-singer, also a poet, whose song is in harmony with nature's vital rhythms.

Thus sang the uncouth Swain to the Oaks and rills,
While the still morn went out with Sandals grey,
He touched the tender stops of various Quills,
With eager thought warbling his Doric lay:
And now the Sun had stretched out all the hills,

And now was dropt into the Western bay:
At last he rose, and twitched his Mantle blue:
To-morrow to fresh Woods, and Pastures new.

(186–193)

The power of song here participates in the movements of life and death
in nature, correlated in sympathy with the passage from dawn to evening. Like the Orpheus who once lived, this poet sings to trees and
rivers, and his song will be reborn with the "fresh" life of the morning
that will succeed the darkness that is now approaching; his mantle,
the color of the clear, daylight sky, already anticipates that rebirth to
new energy of song and joy in "fresh Woods, and Pastures new."

Milton thus splits the Orphic voice into two: a mournful and a
revitalized song. Poetry itself, through its identification with a singer-
hero who suffers, dies, and is reborn, participates in the diurnal (and
by metonymy the seasonal) alternation of life and death. The pattern is
a very old one. It can be traced back to the shepherd-kings and singers
of the ancient Near East such as Tammuz, Enkidu, and David and then
recurs with a more self-conscious reference to the power of poetry and
art, in figures like the dying Daphnis of Theocritus' First *Idyll* or the
dead and resurrected Daphnis of Virgil's Fifth *Eclogue*.[4]

When in somberer mood Milton returns to the figure of Orpheus in
Paradise Lost, a dualism is still present, but the terms have changed.
Invoking the heavenly Urania as his own Muse at the beginning of
book 7, he presents Orpheus' failure as unrelieved. Defeated by the
"barbarous dissonance . . . / of that wild rout that tore the Thracian
bard / in Rhodope," Orpheus embodies the precariousness and isolation of Milton's own poetic voice.

More safe I Sing with mortal voice, unchang'd
To hoarse or mute, though fall'n on evil days,
On evil days though fall'n, and evil tongues;
In darkness, and with dangers compast round,
And solitude; yet not alone, while thou [Urania]
Visit'st my slumbers Nightly.

(7.24–29)

Over against the pagan legend, where, as in *Lycidas*, the Muse could
not "defend her son," Milton sets his own post-Orphic "heavenly"
Muse, with her fusion of Neoplatonic and Christian allegory.

In Rhodope, where Woods and Rocks had Ears
To rapture, till the savage clamor drown'd
Both Harp and Voice; nor could the Muse defend
Her Son. So fail not thou, who thee implores:
For thou art Heaven'ly, she an empty dream.

(35–39)

In the failed poet, Orpheus, art and Muse are unavailing against the sensuality, ignorance, blind violence in men; the living poet must turn to another power, one above the purely aesthetic realm of classical culture, for strength and consolation.

Rilke too experiences the failure of Orpheus vividly in his imaginative consciousness as a poet; but that failure constitutes a challenge to which the answer still lies within the Orphic myth itself, not outside, as in Milton. The poet must seek to understand and incorporate the two polarities of Orpheus.

In the sonnet on Orpheus' death cited above, the poet's defeat and triumph become symbols of modern man's loss and attempted recovery of the spirit of song in a world of alienation, violence, depersonalized and demythicized life.

Schliesslich zerschlugen sie dich, von der Rache gehetzt,
während dein Klang noch in Löwen und Felsen verweilte
und in den Bäumen und Vögeln. Dort singst du noch jetzt.
O du verlorener Gott! Du unendliche Spur!
Nur weil dich reissend zuletzt die Feindschaft verteilte,
Sind wir die Hörenden jetzt und ein Mund der Natur.

In the end they battered and broke you, harried by vengeance,
and while your resonance lingered in lions and rocks
and in the trees and birds. There you are singing still.
O you lost god! You unending trace!
Only because at last enmity rent and scattered you
are we now the hearers and a mouth of Nature.

(Sonnets to Orpheus, 1.26.9–14)

Here Orpheus, the "lost god," is a "trace" of some larger entity or mystery that we must pursue and recover. His gift and sacrifice recreate a lost harmony with "nature," not the nature that wipes out our spiritual creations in death, but nature as the reservoir of vitality and energy, the echo chamber of whatever songs "are singing still."

In this Romantic or post-Romantic spirit, Orpheus becomes the vehicle for nostalgic longing for lost creativity or spontaneity rather in the manner of Schiller's "Die Götter Griechenlands" or Elizabeth Barrett Browning's "The Dead Pan." The mood has its analogue even in antiquity, as in this epigram by the late Hellenistic poet Antipater of Sidon (ca. 120 B.C.):

> No longer, Orpheus, will you lead the oaks under your spell nor the rocks nor the herds of beasts that obey their own laws. No longer will you put to sleep the roar of the winds nor the hail nor the swirl of snowflakes nor the crashing sea. For you have perished, and the Muses, daughters of Memory, have wept over you, and most of all your mother, Calliope. Why do we wail over sons who have died when not even the gods have the power to keep Hades from their children?[5]

In this mood of self-indulgent nostalgia, the magic of Orpheus' creative energy appears as inaccessible. The poet's death or absence symbolizes the faded power of ancient myth and ancient poetry, the death of a living tradition. As in *Lycidas*, the elegiac mood both celebrates the power of Orphic song and regretfully observes its remoteness from the present age.

In Virgil's *Eclogues*, Orpheus symbolizes the capacity of poetry to evoke that sympathy between man and nature which is essential to the pastoral mood. Virgil is perhaps the first poet to exploit for pastoral the songfulness inherent in nature that the Orphic power can call forth.[6] Here the control over nature that the myth of Orpheus may imply yields to sympathy with nature and the expansive joyfulness of singing in harmony with nature. The achievement of this Orphic poetry is to create the peace, trust, and sensitivity in which man can listen to this music of nature and find a place for it in his own life amid the violence of war and the passion of love.[7]

The bucolic fiction operates in a manner analogous to the fanciful magic of the Thracian hero: it persuades us that barriers between man and nature can dissolve in a world full of beauty, song, and love. Yet the very artificiality of the genre reminds us that all of this is only a desiderated ideal, a wishful unreality, its animating spirit of Orphic sympathy as remote from actual life as the dead Orpheus of Antipater or Milton.[8]

In Theocritus' First *Idyll* the landscape is songful.

> Ἀδύ τι τὸ ψιθύρισμα καὶ ἁ πίτυς, αἰπόλε, τήνα,
> ἁ ποτὶ ταῖς παγαῖσι, μελίσδεται, ἁδὺ δὲ καὶ τύ
> συρίσδες. μετὰ Πᾶνα τὸ δεύτερον ἆθλον ἀποισῇ.

> Sweet the whispering, and sweetly sings that pine, goatherd, there
> by the springs; but sweetly too do you play the flute. After Pan you
> will win the second prize. (1.1–3)

The soft sound, alliteration, repetition of the key word, "sweetly . . .
sweetly," suggest a sympathetic accord between the music inherent in
the landscape and the music made by man in nature.[9] In an epigram attributed to Theocritus, the cowherd Daphnis, an Orphic presence in
bucolic song, will practise the magic or *thelxis* of song in a setting of
oak trees, caves, and the rustic god Pan.[10] Another Hellenistic pastoral
epigram, attributed to Plato, makes the dreamlike bucolic setting a virtual symbol of the "magic" (*thelxis*) of this type of poetry.

> Come sit by this high-leafed songful pine, rustling in the Zephyrs'
> frequent breezes; and the pipe, (playing) beside my plashing
> streams, will cause sleep to drop upon your lids as you are cast under
> the magic spell (*thelgomenos*).[11]

The tree in this setting is already "songful" (*phōnēëssan*), and the pipe,
even without benefit of singer, is casting its restful spell through the
liquid imagery of "dripping" (*stazein*), which suggests both the bur-
bling brook flowing by or a drug being poured. The vocal tree, drowsi-
ness, and the language of magical spells create an atmosphere of fluid
interchange between man and nature that, like the elusiveness of
Orpheus' magic itself, is both accessible and distant.

The myth thus contains two diverse aspects of the power of poetry,
which we may label the immanentist and the transcendent respectively.
The two poles are present not only in Milton's *Lycidas*, as we have seen,
but even more markedly in the contrast between Daphnis and Silenus
of Virgil's Fifth and Sixth *Eclogues*, between the Daphnis and Lycidas of
Theocritus' First and Seventh *Idylls*, between Aristaeus and Orpheus of
Virgil's Fourth *Georgic*, and in the shifts between immanence and transcendence throughout Rilke's *Sonnets to Orpheus*. The poet can view his
special form of language as a means of sympathetic participation in and
identification with the struggles and processes of life against death, or
as a privileged medium for viewing that struggle at a distance. On the
one hand the poet is a personal sufferer whose song itself is both the
literal and symbolic participation in the processes of loss, death, and
renewal in nature. On the other hand the poet identifies himself with
the impersonal laws of nature; his song is eternal, reflects the timeless
patterns of the world rather than his own emotional life, and indeed
may serve as a foil to the turbulence of individual emotional life.

These two possibilities find deeper resonances within the events of the myth itself. Although the version in which Orpheus loses Eurydice is the more familiar to us, thanks to the poetry of Virgil and Ovid, another version, current at least as early as the middle of the fifth century B.C., told of Orpheus' success in bringing Eurydice back from the dead.[12] Thus from a very early stage the myth seems to have held a dual possibility: the poet's transcendence of the laws of nature by his magical power, or his defeat by the sternest of nature's necessities.

The version in which Orpheus triumphs over death is only the logical extension of his song's power to move animals, stones, and trees: it mediates between the life-giving joy of human creativity and the creative energies in nature. Hence Orpheus' song, in the literary tradition, contains the knowledge of nature's laws, the forces of union and diffusion, growth and decay that brought the world into being. Here the "religious" and "poetic" traditions converge. The religious texts of Orphism include several cosmogonic poems, of which a parody survives also in Aristophanes' *Birds*.[13] The cosmogony that Apollonius of Rhodes has him sing in the first book of the *Argonautica*, like the cosmogony of the Orphic singer Silenus in Virgil's Sixth *Eclogue*, has a literary rather than a religious function. A drunken brawl threatens to break out among the Argonauts, and Orpheus quells it by singing about the origin of the world from the primal elements, earth, sky, and sea, down to the reign of Zeus (*Arg.* 1.492–511). The heroes listen "with straining ears" and "become quiet at his spell (*kēlēthmos*); such a magic enchantment (*thelktron*) of song did he leave in them" (515). The power of poetic knowledge over external nature in the subject matter of the song here corresponds to a power over inward emotions in the effect of the song.

This double aspect of Orphic power in turn corresponds to a double aspect of the power of language itself: the means to a more vibrant contact with the world or a screen between us and the world, distorting rather than focusing or clarifying reality. The myth oscillates between the power of form to master intense passion and the power of intense passion to engulf form. Whereas the success of Orpheus reflects the power of language, raised to its furthest limits, to cross the boundaries between opposing realms of existence, matter and consciousness, and finally life and death, his failure reflects the inability of the language of art to empty itself of the subjectivity of the artist, to reach beyond emotion and obey the laws of an objective reality outside, in this case the conditions that the gods of the underworld impose for Eurydice's return.

The tale of Orpheus' descent and successful ascent repeats an ancient pattern of fertility myths, the rescue of the Maiden or Kore from the dark realm of death, which restores nature to life after a period of barrenness. Ancient authors were quick to note the similarity between Orpheus's descent and that of Dionysus, in one of his aspects a god of vegetation, who descended to the underworld to raise up his mother Semele, probably originally a goddess of the earth and its crops.[14] Like a vegetation god too, Orpheus' remains are scattered over the fields in winter by maternal figures ("mothers" in Virgil, married women in Hellenistic versions),[15] and universal nature laments his passing. His rejection of heterosexual love and procreation cannot be traced back farther than the Hellenistic period.[16] A homosexual Orpheus perhaps reflects a view of art as pure "artifice," defying the laws of natural reproduction. This relation between art and nature is what one would expect of the Hellenistic poets, with their stress on the importance and independence of art and their programmatic self-consciousness about artifice as an essential component of art.

Here again the myth of Orpheus contains opposing possibilities for the relation between poetry and the external world. On the one hand, Orphic song can reject nature in an insistence on art as the autonomous vehicle of subjective emotion, a purely human sensibility that contrasts with unfeeling nature. On the other hand, Orphic song can embody that universal harmony which unites man with nature, the unifying concord of the cosmos that finds expression in the song that moves birds, beasts, stones, and trees in rhythmic responsion to its own beat and tune. Orpheus' music can express man's participation in that cosmic harmony and also recreate it in the shaped, human terms of art. This conception of Orpheus is implicit in the cosmogonic singer of Apollonius of Rhodes and has its models in the poet of Hesiod's *Theogony* and philosopher-poets like Empedocles. But, as we shall see, it leaves its trace in Virgil and Ovid too.

In his crossing of boundaries, Orpheus also veers between the Apollonian and Dionysiac. In some versions he is the son or protégé of Apollo, protected by this god after his death, the enemy of Dionysus and his followers, who are responsible for his death.[17] In other versions, however, he is the son of a remote Thracian king, Oeagrus, has affinities with Dionysus in his descent to the underworld, founds Dionysiac mysteries, and is the founder of a religious sect in which Dionysus occupies an important role.[18] In an ode of Euripides' *Bacchae*, the Maenads ask whether their god, Dionysus, leads his bands "among the valleys of heavily treed Olympus where once Orpheus, playing his lyre, led together trees through [his art of] the Muses, led together the wild beasts" (560–564). Orphic song is here incorporated into Dionysiac ecstasy on the mountainside. The anaphora of the verb, "led together . . . led together" (*synage . . . synage* [563f.]) and the metrical and syntactical parallelism of the two lines also serve to represent and imitate the magical power of Orpheus in the mimetic mode of lyrical chant, an orally performed and vividly enacted ritual celebration.

As an Apollonian figure, Orpheus appears as a culture hero, such as Prometheus or Heracles, a benefactor of mankind, inventor of poetry, theology, agriculture, letters, a religious teacher, and educator of heroes.[19] But on the other hand his music is totally the extension of his own emotional life. The sympathy he creates between himself and the beasts, trees, and stones that he moves by his song reflects not an attitude of control but a resonant harmony between poet and nature. Even his knowledge of the laws of organic growth and decay, the coming to be and passing away of the world, is an intuitive, playful knowledge. It is interesting that in the religion of Orphism the playfulness of the child has a major role.[20] This Orpheus is nonaggressive, gentle; he communicates with the "lower" forms of vegetative and animal life as he communicates with his own instincts. Though Greeks could regard him as a civilizing hero, his function in most of Western literature and art has been to embody an antirational, anti-Promethean strain in our culture.[21]

II ·

The early Greek vocabulary for the appeal of song draws a parallel between the literally "fascinating" (Latin *fascinum*, "magical charm") power of language and the power of love, between erotic seduction and the seduction exercised by poetry.[22] The word *thelgein*, "enchant," "charm by a spell," for example, describes the Sirens' song, Circe's brutalizing sexual power (*Od.* 10.213, 290f.), and the poet's influence over a whole assembled populace (*Homeric Hymn to Apollo* 161). Calypso's attempt to keep Odysseus on her remote island combines verbal and erotic magic: "By soft and guileful words she was always charming him (*thelgei*) that he might forget Ithaca" (*Od.* 1.56f.). Similarly the love-goddess Aphrodite's beguilement contains "conversation and cozening speech (*parphasis*) which deceives the minds even of those who have sense" (*Iliad* 14.214–217).

The association continues throughout Greek literature. In the story of Deianeira and Heracles told in Sophocles' *Trachinian Women,* the magical power of persuasion by language, the power of love, and the magical potion (drug) of the Hydra's blood are all interchangeable, not merely as metaphors, but as actual equivalents for one another in an age that does not yet consign myth and metaphor to the realm of pale conventions but can still feel them as active, living presences.[23] In the concretely imagistic language of Aeschylus, Aphrodite exerts her power of love through her follower, Persuasion, who is an "enchantress" (*thelktōr Peithō* [*Suppliants* 1040 and cf. 1055]). Later poets often describe poetry as a *pharmakon* or "drug" that can both alleviate and cause the pain of love (for example, Theocritus, *Idyll* 11.1). A fragment of the Hellenistic poet Bion runs as follows:

> May Eros summon the Muses; may the Muses endure Eros. May the Muses give me, who am full of desire, song, sweet song, sweeter than any drug.[24]

The *Praise of Helen* by the Sophist Gorgias, one of the founders of rhetoric as a systematic discipline, not only consistently links the power of language and the power of eros but also seeks to understand the former in concrete, imagistic terms analogous to those of Homer, Aeschylus, and Sophocles.

> The power of the word has the same relation to the organization (*taxis*) of the soul as the organization (*taxis*) of drugs to the constitution (*physis*) of the body. For just as different drugs lead different humors forth from the body and bring cessation to some from sickness and to others from life, so of discourses (*logoi*), some cause pain, others delight (*terpsis*), others fear, while others set their hearer into a state of confident boldness, whereas others by an evil persuasion (*peithō*) drug and bewitch the soul (*ek-goēteuein*). (14)[25]

Plato's view of language challenges this entire poetic tradition. His definition of rhetoric in the *Gorgias* and *Phaedrus* attempts to replace the emotion-arousing, literally "spell-binding" power of language with its logical, poetic function.[26]

In archaic poetry, song, *aoidē,* is closely akin to *ep-aoidē,* "enchantment. The chantlike effects of repetition, alliteration, assonance, or the like reproduce some of the power of this song-as-magic even in highly sophisticated poets like Sappho and the authors of the Homeric Hymns. Sappho's *Ode to Aphrodite* (1 Lobel-Page) uses this incantatory aura not only to compel the presence of Aphrodite, but also to imitate, in its own word-magic, the quasi-hypnotic power of love's sorcery.[27] The Homeric *Hymn to Demeter* uses a highly formalized diction and repetition to evoke the power of witchcraft against which the (disguised) Demeter promises her aid.

> I know an antidote much stronger than herbs;
> I know a goodly cure for baleful witchcraft.[28]

Even a highly self-conscious poet like Pindar, writing at the end of the archaic period, feels poetry as incantatory magic. Songs, *aoidai*, are the "wise daughters of the Muses" and have the power to "lay hold of weary limbs" and "charm away" (*thelgein*) the pain, like a doctor, who in early Greece also practices by means of "enchantments," *epaoidai* (*Nemean* 4.1–3; cf. 8.49–51). Pindar in fact gives us some of the most vivid testimony in early Greek literature to the Orpheus-like magic of poetic compulsion. A fragmentary ode describes how the golden Sirens (literally, "Charmers," *kēlēdones*) adorning Apollo's temple at Delphi so ensorcelled passers-by with their "honey-spirited song" that they forgot their wives and children and failed to return home until the gods decided to plunge the temple into the earth.[29] Two other passages have similar "Orphic" conceptions of poetic magic, enabling the poet to cross the boundaries between the human and natural worlds. In a Parthenion or maiden-song, the chorus leader, speaking in the first person, says,

> I shall imitate in my songs . . . that siren-sound which silences the Zephyr's swift winds when Boreas, shivering with the storms' strength, rushes upon us with his blasts and stirs up the wave-swift sea.[30]

In another passage, unfortunately in a fragmentary context, the singer tells of being "stirred up to song like a dolphin of the seas when the lovely tune of flutes moves in the deep of the waveless sea."[31] Pindar's only reference to Orpheus in the *Victory Odes* interestingly occurs in a poem that vividly describes the magic of love as "persuasion" and "incantation" (*Pythian* 4.213f.). Orpheus here is "sent by Apollo, player of the lyre, father of songs" (176f.).[32]

Although he writes in the language of fifth-century logical argumentation, the Sophist Gorgias is still following the Orphic "myth" of language as magic when he extols *logos* ("language," "word," "discourse") as "a great tyrant" (*dynastēs megas*) in his *Praise of Helen*.

> Inspired song-incantations (*ep-aoidai*) are summoners of pleasure, banishers of pain. For the power of song-incantation, uniting with the opinion (*doxa*) of the soul, charms it (*thelgein*) and persuades it and changes it by sorcery (*goēteia*). Of magic and sorcery the arts (*technai*) are twofold, for the soul is subject to its errors, and opinion is subject to its deceptions. (8)[33]

Not only in the fifth century B.C., but many centuries later, Orpheus' music is a magical spell, a by-word for magical power. Pausanias in the second century A.D. calls him "wondrously skilful at magic" and pairs him with Amphion, legendary builder, by music, of the walls of Thebes, in his ability both to charm wild beasts and in the civilizing power that causes rocks to take their proper place spontaneously in a city wall.[34]

In the figure of Orpheus, however, the primitive magic of enchantment over wind and wave is lifted to a larger conception of the animating and vitalizing power of the beauty and pleasure of song. This development is implicit in the two fragments of Pindar cited above. It is even clearer in the most detailed archaic description of Orpheus' own magic that we possess, a few lines of the late archaic lyric poet Simonides.

> Above his head flutter innumerable birds, and from the dark-blue sea fishes leap straight up in harmony with his lovely song.[35]

The exuberant diction, coloristic lushness of imagery, and delight in movement characteristic of Greek choral poetry here create a vivid pictorial equivalent for the energizing magic of Orphic song.

In the more sober lyricism of a Euripidean chorus (from the lost *Hypsipyle*) Orpheus exerts this magic on wind and wave only indirectly, through the mediation of human response. He propels and steers the Argo by his songful commands to the rowers.

> At the mast in the ship's middle Orpheus' Thracian lyric sang out the boatswain's orders of far-moving strokes to the oarsmen, now for swift motion, now for rest from the pine-wood oar.[36]

By contrasting the poetic diction of the Orpheus myth with the prosaic language of sailing (Euripides writes for an audience whose livelihood and safety depend on Athens' citizen navy), the poet creates a rich interaction, characteristic of his style, between the remote and the everyday. By bringing the magic of the Thracian hero-singer into direct juxtaposition with the realities of contemporary life, he calls attention to the fanciful, romantic elements in the myth but also allows them a plausible new role in a familiar context of maritime realities. He thus exploits the aura of imaginative distance and fantasy in Orpheus while also making the myth accessible to normal experience. In keeping with Orpheus' humanized and practical, civilizing functions in this ode, Euripides also assigns him the task usually given the centaur Chiron of educating young heroes. Losing his usual nonaggressive character, Orpheus here teaches not only the "music of the Asian lyre" but also "the martial arms of Ares."[37]

III ·

In the poetry of early Greece, where Orpheus makes his first appearance perhaps around 600 B.C., he has a more limited, but no less important meaning.[38] Archaic Greece, though literate, is still largely an oral culture. In such a culture poetry is oral poetry. It is therefore closer to its origins in ritual and incantation. The oral poet creates a special kind of rapport with his audience, what E. A. Havelock calls a "mimetic" response.[39] The audience is caught up in a situation of performance in which they are not merely passive onlookers but feel and consciously or subconsciously mimic, in their own bodies, the rhythmic movement and beat of the song. Poetry of this type produces a total response, not just the distanced, intellectual response of the visually oriented, read poetry to which we are accustomed. The highly formulaic and formalized, ritualized patterning and repetition of meter and diction in early oral poetry reinforces this total effect. These formal qualities act through the motor responses and psychosomatic mechanisms of the audience, producing an identification, at the physical as well as mental level, with the rhythmic movements and structure of the poet's song.

Nonliterate audiences feel this "mimetic" effect as a kind of magic. When the poets of early Greece try to describe such effects, as I have noted, they regularly have recourse to the language of magic and incantation. Homer repeatedly describes the poet's song as *thelxis*, an incantatory power that bewitches the hearer even against his conscious will. Such is the effect of the bard Phemius (*Od.* 1.337) and the bardlike Odysseus when he skilfully tells his wondrous tale (11.367–369) or spins his yarns of distant voyages (14.387, 17.514).[40]

The magic of Orpheus' song is particularly appropriate to an oral culture, which is totally dependent on and open to the spoken word for the expression and preservation of its values. In an oral culture one has fewer defenses against the "compulsion" (*anagkē*) of formalized language, be it poetry or rhetorical prose.[41] Hence the power of the accomplished singer can seem almost boundless. Homer shows us the bards of the *Odyssey* reducing strong heroes to tears even at the joyful banquets of hospitable kings (8.520f., 537–541; cf. 1.336–344).

Orpheus himself is the oral poet par excellence. He sings outside, under the open sky, accompanying himself on his famous lyre. His fabled effect upon wild beasts, stones, and trees generalizes to the animal world the mimetic response that an oral audience feels in the situation of the performance by the creative oral singer or his successor, the rhapsode. This compulsive, incantatory power of oral song, the rhythmic swaying that it produces in its human or nonhuman audience, the animal magnetism with which it holds its hearers spellbound all find mythical embodiment in Orpheus. Vase paintings and other visual representations of Orpheus throughout antiquity show his audience caught up in a trancelike, physically responsive movement.[42] Though centuries after the disappearance of a creative oral tradition, Virgil's lines on the Orphic singer Silenus in the Sixth *Eclogue* concentrate still on this essential attribute of rhythmical responsive movement.

> Then would you see the Fauns and wild beasts join playfully in the rhythm (*in numerum*), then the stiff oaks move their tops. Not such joy does the rock of Mount Parnassus take in Apollo nor such wonder do Rhodope and Ismarus feel for Orpheus. (27–30)

When the learned Athenaeus, writing at the end of the second century A.D., links early Greek poetry with Orphic song, he may have in mind its predominantly oral character.

> The ancient wisdom of the Greeks, as seems likely, was wholly given over to music. Because of this they judged Apollo the most musical and most skilful of the gods, and Orpheus the most musical and skilful of the demigods (14.632C).

The stress on music here also suggests those oral rhythmic, performative aspects of poetry we have seen associated with Orpheus.

Along with quasi-erotic "seduction" and magical "spell," "pleasure" or "delight" (*terpsis, hēdonē, chara*) is one of the recurrent attributes poets in an oral culture attribute to song.[43] This *terpsis* regularly characterizes Homer's bards, and of course it is an essential attribute of

Orpheus' song. A mid-fifth-century text interestingly links this form of "pleasure" with Orphic song. After the murder of Agamemnon the usurper Aegisthus tries to cow the recalcitrant Argive elders.

> You have a tongue the opposite of Orpheus'. For he led everything along by his voice with delight (*chara*), but you, all astir with silly barking, shall be led along yourselves, until you are subdued and so shown more tame. (Aeschylus, *Agamemnon* 1629–1632)

Like Euripides and Apollonius after him, Aeschylus associates the beauty and pleasure of Orpheus' verbal magic with the humanizing power of art and civilization. The civilizing Orphic power, however, is a foil to the bestialization of these elders by the murderer. Aegisthus' metaphors of barking and taming ironically resume the bestial imagery that accompanied his vitiation of civilized values when he helped kill the legitimate king.

This mimetic effect of Orphic magic is especially prominent in two famous passages of Plato. In the *Ion*, speaking specifically of the rhapsodes, oral reciters of Homer, he compares the power of poetic inspiration to the magnetic attachment of one iron ring to another in a chain (535E–536B): "Some hang suspended and draw their inspiration from some poets, others from others, some from Orpheus, others from Musaeus." Given the material here studied, it is clear why Plato associates with Orpheus the qualities he (pejoratively) attributes to this traditional oral poetry: magical, quasi-hypnotic effect, emotional response, power to move and compel large audiences.

In the *Protagoras*, Plato half-humorously extends this magical influence of words to the Sophist Protagoras, who leads his followers from all parts of Greece, "charming them with his voice, like Orpheus, and they follow charmed by that voice" (315A–B). He thus associates the rhetorical art of the Sophist with the primitive magic of archaic song. Shortly afterward Protagoras, praising the antiquity of his profession, adduces as his predecessors the old poets, Homer, Hesiod, Simonides, and again, Orpheus and Musaeus (316D). Seeking to substitute his own philosophical training for the older education by the poets—primarily oral poets—Plato vehemently rejects the ancient poetic "magic," which in his view feeds the emotional, irrational faculties of the baser part of the soul. The long uninterrupted monologues of Protagorian rhetoric generate an incantatory, hypnotic acquiescence, unconducive to the philosophical search for truth. Plato will therefore cut them up into the sharp give-and-take of Socratic questioning and irony (cf. 329A–B, 334C–335C).

For Plato the magic of Orphic speech can persuade but cannot attain to truth. As a precursor of the Sophists, Orpheus belongs in the realm of *doxa*, opinion based on the evidence of the senses, not *epistēmē*, knowledge of reality through the intellect. For this reason, when Plato has Phaedrus tell the story of Orpheus and Eurydice in the first speech on love in the *Symposium*, he uses a version that hovers between success and failure but in fact inclines more toward the latter.

> So do the gods honor zeal and heroic excellence (*aretē*) toward love (*erōs*). But Orpheus, son of Oeagrus, they sent back unfulfilled (*atelēs*) from Hades, showing him a phantom (*phasma*) of the woman for whom he came, but not giving the woman herself because he seemed to them to have acted the part of a coward since he was a citharode [singer with the lyre] and didn't venture to die for the sake of love, as did Alcestis, but rather devised a means of entering Hades while still alive. Therefore they laid a just penalty upon him and caused his death to be at the hands of women, nor did they do him honor, as they did Achilles, son of Thetis, whom they sent to the Isles of the Blessed (179D–E).

Presumably Orpheus succeeded in persuading the gods below, but Plato makes no mention of this fact, nor of his song in Hades. The wraith or shadow figure (*phasma*) that he wins keeps his action in the realm of illusion. Plato does not admit the rhetor-poet/singer to the rank of true lovers: his *erōs* (love) is as delusory as his *logos* (speech). Far from stressing his success, Plato dwells upon his death, underlines its unheroic character, and (a rare motif) makes it a just punishment visited upon him by the gods.

The wraith (*phasma*) that the gods show Orpheus indicates Plato's view of the inadequacy of poetry and rhetoric to represent "reality," which in the *Symposium* is reached by the highest eros. This meaning of the myth is not restricted to Plato, for, as we have seen, it can signify the ambiguity of (poetic) language from the beginning. The three great classical poets who treat it extensively—Euripides, Virgil, Ovid—all deal with this ambiguous side.

IV ·

In Euripides's *Alcestis*, Orpheus' rescue of Eurydice from the underworld is a paradigm for Heracles' rescue of the heroine from Death.
Admetus cites the myth as an example of persuasion triumphant over
death.

> If I had Orpheus' tongue and song so that I could by song charm
> (*kēlein*) either Demeter's daugher (Persephone) or her husband and
> take you forth from Hades, I would have descended there, and
> neither Pluto's dog nor Charon at his oar, ferryman of dead souls,
> would have held me back until I had set your life once more into the
> light. Therefore await me there until I die and prepare a house where
> we may share our dwelling. (357–364)

Admetus' language itself imitates the rhetorical force of Orphic persuasion. In striking contrast with the simplicity and directness of
Alcestis' speech just preceding, Admetus uses a carefully constructed
periodic sentence and an elaborate symmetry of clauses ("either
Demeter's daughter or her husband . . . neither Plato's dog nor
Charon at his oar"). One wonders, however, if the subterranean
domestic felicity envisaged in line 364 is not a deliberate touch of irony
undercutting the tragic tone of the myth.

Euripides here combines the Orphic allusion with a mythic paradigm one stage removed, the descent and return of Persephone (Kore,
358) from the dead. This sets the personal grief of Admetus against a
larger pattern of loss and renewal. When Orpheus recurs in the last
ode of the play, however, it is to exemplify the ineluctable power of
Necessity (*Anagkē*), particularly death, in a context much concerned
with language. The chorus tells how it has searched through many
songs and discourses but has found nothing more powerful than
Necessity, "nor any drug [for it] in the Thracian tablets inscribed with
[the sayings of] Orphic song, not even among all those drugs that
Phoebus Apollo gave to the sons of Asclepius as cures for much-
suffering mortals" (962–971). The power of Orphic song as a magical
drug (*pharmakon*) against death has a second paradigm in Apollo's gift
of the power of healing to his son, Asclepius. In both cases, however,
there is an ambivalence between the conquest of death by art and the
failure of art before death. Apollo opened the play with this tale: Zeus
has killed Apollo's son, Asclepius, precisely because he brought
mortals back to life (3ff.). As a result of Apollo's vengeance, Zeus'

"necessity" (*anagkē*) made him serve Admetus, and that service results in Alcestis' death in his behalf (5–21).

The first ode in the play connects the myth of Apollo and Asclepius with Alcestis.

> If only Apollo's son were to see this light of life with his eyes, she (Alcestis) would have left the dark abode and gates of Hades. For he raised up those subdued by death, until the Zeus-hurled bolt of lightning's fire destroyed him. But now what hope do we have still left of [her] life? (122–131)

Asclepius' power over death, however, like the power of Orpheus in Admetus' speech, appears in a contrary-to-fact condition, as something wished for, but unreal. Thus the myth of Orpheus gradually takes its place in a series of mythic mirror images reaching back from the present to the nearer and more distant past (Asclepius and Persephone respectively.) Each mythic paradigm reflects the hopelessness of a victory over death in the present. Then, in a surprising reversal, Heracles does succeed in defeating Death and bringing the lost Kore figure, the veiled bride of Admetus, back from Hades. He does so, however, not by persuasion and art, but by their exact opposite, brute force.[44]

Thus at every turn the myth of Orpheus is both validated and denied. Ostensibly using the legend of Orpheus' success as a paradigm for Alcestis' return, Euripides places it in a context where Necessity, not flexibility, Death, not the renewing power of language and poetry, seem to be irresistible—only to reverse the relationship in the surprise ending of Heracles' descent and return. By setting the Orpheus myth within a group of interlocking and potentially contradictory paradigms—Asclepius, Persephone, Heracles—he keeps the Orphic power ambiguous. This ambiguity, however, only exploits the vacillation, inherent in the myth, between the power of language and its futility in the face of the "necessities" of existence.

The ambiguity of Orphic magic in language has a small but interesting role in one of Euripides' last plays, the *Iphigeneia at Aulis*. Pleading for her life before her father, Agamemnon, the young Iphigeneia begins her speech as follows:

> If I had Orpheus' speech, my father, to persuade by magic song (*peithein epaidousa*), so that the rocks would follow me, and to charm whomever I wished by my words, I would have come to that point. But now I shall offer the wisdom I have, my tears. For that is all my strength and skill. (1211–1215)

She mentions Orphic art (cf. *sopha*, 1214), only to abandon it for the completely emotional plea of a daughter falling on her knees before her father, touching his hand and beard (1216ff.). The contrary-to-fact condition, the allusion to Orphic incantatory music, and the fantasy of stones moved by song suggest a certain lyrical remoteness, a fabled world where nature responds to human music and human feeling. That mood, however, is quite at variance with the harsh reality of the world depicted in the play.

Symbol of artful persuasion par excellence, Orpheus has his place in a familiar rhetorical topos (a variant of "Unaccustomed as I am . . ."). But in Iphigeneia's situation—a daughter begging her own father for her life—elaborate formal rhetoric is bizarrely inappropriate and hideously jarring. It only points up the perversion of the closest human ties and the dehumanization of this society. Iphigeneia's plea for survival needs no rhetoric. It is a young being's instinctive cry for life. Her brief peroration begins, "This light is the sweet thing for men to look upon" (1250). She possesses "Orphic" power, as it were, through the natural gifts of youth: frankness, innocence, simplicity, truth. But for all her natural eloquence and the magic of her speech, she does not persuade. Purity can have no effect on the corruption to which she falls victim.

It is not accidental, therefore, that her reference to Orpheus's magic omits beasts and trees and mentions only stones. The most fantastic effect of his song is, ironically, the most appropriate here, given the hopelessness of her situation. The sequel soon reveals how frail and brittle is the mythic remoteness of Orpheus in her imagined hopes. As in the later versions of the legend of the arch-poet himself, the power of persuasive speech rests not with harmonious song nor with the pathetic cry of the young girl who invokes him, but with the unreasoning roar of an impassioned mob lusting for blood (cf. 1346–1357).

V ·

In Virgil's version at the end of the Fourth *Georgic*, the two sides of this tension between the omnipotence and the helplessness of language and art are embodied in two separate characters.[45] The creative, life-giving power of Orpheus, his ability to awaken the dormant life of nature, is represented in the shepherd-god Aristaeus, whose descent accomplishes the rebirth of his bees, the renewal of life. The tragic side, the fragility of art in the face of death, is enacted in Orpheus himself, whose descent to the lower world, though initially successful, results in hopeless loss: forgetting his promise to Persephone and yielding to passion. Orpheus turns around and Eurydice slips back to Hades. He can then use his power of song only to lament his failure in the sterile, frozen landscape of the north, where the inverted fertility rite of his death only underlines his inability to recover the life he sought (G.4.485–527). Virgil stresses less the magic power of Orpheus' song than the harsh, inexorable "law" of the underworld deities (489ff.) and the disastrous passion, the *furor* or desperate madness of love, which violates that law and is punished by eternal separation (494–501).

This division of the power of Orphic art into two figures, however, does not mean that Aristaeus is entirely positive. Though he succeeds in his task of restoring a part of dead nature to life, he has his own destructive passion and violence in his (presumably) amorous approach to Eurydice, which causes her flight and thus her death (cf. 457–459). The resultant curse from Orpheus and the Nymphs destroys his bees; to expiate his crime he must descend to his goddess-mother, Cyrene, at the source of all rivers and endure the trial of his encounter with Proteus.

Sympathetic accord with nature and mysterious knowledge of its laws lie not with Orpheus, nor with Aristaeus, but rather with this wise old man of the sea who "transforms himself into all the wondrous shapes of things" (441). Proteus' wisdom mediates between the two mortal heroes, as also between brute nature and divinity, fire and water, earth and sea. Thus it is he who tells Aristaeus the tragic tale of Orpheus. His knowledge of past, present, and future (392f.) includes not only the mystery of the changefulness of matter in nature but also the dark forces of hatred, vengefulness, destructive anger. With the grey light of his blazing eyes (451) and his "heavy gnashing" of teeth (*graviter frendens* [452]; cf. Orpheus' "heavy wrath," *graviter . . . saevit*, four lines later [456]), Proteus embodies the resistant, intractable otherness of nature over against its generosity and helpfulness suggested in the female divinity of sea and nature, Cyrene. In this aspect, Proteus is associated not only with the mystery of a world order that yields up its secrets through violence, but also with the necessity of violence in the post-Saturnian world (cf. 1.120ff.) that leaves human life under a curse, the theme of Proteus' first words (453–456). Orpheus has Proteus' sympathy perhaps because the doomed poet, crossing between life and death, is closer to nature's mystery. He identifies with nature rather than forcing it and projects his inward life into its rhythms. If Aristaeus embodies the capacity of human intelligence to use nature for his own needs, Orpheus embodies the equally unique human capacity to sympathize with nature and express a sense of violation and loss analogous to that of nature itself. Hence the comparison of his song to the bereft nightingale (511–515) and nature's echoing of his grief (523–527). Hence too Proteus, even captured as he is, in the end eludes his captor. He slips away back into his watery element before giving Aristaeus exact instructions about mollifying the wrath of the Nymphs (528f.). This crucial knowledge comes as a spontaneous gift from his mother (503f.). The maternal figure, destructive for Orpheus (*matres* [520]), is thus helpful and life-giving for Aristaeus (*mater, Cyrene mater* [321]).

Orpheus, however, for all the disastrous results of his passion, has the sympathy of the narrator and presumably of the Nymphs, spirits of nature, who take up his cause (cf. 460ff., 532–536). Although he fails in his attempt to restore life by descending to the underworld, he still exerts his magical persuasion of song over the infernal realm (469–484). Even after death he has the power of a "divinity" (*numen* [453ff.]) to curse. But where Aristaeus, the practical man of action, succeeds in his "art" (315), Orpheus, the poet, fails. The wild passion of his love neutralizes the magical, potentially revivifying power of his song. He is a victim of his own emotional violence and of the violence of others, the fury of the *matres* who kill him (520–522).

Orpheus here embodies an aspect of poetry that is tragically self-indulgent, centered upon itself and upon the personal emotion of the poet, prodigally passionate, wasteful of its own energies. Although Aristaeus has his violence and egotism too (cf. 321ff.), it is he who acts to implement the hidden lore of the nature deities, Proteus and Cyrene, and after heroic trial, including a descent and ascent parallel to Orpheus', reaps the reward. His effort, unlike the purely private goal of Orpheus, bestows on subsequent generations a rite of renewal that Orpheus could not achieve, bringing forth life from its mysterious repositories deep in the earth.

It is characteristic of Virgil, however, to give full expression to the *cost* of this regeneration. The unresolved suffering of Orpheus and Eurydice and the violence done to the animals in their sacrificial death are the price of the bees' renewal.

Here they behold a sudden and wondrous prodigy: in that entire womb the bees buzz throughout the cattle's putrefied entrails (*liquefacta boum per viscera*) and seethe forth from the smashed ribs (*ruptis . . . costis*). (554–556)

Nor are we shown any emotional recognition or inward repentance on Aristaeus' part. Cyrene had mentioned suppliant gestures, seeking peace, prayer, the violated divinities' granting of pardon and relinquishing of wrath (534–537). In Aristaeus' performance of the rite, the note of contrition is absent: these are simply necessary acts to be done in an efficient, objective, step-by-step manner.

Haud mora: continuo matris praecepta facessit;
ad delubra venit, monstratas excitat aras,
quattuor eximios praestanti corpore tauros
ducit et intacta totidem cervice iuvencas.

There is no delay. At once he performs his mother's instructions. He comes to the shrine, stirs to life the altars shown him, and brings four splendid bulls of surpassing form and as many heifers, with necks untouched [by the yoke]. (548–551)

The style is clipped and matter-of-fact. Those beautiful bodies of bulls and heifers (550f.) will soon be a formless mass of rotting entrails and broken bones (*liquefacta . . . viscera, ruptis . . . costis* [555f.]).

This Orpheus is not the culture hero found in other parts of the tradition. His "art," unlike Aristaeus', is entirely in the service of his private grief, a protest against the larger order of nature that embraces renewal as well as loss. The simile that compares him to a grieving nightingale whose nest and fledglings the "harsh farmer" has destroyed (511–515) presents Orpheus as the victim of an Aristaeus-like figure of work and effort who, like Aristaeus, symbolizes the necessary violation of nature that man's survival has always entailed. Whereas Aristaeus' story moves to energetic action in the context of the civilized arts of ritual, animal husbandry, and apiculture (528–558), the magic of Orpheus' song remains outside the limits of civilization, in the deserted places of the wild, "soothing tigers and leading oak trees" (508–510).

The other side of Orpheus' poetic power, the humanizing capacity of song that encompasses and transmits a deep knowledge of nature's laws, appears briefly in Virgil's epic.[46] On his descent to the underworld, Aeneas, the future founder of Rome, meets the poet in the

Elysian fields, dressed in the solemn robes of a priest or prophet, playing upon his lyre (*Aen.* 6.645-647).[47] His immediate companions are the founders of Troy, "great-hearted heroes" (648-650). Nearby are those who have sacrificed their lives for their homeland, pious priests and inspired prophets, and "all those who cultivated their lives in the discovery of the arts or who by their deserving acts won a place in others' memory" (660-664). Orpheus' song, then, is here reunited with that other, civilizing task, which in the *Georgics* rests with his alter ego, Aristaeus, the hero who "hammers out art" for later generations (cf. *G.*4.315).

In Ovid the individualistic, private side of Orphic poetry as the voice of passionate love reemerges as the dominant trait. Ovid divides the tale between books 10 and 11 of the *Metamorphoses*. The episode of book 10 recounts Eurydice's death, Orpheus' descent, and his second loss of his bride; book 11 tells of the poet's death at the hands of the Maenads and his subsequent reunion with Eurydice in the lower world. In between are a number of tales, mainly of homosexual or incestuous love, presented as the songs of the grieving Orpheus (10.148-739).

Ovid makes a number of major modifications of Virgil's version.[48] He totally eliminates Aristaeus, thereby removing the tension between private emotion and external action implicit in the *Georgics*. Orphic power here centers entirely upon emotion: it is the power of poetry inspired by love and expressing love. Orpheus is a lover-poet whose irresistibly beautiful song wins even the bloodless inhabitants of the underworld over to love. Love itself has a persuasive power. Orpheus' appeal is based not upon the power of song, as in Virgil (*cantu* [*G.*4.471]), but upon his frank avowal of his total submission to Amor.

> I wanted to be able to endure [the loss], and I can affirm that I tried. Love won out (*vicit Amor*). This god is well known in the upper world. Whether he is known here too I am uncertain, but I suspect that he is; and if the tale of the ancient rape [of Persephone] did not lie, Love joined you too (*vos quoque iunxit Amor*). (*Met.* 10.25-29)

Ovid then expatiates, far beyond Virgil, on the underworld audience reaction (*Met.* 10.40-48; cf. *G.*4.480-484). His own highly rhetorical style admirably suits this characterization of Orpheus.

If Virgil's Orpheus, then, symbolizes that poet's conflicts between poetry as a civilizing, socially responsible task, in touch with the life-forces of nature, and poetry as an expression of private emotion,

introspective and ultimately tragic in its futile reflection on the hopelessness of the human condition, then Ovid's Orpheus reflects a
poetry of rhetorical artifice centered entirely upon the personal concerns of love and the inner emotional life and essentially uninvolved
with external issues of social or moral responsibility.

It is for this reason, perhaps, that Ovid devotes twenty lines to list-
ing the trees which the "vocal strings" of Orpheus' lyre attract (*Met.*
10.86–105). Although these trees give him an opportunity to relate the
myth of Cyparissus, they also form a *locus amoenus* characteristic of
poetry, adorned by the "shade" (*umbra* [88]) that marks the peaceful
setting of creative leisure in Augustan poetry.[49] This Orpheus, in other
words, uses his magical art of song to create his own symbolic context
of poetry. He thus functions in a way analogous to the Orpheus of
Virgil's *Eclogues*, a symbol of the aesthetic aims and spirit of the poet
himself. When he sits down amid the birds and beasts that his song
draws, he waits until he "felt the different notes, though diverse in
sound, coming together in harmony" (*et sensit varios quamvis diversa
sonarent,/concordare modos, hoc vocem carmine movit* [10.146f.]). He is an
artist sensitive to the technical aspects of his craft.

In bringing the "different measures" together in harmonious
sound, he reflects the theme and poetic task of the *Metamorphoses* as a
whole.[50] Indeed the poem opens, after a brief reference to the theme of
transformation, with the "Orphic" account of a cosmogony in which
uniting or separating elements, harmoniously or inharmoniously
joined, form a major topic (cf. 1.7f.). Physical creation, a microcosm of
poetic creation, "bound together in harmonious peace things kept
apart in [separate] places" (*dissociata locis concordi pace ligavit* [1.25]).
Ovid, however, refuses to take his art as seriously as does Virgil. The
actual Orpheus of the tenth book, therefore, unlike the cosmogony-
singing poet of Apollonius or the "Orphic" singer of Virgil's Sixth
Eclogue, deliberately spurns cosmic themes like gigantomachies in
favor of stories of the "illicit passions" of girls and boys that he will
treat "with lighter lyre" (10.148–154).[51] The "power of Jove" that
defeated the Giants and "scattered victorious thunderbolts over the
Phlegrean fields" (151) now dwindles to the "false feathers" of the
eagle which "beat in the air" (*percusso mendacibus aere pennis* [159]) to
carry the fair young Ganymede rather than thunderbolts (158–161).

Though Ovid's Orpheus, like Virgil's, meets his death at the hands
of the enraged Maenads, even here the life-giving, animating force of
the poet's song predominates. It tames the missiles hurled by the

maddened women and holds them at bay until the wild shouting finally drowns out his voice (11.9–19). His death thus becomes the defeat of art's capacity to persuade, humanize, and soften man's darker impulses to blind hatred and lust for blood. This is the first time his song fails to move.

> et in illo tempore primum
> inrita dicentem nec quicquam voce moventem
> sacrilegae perimunt, perque os, pro Iuppiter, illud
> auditum saxis intellectumque ferarum
> sensibus in ventos anima exhalata recessit.

> And as then, for the first time, he spoke in vain and moved nothing with his voice, the impious women killed him, and through his mouth, by Jupiter, that voice, heard by the rocks and understood by the sense of wild beasts, departed as he breathed forth his life into the winds. (11.39–43)

The failure of song, however, is in a sense only temporary, for the natural world at once mourns his passing in a rich elegiac lament like that over Milton's Lycidas (44–49).[52] Apollo intervenes to protect the severed head from a threatening serpent, and Bacchus punishes his guilty worshippers and abandons the area (55–60, 67–89).

By having Orpheus' head murmur only "something mournful" (*flebile nescio quid* [52f.]), rather than calling "Eurydice," as in Virgil (*G.*4.525f.), Ovid cleverly introduces an element of suspense that prepares for his surprise ending. He last mentioned Eurydice some 750 lines before. His Orpheus has shunned "female Venus" in favor of young boys (*Met.* 10.79–85). Perhaps, then, he has forgotten all about Eurydice, whose name is so conspicuously absent from his final lament. Suddenly it proves not to be so. His Orpheus and Eurydice are now reunited in the underworld (11.62–66). The lovers walk arm in arm, and now "Orpheus looks back with impunity on his Eurydice" (66). The second loss of his bride is balanced by the regain of his second descent (cf. 61f.). Ovid thus manages to interweave the pathos of the tragic Orpheus with the happy ending of the successful Orpheus,[53] and with this tour de force he reconciles the contradictory versions of the mythic tradition.

Whereas Ovid's Orpheus is primarily the poet of private emotion and devoted passionate love, he does not entirely overlook the other side of Orpheus, the civilizing founder of poetry and religion. The intervention of Apollo obliquely alludes to this side of the myth, for in other versions the god endows the severed head, safely arrived on Lesbos, with prophetic and music-inspiring power.[54] Shortly after, in fact, Ovid's Orpheus appears as the founder of a mystical cult in Phrygia and Athens (92–94).

Ovid further defines the power of Orphic song by parallels or contrasts with similar myths, particularly those of Pygmalion and Midas. Orpheus himself sings the former tale (10.270–297); the latter follows almost directly upon Orpheus' own story (11.90–193).

Like Orpheus, Pygmalion is a consummate artist, though his medium is stone, not words; and like Orpheus he is also (temporarily) hostile to women. Like Orpheus too his art gives him the magical power of crossing the boundaries between inert matter and living consciousness.[55] Yet this power does not come from his own artistry, but from outside, as the gift of Venus granting the fulfillment of his secret desire. In terms of the "Orphic triangle" sketched above, the axis between love and death, crucial for the poignancy of Orpheus' story, has no place here at all; and this artist is himself the surprised victim of his own skill (*ars adeo latet arte sua,* "To such a degree does art lie hidden in his own art" [10.252]).

This artist creates the ideal image of his own love (243–249), in contrast to the ugly reality of the women around him, and then endows that object with a beauty inappropriate to it (259–269). Even though he dresses it in jewels and purple, he can make it no more beautiful than it was in its original, sculptural form (*nec nuda minus formosa videtur,* "nor did the nude state seem any less beautiful" [265]). The Pygmalion episode explores the confusion of art and life. It depicts the creative capacities of artistic imagination on the one hand but also shows the self-deceptive possibilities of that imagination on the other. The imagination that creates the lovely statue is dangerously akin to the "crystallization" of love that endows the beloved with unreal charms, makes her an object of the aesthetic imagination. In Pygmalion the mimesis of nature through art reveals a dangerous affinity with the self-deceptiveness of romantic love.

Orpheus' power of giving sense to senseless matter has a foil in both the punishment of his killers, who are rooted to the earth as trees (11.67–84) and in the story of Midas, the foolish king whose contact with Silenus wins him the golden touch.[56] He wins this gift, however, not by any creative or intellectual energy of his own, but through the accidental find of his servants and his own lavish hospitality. The golden touch, robbing living beings of their life, is, of course, exactly the reverse of Orpheus' power and also proves to be a misuse of the god's generosity (100–102).

The second half of the Midas episode invites an even more direct comparison with Orpheus. Not having learned his lesson, the foolish king prefers the music of Pan to that of Apollo (146–163). In the contest that decides the issue, the judge, Mount Tmolus in Lydia, proves the superiority of Apollo's song by moving its forest in rhythm to the song (*vultum sua silva secuta est* [163f.]). Apollo's song, in other words, repeats the effect of Orpheus', raising nature up to the level of human sensibility. Midas' bad taste in music, however, has just the opposite effect: it lowers him to the level of the beasts in that part of his body that betrayed his folly: "Apollo did not permit his stupid ears to retain their human form" (174f.). Like the rustic god whose music he preferred, Midas now combines human with subhuman traits.[57]

Through Orpheus and the tales related to Orpheus, Ovid suggests an implicit poetics of metamorphosis. True Orphic song crosses the boundaries between matter and spirit in an upward direction: it brings life and sensitivity where before there was only inert matter. The enraged Bacchantes and the foolish Midas undergo downward metamorphosis, from human to bestial or plant forms. The deity presiding over these latter changes is not Olympian Apollo, protector of Orpheus, but the god of the drunken revel, Bacchus, whose Maenads destroy Orpheus, his half-bestial companion Silenus, and the goat-footed god of the wild countryside, Pan (cf. 146–149). Over against the ever-present possibility of human degradation to bestiality in this world of sudden, arbitrary change and unstable identity, therefore, stand this Apollonian-Orphic poetry and its upward movement from matter to spirit, from lifeless stone or tree to human sensitivity.

VI ·

For Rilke, as for Ovid and Virgil, Orpheus symbolizes the very essence of poetry. He compels the elemental forces of love and death to confront each other in art. Rilke's conception of Orpheus goes back to the notion, inherent in the earliest stories of Orpheus, of the basic interrelatedness of all parts of the world. The magic of the poet's song makes visible and communicable that hidden harmony; it reveals the unity in which life and death appear as ultimately parts of the same continuum. Of the poets here discussed, Rilke's greatest affinity is perhaps with Virgil in his recognition of the tragic dimension of art, never able to close the gap between image and object, eternal form and changing substance.

This tragic aspect of Orpheus is perhaps strongest in the long poem *Orpheus. Eurydike. Hermes,* written in 1904.[58] The poet, painfully descending into the mysterious subterranean landscape, "the unfathomable mine of souls," is almost alienated from his own being,

> no longer conscious of the lightsome lyre,
> the lyre which had grown into his left
> like twines of rose into a branch of olive.
> It seemed as though his senses were divided.
>   (*Orpheus. Eurydike. Hermes,* stanza 4)

Viewed in the light of the inaccessibility of the dead beloved, the poet's magic is a poetry of grief, transforming all of nature into a "world of lamentation," *eine Welt aus Klage.*

> She, so belov'd, that from a single lyre
> more mourning rose than from all women-mourners,—
> that a whole world of mourning rose, wherein
> all things were once more present: wood and vale
> and road and hamlet, field and stream and beast,—
> and that around this world of mourning turned,
> even as around the other earth, a sun
> and a whole silent heaven full of stars,
> a heaven of mourning with disfigured stars:—
> she, so beloved.
>   (stanza 5)

Like Virgil, though with greater psychological detail, Rilke focuses on the poet's fatal mistrust that causes the irrevocable loss of his beloved.

Shifting the emphasis from Orpheus to Eurydice, as modern poetry tends to do,[59] Rilke draws upon her ancient affinities with the Bride of Death, the Kore figure, like Persephone. Her death gives her a kind of second virginity in which she is untouchable, unreachable.

> She had attained a new virginity
> and was intangible; her sex had closed
> like a young flower at the approach of evening,
> and her pale hands had grown so disaccustomed
> to being a wife, that even the slim god's

endlessly gentle contact as he led her
disturbed her like a too great intimacy.

Even now she was no longer that blonde woman
who'd sometimes echoed in the poet's poems,
no longer the broad couch's scent and island,
nor yonder man's possession any longer.

She was already loosened like long hair,
and given far and wide like fallen rain,
and dealt out like a manifold supply.

She was already root.

(stanzas 7–10)

Now, instead of the direct response of either impassioned accusation or loving forgiveness (Virgil, G.4.494–498 and Ovid, Met. 10.60–62 respectively), this Eurydice makes no response at all and scarcely notices Orpheus' disappearance. She discerns only the distant, indistinguishable countenance of "someone" in the distance, "dark in the bright exit." She herself, her movement impeded by the long funereal shrouds, returns to the dead, "uncertain, gentle, and without impatience."[60]

Rilke returns to this myth two decades later in the fifty-five *Sonnets to Orpheus.* The figure of Orpheus now becomes pure symbol, symbol of the poet's hesitation between the wish to immortalize and the plunge into the flowing, transient moment of beauty that can never be recaptured. This Orpheus occupies a place of fundamental and irreconcilable contradictions.

Ein Gott vermags. Wie aber, sag mir, soll
ein Mann ihm folgen durch die schmale Leier?
Sein Sinn ist Zwiespalt. An der Kreuzung zweier
Herzwege steht kein Tempel für Apoll.

A god can do it. But how, tell me, shall
a man follow him through the narrow lyre?
His mind is cleavage. At the crossing of two
heartways stands no temple for Apollo.

(Sonnets to Orpheus, 1.3.1–4)

The book of *Sonnets* is dedicated as a "monument" to "Eurydice," a young girl, Vera, a dancer, who died at nineteen. One sonnet, however, admonishes against erecting monuments and views Orpheus as

the spirit of song, which can hold and accept the endless transformations or "metamorphoses" of life.

> Set up no stone to his memory.
> Just let the rose bloom each year for his sake.
> For it is Orpheus. His metamorphosis
> in this one and in this. We should not trouble
>
> about other names. Once and for all
> it's Orpheus when there's singing. He comes and goes.
> Is it not much already if at times
> he overstays for a few days the bowl of roses?
>
> (1.5.1–6)

On the other hand, Orpheus' song is also "pure transcendency," and
this Orphic magic opens the book of *Sonnets.*

> There rose a tree. O pure transcendency!
> O Orpheus singing! O tall tree in the ear!
> And all was silent. Yet even in the silence
> new beginning, beckoning, change went on.
>
> Creatures of stillness thronged out of the clear
> released wood from lair and nesting-place;
> and it turned out that not from cunning and not
> from fear were they so hushed within themselves,
>
> but from harkening. Bellow and cry and roar
> seemed little in their hearts. And where before
> hardly a hut had been to take this in,
>
> a covert out of darkest longing
> with an entrance way whose timbers tremble,–
> you built temples for them in their hearing.
>
> (1.1)

The power to instill consciousness in trees and stones now becomes
inward, "high tree in the ear" (line 2) or, in the last line, "temples in
their hearing."

The power of Orpheus, then, is no longer the power of magical
compulsion or persuasion, nor even the power to unite animate and
inanimate nature in the rhythmic sympathy of song, but rather the
capacity to grasp the changeful, death-bound beauty of life while
simultaneously surrendering any claim on its permanence.[61] In the last

of the *Sonnets*, the poet addresses Orpheus as a "friend" both close and remote, and asks him to be thoroughly immersed in "metamorphosis" (*Geh in der Verwandlung aus und ein* [2.29.6]). It concludes:

> Be, in this immeasurable night,
> magic power at your senses' crossroad,
> be the meaning of their strange encounter.
>
> And if the earthly has forgotten you,
> say to the still earth: I flow.
> To the rapid water speak: I am.
>
> (2.29.9–14)

In this very willingness to accept totally life as the "crossroad" where being and transience meet, the poet transforms the fear and pain of loss and change into something joyful and vital: *Ist dir Trinken bitter, werde Wein*, "Is drinking bitter to you, turn to wine."

Sonnets 2.13 expresses this paradox of poetry between monument and metamorphosis in the brilliant image of the glass that breaks at the moment of its highest note (*Sei ein klingendes Glas, das sich im Klang schon zerschlug*). Significantly this image occurs in the context of the dead Eurydice for whom no return is foreseen or even desired.

> Be ever dead in Eurydice–, mount more singingly,
> mount more praisingly back into the pure relation.
> Here, among the waning, be, in the realm of decline,
> be a ringing glass that shivers even as it rings.
>
> Be–and at the same time know the condition
> of not-being, the infinite ground of your deep vibration,
> that you may fully fulfil it this single time.
>
> (2.13.5–11)

As both the sufferer and the poet who monumentalizes/transforms the suffering, Orpheus can both sing and enact a poetry that is simultaneously the subject and the symbol of the tragic nature of life itself. He–like the poet/poetry of the *Sonnets*–is both the shivering glass and the ringing note. Between humanity and divinity, he also mediates two sides of poetry.

> Gesang ist Dasein. Für den Gott ein Leichtes.
> Wann aber *sind* wir?

Song is existence. Easy for the god.
But when do we *exist?*

(1.3.7–8)

Orpheus can symbolize the paradoxes of both life and art because he
owes his very existence as a mythic symbol to this need to find a form
that can hold contradictions.

Does he belong here? No, out of both
realms his wide nature grew.
More knowing would he bend the willows' branches
who has experienced the willows' roots.

(1.6.1–4)

In Rilke more than anywhere else he symbolizes the power of language
to signify while yet spanning opposites, suspended over paradoxes.

The next-to-last of the *Sonnets* identifies the dead Vera-Eurydice's
dance with Orpheus' song, conjoined by the paradox of "fleetingly
transcending (*vergänglich übertreffen*) dumbly ordering nature."

O komm und geh. du, fast noch Kind, ergänze
für einen Augenblick die Tanzfigur
zum reinen Sternbild eines jener Tänze,
darin wir die dumpf ordnende Natur

vergänglich übertreffen. Denn sie regte
sich völlig hörend nur, da Orpheus sang.

O come and go. You, still half a child,
fill out the dance-figure for a moment
to the pure constellation of one of those
dances in which we fleetingly transcend

dumbly ordering Nature. For she roused
to full hearing only when Orpheus sang.

(2.28.1–6)

The figure of oxymoron in *vergänglich übertreffen*, heightened by its
enjambment at the beginning of the second stanza, creates a linguistic
equivalent, on the level of the syntactical construction itself, of the contradictions inherent in art: the contrast and the identity between the
momentary "dance-figure" of the mortal girl, now dead with Eurydice,
and the "pure star-figure" (*reinen Sternbild*) of the remote constellation.
It is Orpheus' song that pulls the two together. *Ein für alle Male / ists*

Orpheus, wenn es singt, "Once and for all / it's Orpheus when there's singing" [1.5.5f.]).

VII ·

During the two and a half millennia in which Orpheus has been alive in myth and art, each age has actualized a different aspect of this plastic figure. In archaic Greece, when the word is still a thing to conjure with, Orpheus appears as a magician, the practitioner of a mysteriously compelling incantatory force, but also as a religious teacher and prophet. In fifth-century drama he exemplifies the force of persuasive speech per se. Hellenistic authors such as Apollonius of Rhodes stress his civilizing power, make him a learned singer of cosmogonies or else — a direction to be followed by Ovid — dwell upon the pathetic or erotic aspects of the myth, the emotions of loss, homosexual love, grief without end. In Virgil's early work he is a symbol of the lyrical, inspired quality of poetry itself; but the *Georgics* present a fully tragic Orpheus balanced precariously between the creative and the self-delusive capacity of language. In Ovid's Orpheus, however, tragedy gives way to the celebration of the power of love and poetry to move its audience, be it the monsters of Hades or the readers of the *Metamorphoses*. Personal, amorous, a lover-artist in a world in which love ultimately conquers all, this Orpheus mirrors some of the essential poetic aims and qualities of the *Metamorphoses*.

As a potent mythic symbol, Orpheus spans life and death; order and emotionality; animate and inanimate forms; fertility and sterility; man's control over nature and sympathetic fusion with nature; the power of art over death and its futility before death; the malleability of the world to language and the inability of the poet to deal with reality; harmony with natural processes and hopeless protest against the most basic law of existence; the transience of human creation and the yearning for participation in eternal forms. Located at the fringes of the civilized world, the son of the god of order and light or of an obscure Thracian barbarian, he embodies the marginal, "liminal" position that art and the artist, and artful language too, have always held. Akin to the trickster who defeats death by his wiles, he crosses the boundaries not only between life and death and between man and nature, but also between truth and illusion, reality and imagination. His descendants are the bearers of Mozart's Magic Flute or the recurring magician figures in Mann's fiction, Hesse's "Magic Theater" (*Steppenwolf*),

Fellini's *8½*. Like Pygmalion he not only possesses the autonomous power of imagination that allows life to flow into inert matter, but he can also admit his instinctual, erotic life into the domain of his art and thereby transform both.

Underlying all these antinomies is the intimation of a fundamental unity, a mythic vision of the unity between life and death as the inseparable poles of a single reality. It is this unity that enables the Orphic voice to cross from the living to the dead, to move both men and stones. In this respect, as Mircea Eliade has suggested, Orpheus is a manifestation of the "Great Shaman," able to transcend the physical limits of his body, stretch his consciousness to states unknown to most men, and bring a soul back from the realm of the dead. Commenting on the myth in the light ot its (often developed) Christian affinities, Peter Dronke locates its basic and universal meaning in

> the intimation that the here and the beyond are not irrevocably opposed to each other, that they form one world, that one who is endowed with a more-than-human power of vision (expressed in the figure of prophetic, quasi-divine song) or endowed with a more-than-human power of love, can know this greater whole, can pass from here to beyond and back again, and can "redeem" others, giving them this same power, giving them a "new life."[62]

This sense of the wondrous and fearful unity of being is one of the gifts bestowed by language when intensified by the "magic" of Orpheus' power. This aspect of the myth—the drive to transcend the limits of physical matter, but also the imagination and intensity that encompass being and transience in a unitary vision—informs the most significant modern reinterpretation, Rilke's *Sonnets to Orpheus*.

Above all, it is the paradoxes and contradictions inherent in language itself that generate the ambiguities and conflicts in the various versions of the myth: the capacity of poetic language to encompass the unsayable and its futility in the face of ineffable joy, beauty, or suffering; its ability to clarify or to distort; its power of self-transcendence and also of self-deception.

Orpheus and the Fourth *Georgic*
Virgil on Nature and Civilization

I ·

The fundamental theme of Virgil's *Georgics* is the relation between man and nature. Though the poem is ostensibly concerned with giving practical advice to farmers, probably as part of the renewed Augustan interest in the soil and farming, it is far more than a didactic poem in the narrow sense of the term. As any sensitive reader of the *Georgics* will feel, Dryden's celebrated judgment, "the best Poem of the best Poet," is not to be taken lightly. The agricultural instructions are only the framework for the poet's deep exploration of larger matters: the alternation between creativeness and destructiveness, gentleness and force in the world; the pessimistic sense of human sinfulness and the hope for regeneration; the possibilities, positive and negative, for human civilization against the flawed backdrop of human history and the elemental violence of nature's powers.

These relations are expressed in part in certain contrasts of mood between the four books. Hence book 1 ends with a long, gloomy excursus on the Civil Wars, pervaded by a sense of the perversity of human nature and absorbed with sin and expiation.

> satis iam pridem sanguine nostro
> Laomedonteae luimus periuria Troiae.

> Long since have we paid with our blood for the perjuries of Laomedon's Troy. (G.1.501–502)

And it ends with an image of violence unleashed and out of control.

> saevit toto Mars impius orbe;
> ut cum carceribus sese effudere quadrigae,

addunt in spatio, et frustra retinacula tendens
fertur equis auriga neque audit currus habenas.

Wicked Mars rages over the whole world; just as when four-horse
chariots pour forth from the starting gates, they enter the course, and
the charioteer, pulling back on the reins to no avail, is carried along
by the horses, and the chariot pays no heed to the reins. (511–514)

The second book strikes a positive note with its description of a
Golden Age and praise of a simple life of peace, work, reverence. The
third book returns to violence again, with the theme of love, and ends
amid desolation: a scene of winter barrenness and brutality (3.349–383)
and finally a long description of a plague that reduces man to a pre-
civilized condition, leaving him scratching at the earth with bare hands
(*ipsis / unguibus infodiunt fruges*, etc. [3.534ff.]). The fourth book reaffirms order and regeneration with its account of the bee community
as a model of harmony and good government.

In recent years several suggestions have been given for understanding the unity of the four books. Such schemes as Labor (1)–Life (2)–
Love (3)–Law (4) or War–Peace–Death–Resurrection or the balance
between nature's resistance to man in 1 and 3 and her cooperation in 2
and 4 have much to recommend them,[1] although, as always with such
structural analyses, there is a danger of oversimplifying and perhaps
overintellectualizing a rich and complex work of art.

The Fourth *Georgic* has its special problem. Servius, in his commentary on the poem, says that the second half of the book, the
Aristaeus-Orpheus story, was added later by Virgil to replace an earlier
passage that praised Gallus, a close friend and fellow poet of Virgil
who came to a bad end as prefect of Egypt and committed suicide in
27 or 26 B.C. Servius says that Virgil made the change at the orders of
Augustus (*iubente Augusto*). This problem has been one of the most
widely discussed questions in Virgil and unfortunately has deflected
attention away from the crucial issue of the meaning of book 4 (in its
present condition) as a whole. There has been a growing tendency
among scholars, since Eduard Norden lent his great authority to the
idea in 1934,[2] to discount Servius' remarks as an exaggeration and to see
the Aristaeus-Orpheus episode as part of Virgil's original intention.
This position has been carefully and on the whole successfully argued,
and there is no need to rehearse the familiar.[3] Indeed, even if one were
to grant that the Aristaeus-Orpheus portion is a later addition, its
thematic connections with the other books are so just and rich that one

would be almost compelled to the conclusion that the "addition" is a masterstroke that naturally completes the movement of the preceding parts of the poem.

Allowing that Virgil may have made *some* revision after Gallus' disgrace (for Servius' remarks cannot be simply disregarded), possibly the excision of some twenty lines at most,[4] we must recognize that the poet still let the book be published as it stands. And we should not forget that Virgil was a perfectionist (he worked for seven years on the *Georgics*, a poem of little over two thousand lines), a poet intensely concerned with structural relationships, thoughtful and infinitely suggestive contrasts and balances. There is no question in the *Georgics*, as there is in the *Aeneid*, of editorial bungling and posthumous publication. The poem was given to the public as Virgil wanted it to appear. And finally the structural complexity of the work is too great, Virgil's sense of "architecture" already too well developed, to permit us to think that the work was not meant so to stand and that the contrasts and structural difficulties it contains (or seems to contain) were not intended to be significant.

Why then does Virgil juxtapose the Aristaeus-Orpheus episode with his account of the bees, and why has he chosen to end the work in this way? In what sense is book 4 a unity, and how does that unity reflect on the entire poem?[5] These are the questions to which I shall address myself here. As I hope will appear, these questions are of some importance—*res est non parva*—for on them turn the larger questions of the tone and meaning of the poem as a whole and hence of Virgil's views on man's place in the frame of nature and the value and difficulty of man's higher achievements, of civilization itself.

II ·

More than any of the three previous books, the Fourth *Georgic* is only marginally concerned with practical advice per se. The significance of the bees lies, as H. Dahlmann has shown, in their similarity to and difference from man and man's political community.[6] The metaphor that describes bee society in terms of human society is the controlling element of the first half of the book. But here emerges the significance of the second half: bees are *not* men; the metaphor does not hold. And where the metaphor gives way, the human narrative, with human values and human suffering, breaks through.

Hence the selfless and sexless love of the bees contrasts with the passionate and all-absorbing love that man can feel. The bees' *amor* is aimed entirely at productivity (*amor . . . habendi* [177]; *tantus amor florum et generandi gloria mellis,* "so much love of flowers and glory of creating honey" [*G.4.205*]). Even procreation is seen in terms of this productivity. There is no passion, only work: *neque concubitu indulgent, nec corpora segnes / in Venerem solvunt,* "They neither take pleasure in lying together, nor do they sluggishly loosen their bodies for Venus" (198–199). The adjective *segnes* is significant: Venus, sexual desire, would make them "sluggish," prevent them from work. And as they remain free of the involvements of sexual reproduction, so death holds no tragedy for them.

> ergo ipsas quamvis angusti terminus aevi
> excipiat (neque enim plus septima ducitur aestas),
> at genus immortale manet, multosque per annos
> stat fortuna domus, et avi numerantur avorum.

> Therefore though but the limit of a narrow lifetime contains them (for their age does not reach beyond a seventh summer), still the race remains, immortal, and over many years the fortune of the house stands strong, and the grandfathers of grandfathers are counted. (206–209)

Bees, then, are totally reconciled to their function. Their lives subserve the ends of nature. Human as they may seem to be, they look not beyond these aims.

But the tragedy of Orpheus in the second part of the book is the tragedy of man and the tragedy of civilization. Unlike the bees, man cannot reconcile himself to the conditions of life and nature, does not accept the fundamental facts of existence, challenges death itself, even then loses the fruits of his victory because of *dementia* and *furor* (488, 495), yet is still unreconciled, still finds the laws of nature brutal, unfeeling, unjust: *ignoscenda quidem, scirent si ignoscere manes,* "Things worthy of pardon, if the shades knew how to pardon" (489). And for man the disappearance of sexual desire marks not a wholehearted accord with nature's purposes but despair and death: *nulla Venus, non ulli animum flexere hymenaei,* "No Venus, no marriage rites turned his mind" (516). This line, of the doomed Orpheus, stands in pointed contrast to the happy activity and chaste energies of the bees: *nec corpora segnes / in Venerem solvunt,* "They do not loosen their bodies for Venus" (198–199). Instead of the unindividuated confidence in the *genus immortale,* we meet in Orpheus an individual, deeply human, who loves, suffers, dies. And what survives him is precisely that which arises out of his suffering and his love, the cry after his lost beloved that echoes over the natural world, the world that, as always, outlasts human grief.

> tum quoque marmorea caput a cervice revulsum
> gurgite cum medio portans Oeagrius Hebrus
> volveret, Eurydicen vox ipsa et frigida lingua
> a miseram Eurydicen! anima fugiente vocabat:
> Eurydicen toto referebant flumine ripae.

> Then too, when the Oeagrian Hebrus carrying [him] whirled in the middle of its stream the head torn away from the marble neck, the voice and cold tongue cried out "Eurydice," as his life-breath fled, "Ah, unhappy Eurydice"; "Eurydice" reechoed the banks along the entire stream. (523–527)

If looked at in these terms, the Orpheus episode takes on a larger significance and raises the difficult question, which interpreters of the poem have not generally asked, namely, to what extent does Virgil's ending qualify the poem's persistent hope for the reconciliation between passion and work, *amor* and *labor*.

Brooks Otis makes the excellent observation of the difference between the styles of the Orpheus and the Aristaeus sections of the second half of the book: the style of the *Orpheus* is "empathetic," full of feeling and sympathy; that of the *Aristaeus* is objective, less emotional, less personally involved and involving.[7] But Otis does not draw from his analysis the logical conclusion, that is, that Virgil means us to sympathize deeply with Orpheus as we do not with Aristaeus. It is not just that tragedy is more moving than success, but that the sufferings of Orpheus touch upon the greater complexities of the human condition and hence raise deeper questions. Aristaeus is still vaguely akin to the world of nature, to the bees he rears and regards as the glory and pride of human life (*ipsum vitae mortalis honorem* [326]). He completes the purposes of nature and is helped by its elemental powers: the sea- and river-gods to whom he is akin and even Proteus, the possessor of the *miracula rerum* (441), the things that are wondrous in the world.

Orpheus, on the other hand, is distinctly and nakedly human. No mention, in his case, of divine parentage or divine aid. He takes on himself, alone, both action and atonement. Aristaeus does almost nothing unaided and has to be told, *magna luis commissa*, "Great are the crimes you are to expiate" (454). Not only do we "not quite realize," as Otis observes, "the crime of Aristaeus,"[8] but we are left to wonder whether *Aristaeus himself* realizes it.

This sharp contrast between the two heroes helps account for the difficult ending of the Orpheus section. Proteus concludes his account of Orpheus in line 527, and Virgil at once resumes the Aristaeus story in his own person.

> Haec Proteus, at se iactu dedit aequor in altum,
> quaque dedit, spumantem undam sub vertice torsit.
> At non Cyrene; namque ultro adfata timentem:
> "Nate, licet tristis animo deponere curas. . . . "

> So much Proteus [spoke], and he leapt into the deep sea, and where he leapt he sent the water foaming up under his eddying plunge. But not Cyrene; for she at once addressed her frightened son: "My child, you may put sad cares out of your mind. . . . " (528–531)

The abruptness of the transition has puzzled many critics. But may not this abruptness be intentional? The syntactically awkward "But not Cyrene" (530) (which even Otis thinks a mark of unskilful or incomplete revision)[9] would then be part of this deliberate contrast, this intention to make the difference between the two heroes and their two descents—one into life, the other into death—as sharp and harsh as possible. Orpheus, the fully human figure, is left his full measure of suffering. Aristaeus is hastily protected from grief (531), told that the Nymphs are easily amenable to supplication (535–536), and given the necessary instructions (537–547): which he speedily (*haud mora*, [548]) and efficiently carries out (548ff.). That is all we hear of Aristaeus; and at once, with the bursting out of the bees as from a womb,

> liquefacta boum per viscera toto
> stridere apes utero et ruptis effervere costis,
> immensasque *trahi nubes,*

> through the liquefied vitals of the oxen, in the entire womb, the bees buzzed and seethed forth from the broken sides, and were borne aloft in vast clouds (555–557)

we are back in the first half of the book, amid the tireless, mysterious, determined cycle of nature's life and processes.

> hinc ubi iam emissum caveis ad sidera caeli
> nare per aestatem liquidam suspexeris agmen

obscuramque *trahi vento mirabere nubem*,
contemplator.

Here when you look up to see the swarm, issuing forth from its
hollows to the heaven's stars, and wonder at the dim cloud being
borne aloft on the wind, stand and behold. (58–61)

This significant verbal echoing between the two halves of book 4 is
only one of many links between them.

III ·

The contrast between Orpheus and Aristaeus, then, is crucial to the
broader meanings of the Fourth *Georgic* and of the *Georgics* as a whole.
On these two center the recurrent themes of the poem: the interplay
between man's control over nature and nature's independence—often
destructive independence—from man. In them meets and culminates
the poem's opposition between work and wonder; and from this
opposition derives a still more pervasive tension, both stylistic and
thematic, in the *Georgics*, that between practical advice and poetical
description, toil and beauty. Hence of the two heroes, the one is an
agricultural figure, a *pastor*, and, according to the literary tradition, an
agricultural god; the other is an artist, indeed the artist *par excellence*,
often used by Virgil himself in the *Eclogues* as the symbolic prototype
of the poet (see *Ecl.* 3, 46; 4, 55; 6, 27–30 and 82ff.).

But these oppositions are brought together only in a third person. It
is through the traditionally elusive figure of Proteus that the two
heroes confront each other symbolically in the narrative, that their
separate and opposed destinies are interwoven. Proteus is an evasive
but essential key to the poem, indeed more important than most
commentators have seen. In order to understand book 4 fully, we must
here consider his role and character.

As far as the narrative itself is concerned, Proteus is really super-
fluous.[10] Aristaeus' mother, Cyrene, does indeed say (398) that Proteus
will give *praecepta*, the needed practical instructions. But, as has been
seen above, he leaps abruptly away at the crucial moment (527ff.), and
it is Cyrene who in fact gives the *praecepta* (531ff.), which forthwith
prove their efficacy. Thus Cyrene has known what to do all along. She
has not needed Proteus at all.

Virgil, then, has another reason for introducing Proteus and making
him the narrator of the moving tale of Orpheus. First, obviously, Aris-

taeus is required thus to prove himself by a difficult ordeal. But, more important, Proteus' role as narrator sets him in different relations to Aristaeus and Orpheus respectively. To Aristaeus, by whom he has been forced to speak, he stands in the relation of an accuser, almost a judge; and his first words are words of accusation, a demand for atonement.

> Non te nullius exercent numinis irae;
> magna luis commissa: tibi has miserabilis Orpheus
> haudquaquam ob meritum poenas, ni fata resistant,
> suscitat, et rapta graviter pro coniuge saevit.

> The wrath of some divinity drives you; great are the crimes that you atone. Against you Orpheus, woeful for reasons he did not deserve, is stirring up these punishments—(and they would be fearful) unless the fates should resist, and rages heavily for his wife who was snatched away. (453–456).

Toward Orpheus, on the other hand—*miserabilis Orpheus* is, significantly, Proteus' way of introducing him—he is warmly sympathetic and full of pity, an admirer, and a vindicator of his rights. Here, then, emerges the significance of the different styles—the "empathetic" and the "objective"—of the two narratives.

Proteus' divided relationship takes on further meaning in the light of his symbolic associations, both those inherent in his figure and those Virgil has particularly exploited. The mysterious, symbolic aura around him goes back to the *Odyssey*; and if any figure in the *Georgics* is symbolic, it is he. He seems to occupy a middle ground between god and animal and to exist in a realm between myth and nature. He is connected with the primal forces of nature, and like them he is ambiguously both helpful and recalcitrant. He is a god, held in the highest reverence, endowed with profound and mysterious knowledge, a seer and a prophet.

> hunc et Nymphae veneramur et ipse
> grandaevus Nereus: novit namque omnia vates,
> quae sint, quae fuerint, quae mox ventura trahantur.

> We Nymphs adore him, and so does aged Nereus himself, for as a prophet he knows all things, those which are and which were and which are to come. (391–393)

As a *vates*, a word meaning "poet" as well as "seer," he has some affinity with Orpheus, the inspired poet. Yet he belongs to the animal world too: he seeks shelter in caves (429), companionably pastures his foul-smelling seals (395), and dwells with "the wet tribe of the vast sea" (*vasti circum gens umida ponti* [430]). His ability to change into the basic substances of fire and water connects him with nature's elemental processes.

> omnia transformat sese in miracula rerum,
> ignemque horribilemque feram fluviumque liquentem.

> He changes himself into all the wonders of things, fire and a fearful wild beast and a flowing stream. (441–442).

These *miracula rerum* (a deliberately ambiguous and suggestive phrase) are perhaps to be associated with the wonder of life that surrounds the bees in the first part of the book (see *admiranda spectacula rerum* [3]; *mirabere* [60 and 197], etc.).[11]

Proteus, then, has about him something of the ambiguity, wonder, ungraspable mystery of life itself. One should not try to give too narrow or definite an interpretation to his role, for his dominant characteristic, after all, is changefulness of shape; and only bold and desperate heroes have sought to lay hold of him until he should return to his true and enduring form.

It is this mysterious figure whom Aristaeus is commanded to force. He is explicitly told that he must use violence.

> nam sine *vi* non ulla dabit praecepta, neque illum
> orando flectes; *vim* duram et vincula capto
> tende; doli circum haec demum frangentur inanes.

> For without force he will give no instructions, nor will you bend him by prayer. Use hard force and chains when he is caught. Only then at last will his wiles be broken and become empty. (398–400)

The language of the attack itself puts the reader on the side of Proteus rather than of the hero. Virgil seems sympathetic to Proteus and emphasizes the violence done him: he is old and tired, and the youthful attacker's *clamor* comes abruptly and harshly upon his midday rest.

> cuius Aristaeo quoniam est oblata facultas,
> vix *defessa senem* passus componere membra
> cum *clamore* ruit *magno*, manicisque *iacentem*
> occupat.

When the opportunity presented itself to Aristaeus, scarcely permitting the old man to settle his weary limbs, he rushes on him with a great shouting and, as he lies there, clasps him in chains. (437–440)

And the calm of the preceding simile (433–435), the comparison of the seals to sheep bleating in their mountain steading toward evening, makes Aristaeus even more of the violent and pitiless intruder.

Proteus' first words are in keeping with this tone of outraged peace, for he calls Aristaeus *iuvenum confidentissime* (445), "O most audacious of youths" (*confidens* seems to have a predominantly negative, rather than positive, sense from the time of Cicero). There is a subtle economy of narrative here, for Virgil, in showing us Aristaeus in action against Proteus, perhaps points retrospectively to that same quality of boldness, enterprise, trust in his power to act and compel that led him to pursue Eurydice and indirectly caused her death. Virgil tells us very little of Aristaeus' crime—the crime for which he is consulting Proteus—scarcely more than that Eurydice "fled from him headlong" (*dum te fugeret per flumina praeceps* [457]) and in her flight was bitten fatally by the snake. Yet the sketchy indication of Aristaeus' *confidentia* in the Proteus episode is enough to provide a delicate hint at a quality of mind that separates him from Orpheus.

Aristaeus' treatment of Proteus, then, has larger ramifications within the framework of the *Georgics*. Aristaeus is the man of work and action; and his attack upon Proteus symbolically reflects man's confidently active effect upon the quiet and mysterious powers of nature, the realm of the *miracula rerum* wherein Proteus exists (441).

Orpheus, on the other hand, stands at the opposite pole from Aristaeus in his gentler relation to the world. He makes no attempt to use nature for his own ends, to work upon it. His task as poet is not work, but beauty; not control, but sympathy. This difference is essential to the meaning of the Fourth *Georgic*. It is strongly and beautifully conveyed in the simile of the grieving nightingale to which Virgil, toward the end of his narrative, compares the mourning Orpheus.

> qualis populea maerens philomela sub umbra
> amissos queritur fetus, quos durus arator
> observans nido implumis detraxit; at illa
> flet noctem, ramoque sedens miserabile carmen
> integrat, et maestis late loca questibus implet.

> Just as the nightingale, grieving beneath a poplar's shade, laments its
> lost offspring which a hard farmer, seeing them in the nest, carries
> away, unfledged as they are; but she weeps all night and sitting on
> a branch renews her mournful cry and fills the places far and wide
> with her sorrowful plaints. (511–515)

The second and third lines (512–513) are especially significant, for the
bird is seen as a victim of man's vigilant and unfeeling work upon
nature, a victim of the *durus arator*.[12] Hence Orpheus, through the bird
simile, reveals a perspective on the world different from that of Aristaeus. He shows us the relation between man and nature from the
point of view of *nature*, not man. Through him animate nature, given
a voice, renders back the nature-centered, not the man-centered view
of things. So it is that even at his death Orpheus stands in a special
intimacy with the natural world: the river carries his head and the
banks reecho his lament (523–527).

Yet it is Proteus, the wise and far-seeing narrator, the *vates*, who is
the fulcrum for this basic difference between the two mortal heroes
and the attitudes they embody. In his symbolic connection with the
primal quietudes of life, he is violated by the bold and demanding
energies of the man of work and productivity, *pastor Aristaeus*.

From Aristaeus Orpheus is strongly differentiated by his "unpro-
ductive" way of life, his gentler relation to the world, and the implications of the nightingale simile. And not only is he not connected with
productivity, but he is soon to relinquish entirely that concern with life
and procreation which it is Aristaeus' concern to foster (*nulla Venus,
non ulli . . . hymenaei*, "No Venus, no marriage rites turned his mind"
[516]). He too, like Proteus, like his own Eurydice, like the nightingale,
is a victim of Aristaeus and what Aristaeus stands for: he suffers from
man's aggressive behavior toward his world.

But Orpheus' sufferings are not due entirely to Aristaeus. He too is
expiating a wrong of sorts that he has committed. Indeed, that part of
his own nature which is active, restless, demanding, is the cause of his
deepest unhappiness. In the *dementia* and *furor* that cause him to look
back and hence lose Eurydice (488, 495), he shows his kinship (faint
though it may be) with Aristaeus: a lack of that quiet trust in the
processes of nature which plants and animals have. Aristaeus, with all
his rashness—and in part *because of* this rashness—still has perhaps
something of this trust, a trust that befits an Arcadian shepherd and is
the positive side of his *confidentia*. Hence he succeeds in his attempted

"rebirth" (the regeneration of the bees) as Orpheus fails in his (the revival of Eurydice).

There seems at first to be a contradiction here, but it is a contradiction inherent in the nature of things, one that Virgil does not oversimplify. It is the essence of his mythic form that it enables the poet to present life's eternally conjoined polarities in all the truth of their complexity. Mythic poetry of this caliber celebrates life's generous and mysterious wholeness: life embraces and surmounts the opposites it contains.

So it is with the contrasts between Orpheus and Aristaeus. There is, on the one hand, the saving simplicity in Aristaeus' *confidentia* that manifested itself earlier in his boyish complaint about the dead bees (326–332). And what he is asking is, after all, in accordance with nature's laws, the alternation of death and regeneration, barrenness and fruitfulness. Orpheus, the more complex and inward figure (Virgil significantly keeps him silent, save for his final *a miseram Eurydicen* [526]) makes demands that are counter to these laws. Aristaeus' rashness and energy, then, are still ultimately in the service of nature. Orpheus, more fully human and hence more tragic, seeks the fulfilment only of an intensely personal, peculiarly human need – the passionate and individualistic love from which Aristaeus' bees, nature's most efficient creatures, are singularly free (197ff.).

Through the contrast with Aristaeus, then, Orpheus is linked, also for contrast, with the bees of the first half of the book. Aristaeus and the bees on the one side, Orpheus on the other stand in a complementary relation: Orpheus' *amor* does not further nature's aims of reproduction. He has *amor* without procreation, a peculiarly human, inward and soulful form of *amor*; the bees have procreation without *amor* (in the human sense).

Yet the sad fate of Orpheus and the *furor* and *dementia* associated with him (488, 495) indicate that Virgil's attitude is more complex. Neither Aristaeus nor Orpheus is a faultless model for the right relation to nature. Indeed the Ciconian matrons who tear Orpheus apart are not condemned outright. The narrative suggests shock and horror, to be sure, but not condemnation.

> spretae Ciconum quo munere matres
> inter sacra deum nocturnique orgia Bacchi
> discerptum latos iuvenem sparsere per agros.

The mothers of the Ciconians, scorned in this office, tore him apart
amid the sacred rites of the god and the revels of nighttime Bacchus
and scattered the torn youth far and wide over the fields. (520–522)

The *matres* (and the fact that they are *matres* is significant in the light of
the key theme of reproduction and the continuity of life) do not simply
commit murder: they perform a religious act of a sort (*inter sacra deum,*
etc. [521]) and vindicate nature's laws. The question of condemnation
does not arise, for they are instruments of nature's irrepressible surge.
Hence they reveal too the brutality and horrifying elemental force with
which nature can reclaim its own.

There is perhaps another implicit criticism of Orpheus' behavior in
the lines that immediately precede this description of his death.

nulla Venus, non ulli animum flexere hymenaei:
solus Hyperboreas glacies Tanaimque nivalem
arvaque Riphaeis numquam viduata pruinis
lustrabat.

No Venus, no marriage rites turned his mind: in solitude he roved
over the Hyperborean ice and the snowy Tanais and the fields that
were never widowed of the Riphaean frosts. (516–519)

The juxtaposition of *nulla Venus* and the barren winter waste is suggestive. Orpheus' rejection of Venus, the life force, associates him with
the sterility of winter. It is into the desolate wintry landscape that he
goes to escape Venus and to live out his own "widowed" life (note
viduata, of the snowy fields [518]). The passage recalls the powerful
description of winter in book 3 (3.349–383), especially lines 381–382.

talis Hyperboreo septem subiecta trioni
gens effrena virum Riphaeo tunditur Euro.

Such was this savage race of men, placed beneath the Hyperborean
North Star, beaten by the Riphaean wind.

The contrast between the life and activity of book 4 and this lifeless
inertia of book 3 is one of the important structural contrasts of the
poem. Hence Virgil, without suggesting anything so strong or specific
as that Orpheus' attitude may bring a recurrence of such barrenness,
yet points to a subtle connection between an aspect of Orpheus and
the harshness and barrenness from which book 4 has moved away.

Neither Aristaeus nor Orpheus, then, represents in himself a fully
valid image of man in his relation with his world. The ideal lies, if

anywhere, in a balance between them. But Virgil is seeking not to define an ideal, but to state a basic reality. And over against both Orpheus and Aristaeus, the two men who have such different relations to nature, stand the bees of the first half of the book, full of self-restraint and self-sacrifice, partaking, with unthinking and untroubled instinct, of the given morality of nature. What emerges is the sense of the complexity of man between the two extremes of Aristaeus and Orpheus, external effectiveness in the realm of nature and devotion to man's peculiar inward capacities: emotion, art, love.

If this analysis of the differences between Orpheus and Aristaeus is valid, there appears another explanation for the apparent contradiction in the narrative. Proteus, it will be recalled, tells Aristaeus that he must expiate his crime against Orpheus (4.453ff.); but Cyrene, who gives the actual *praecepta* (530ff.; cf. 398), says nothing of Orpheus and mentions only the anger of the Nymphs (*irasque remittent* [536]; cf. Proteus' *irae . . . Orpheus* [453–455]). Is it again possible that this change is intentional? If so, what purpose does it serve?

The answer suggested by the foregoing analysis is that Virgil at the end wishes to separate the two heroes whose fates have become so closely intertwined in Proteus' narrative. Aristaeus, who reaches an accord with nature's aims, is not, ultimately, to be pulled down by the suffering and unreconciled humanity of Orpheus. Life as work and possibility will not be destroyed by life as tragedy. The positive attainments of *labor* will not be canceled by the negative effects of *amor*. Hence Cyrene, the beneficent goddess-mother, reenacts her sheltering role and keeps her son from a final confrontation with the tragedy of Orpheus. She performs for her son what her Homeric counterpart and literary ancestor, Thetis, cannot do for hers. Hence she mentions the appeasement of Orpheus only late in her instructions and almost parenthetically (545; cf. 553). Instead, she turns the narrative away from tragic loss and failure, the underworld descent, mortality and death, to the Nymphs, the happy and fruitful powers of life, and to nature, which restores and repairs without brooding over the past. Thus her reappearance (530ff.), though technically contradicting the pronouncement of the mysterious and ambiguous Proteus (542ff.), marks a return to a positive and hopeful future.

Yet there is still the contradiction, still no full resolution of the dissonances implied in Proteus' narrative. We are still reminded at the very end that the bees' rebirth takes place out of violence, putrefaction, death: "The bees buzzed over the whole womb throughout the *lique-*

fied vitals of the cows and *bursting* the sides swarmed out" (liquefacta *boum per viscera toto / stridere apes utero et* ruptis *effervere costis* [555–556]). Characteristically Virgil leaves us with the full complexity of the situation. This is part of his deep truthfulness and his greatness. How should the poet, after all, resolve what life does not?

It may be helpful to sum up here the implications of our results for the *Georgics* as a whole. Far from being an irrelevant digression, the Aristaeus-Orpheus episode is intimately connected with the poem's main themes. In a sense it appears as *necessary* to complete the *Georgics*, for it ties together, with the complexity demanded by the subject itself, the delicate and complicated relations between human aggression and nature's resistance or acquiescence; between human destructiveness and nature's creativeness (and the reverse); between man's power over nature and nature's power over man. And while both Aristaeus and Orpheus have, as men, some measure of control over and independence from nature, both are united as parts of nature's realm in their participation in the renewal of life, the most mysterious and least humanly controllable (as both learn) of nature's processes.

IV ·

Despite the apparently limited frame of the *Georgics*, then, their riches and complexities are profound, and Virgil already exhibits that depth and fineness of insight that characterize the *Aeneid*. In the Fourth *Georgic*, in fact, he is already dealing with some of the issues of the *Aeneid*. To equate Aristaeus with the active Augustan ruler and Orpheus with the poet or artist is an oversimplification (though it is with this contrast – the poet in his leisure, Augustus winning battles and giving laws – that Virgil ends the *Georgics*). But the *Aeneid* too is concerned with the delicate balances between inner life and external effect on the world, there rephrased in part to a contrast between humanity and duty. In the single character of Aeneas, Virgil fuses together (though does not always resolve) the opposites that in the *Georgics* are separated into two in the figures of Orpheus and Aristaeus. The Aeneas who suffers loss and through loss feels the inestimable preciousness of his human ties, the precariousness of life, the futility of success without love – the Aeneas who comes to sense the *lacrimae rerum,* "tears for things," and who describes (in lines partly taken from the *Orpheus* of the Fourth *Georgic*) the pain of his final parting from his wife, a disappearing ghost now infinitely beyond him, *par levibus ventis volucrique simillima somno,* "like to the light winds, most resembling winged sleep" (Aen. 2.794)—this Aeneas is foreshadowed in Orpheus. But the Aeneas who is aided by his goddess-mother, who confidently lifts the shield of Rome's destiny on his shoulders (8.731), who at the end seems to submerge his *humanitas* in the act of bloodshed that seals the success of his mission—this Aeneas is anticipated in Aristaeus.

And just as Virgil in the Fourth *Georgic* has separated what is later to be fused with greater complexity into a single figure, so his style is divided: the heroic, "objective" style of success, Homeric achievement and impact on the world for Aristaeus; the subjective, "empathetic" style for the private tragedy and aloneness of Orpheus. It is the essence of Virgil's *humanitas* that he gives us both figures, just as he gives both Aeneases. If one may paraphrase a modern parable, the two figures, the successful hero and the tragic lover and poet, the hero who serves destiny and mankind and the individual who suffers within himself, are "two locked caskets, of which each contains the key to the other."[13]

The Fourth *Georgic,* then, poses the question to be put more sharply and more profoundly in the *Aeneid:* the question of happiness for a being whose life moves both in an inner and an outer world, the value of success in the service of nature or destiny as weighed against the continual losses within the personal realm—losses of loved ones, friends, feeling itself—losses that are the price of conquest and achievement.[14] In contrasting the two journeys and the two styles, Virgil suggests the largeness and complexity of man's condition both as a creature of the natural world and as a being endowed with an inner life; both as a creature who furthers nature's ends, throws himself into the struggle for life, and as a being who negates those ends by his equal capability for unreasoning passion and for love, art, devotion.[15] But, more profoundly, what the Orpheus-Aristaeus episode does is to suggest—and Virgil's way is always to suggest—that human life framed between the two figures may be *essentially* tragic. And here emerges the significance of the first half of the book, the bees: instead of collectively selflessly devoted to the *genus immortale,* we have in the second part individuals engaged in their personal emotions almost to the exclusion of everything else, individuals who not only do not continue the race but themselves die when their intensely personal passion is frustrated. Even Aristaeus feels the loss of his bees with an intensity that blindly blots out the rest of life, throws to the winds nature's demand for continuity and self-preservation.

> quin age et ipsa manu felicis erue silvas,
> fer stabulis inimicum ignem atque interfice messis,
> ure sata et validam in vitis molire bipennem,
> tanta meae si te ceperunt taedia laudis.

> Go on then, and uproot the fertile forests with your own hand, bring hostile fire to the stables and destroy the harvest, burn the crops and ply the strong ax against the vines if such weary unconcern about my honor has taken hold of you. (329–332)

If Aristaeus is seen from this point of view, the differences between him and Orpheus become less than the difference between both of them, taken together as men, and the world of the bees.

This thematic contrast of man and bees involves also a stylistic contrast between the two main halves of the book, analogous to that within the second half itself: the language of the first half is highly Lucretian; that of the second, more Homeric and characteristically Virgilian.[16] The difference suits the contrast between the sure, unquestioned, eager fulfillment of nature's processes and the feeling realm of humanity with its passions, hesitations, failures. This difference corresponds also to that between the light and humorous tone of the first half of the book and the tragic coloring of the second half. It is a contrast between the didactic and the mythic styles, but with a curious inversion: the "real" world of bees and practical instruction is lively and happy; the "ideal" world of myth and poetry is filled with death and disaster. Yet this "poetic" world is simultaneously the highest point artistically to which the *Georgics* attain; and, as Otis has suggested, the emotional, "empathetic" coloring of the Orpheus episode is a kind of stylistic culmination of the work. But the price of feeling is separation from nature, challenge of its laws, refusal to heed the universal demand for the preservation and continuity of life.

It is curious then, that Virgil should end the *Georgics* with the alienation from nature that man's very humanity creates. This alienation is anticipated in the ending of book 3, where a subhuman brutality brings a fearful coarsening of the relation between man and nature (see 3.373–380).[17] Book 4 carries the problem to a profounder level, to the question of whether such a separation may not be inherent in the nature and condition of man. To have arrived at this view and then to

look back at the simple and joyful world of the *Eclogues* in the closing
lines of the *Georgics* is a touch of poetic genius.

> illo Vergilium me tempore dulcis alebat
> Parthenope studiis florentem ignobilis oti,
> carmina qui lusi pastorum audaxque iuventa
> Tityre, te patulae cecini sub tegmine fagi.

> At that time sweet Parthenope (Naples) nurtured me, Virgil, as I
> flourished in the pursuits of unheroic idleness, I who played at the
> songs of shepherds and bold in my youth "sang of you, Tityrus,
> beneath the covering of a spreading beech." (4.363–366)

The poet who could confide in that trustful and easy interchange
between man and nature that characterizes the pastoral view looks
back on himself from the higher, but more somber and clouded
vantage point of the *Georgics* as indeed *audax iuventa*.

This more personal and gentle ending mitigates the tragic and negative elements in book 4, as does, to be sure, the success of Aristaeus'
atonement. But the irreconcilables, the unbridgeable gulf between soul
and instinct, nevertheless remain. They give the poem a perhaps more
pessimistic coloring than many commentators would admit.[18] All is not
confidence in Augustan renascence. Pessimism, however, is too crude
and inadequate a word. It is rather that a deep perception of an eternal
truth underlies and qualifies whatever hope for the specific, immediate
present the poem seems to contain. Otis has suggested that we can
regard the four books as contrasting movements of a musical composition:[19] allegro maestoso – scherzo – adagio – allegro vivace. The analogy is suggestive, but perhaps we should more fittingly label the final
movement allegro, ma non troppo.[20]

3

Ovid's Orpheus and
Augustan Ideology

I ·

Precisely where Ovid seems most Virgilian does one best grasp what is most characteristically Ovidian in him. This observation of Franz Bömer is nowhere so true as in Ovid's handling of the story of Orpheus and Eurydice and of Orpheus' death (*Met.* 10.1–85; 11.1–66).[1]

Curiously enough, most critics of Ovid have been unenthusiastic about this episode. Even so sensitive a lover of Ovid as Hermann Fränkel confessed that "from my boyhood days I have never responded to it."[2] To an Italian critic who made a close study of the episode in the two poets, Ovid seemed to lack "the accent of sincerity,"[3] to suffer from "the conventionalism of imitation ," and to have rendered Virgil's narrative "emptied of content and impoverished."[4] Brooks Otis has rightly resisted regarding the episode "simply as an instance of Ovid's woeful inferiority to a great poet," but he does not credit him with aiming at anything more substantial than "parody and comedy."[5]

There is little doubt that Ovid deliberately dissolves the "high ethos" of Virgil into lower terms.[6] Yet, as Bömer observes, Ovid is not merely a poet of the *pueriles ineptiae* with which Seneca reproached him; he is also, as Seneca appreciated, *poetarum ingeniosissimus.*[7]

It was Eduard Norden who most fully realized that Ovid's divergences from Virgil in the treatment of Orpheus did not just result from his lack of Virgil's "tragic ethos"[8] but stemmed from a deliberate intention to challenge Virgil's style and outlook with his own.[9] Yet Norden examined only a few lines in each episode, and his criticism remained largely negative. He censured Ovid's "lack of participation in the material and in the bearers of the [mythical] events."[10] His touchstone was still the high pathos and heroic suffering of the classical tradition, and hence Ovid's restriction of "participation" appeared as a fault. He did not entertain the possibility that Ovid was deliberately setting out to be "anticlassical" and antiheroic.[11]

This possibility merits serious consideration. Ovid may be taking a special delight in filling the Virgilian outline with a spirit that directly challenges the lofty, tragic style that Virgil created for the Roman epic.[12] As he does later in the story of Aeneas in book 14, Ovid challenges Virgil on his own ground, with his own material. In the Orpheus episode, it is not only the heroic style and the solemnity of tragic suffering and conflict that draw his fire, but also the self-importance of sacrifice and devotion to vast, transcendent purposes. Ovid continues a direction in Roman literature firmly established by Catullus and continued by Horace (or one side of Horace) and the elegists. Here the individual voices his claims to privacy, autonomy, and even to inactivity and directionlessness.

On this view, Ovid is a poet in revolt. The revolt is subtle, and its weapons are wit and irony; but it is none the less real, as Augustus seems to have recognized when he exiled the poet to Tomi. As Leo Curran has written, Ovid recognized the "fluidity, the breaking down of boundaries, lack of restraint, the imminent potentiality of reversion to chaos, the uncontrollable variety of nature, the unruliness of human passion, sexual and personal freedom, and hedonism."[13] He seeks to vindicate individual sentiment and the individual emotional life. He is aware of the chaos to which the passions may lead. And yet erotic love is not all destructive *furor*, as it tends to be in Virgil. Rather, it has a valid place in a world where the person runs the risk of being crushed by a vast, impersonal order. That risk, already subtly and fleetingly hinted at by Virgil, is far more ominous in Ovid.

In Virgil's *Georgics* the story of Orpheus is a tragedy of human passion. Man disobeys the inexorable laws of nature and suffers accordingly. The cosmic order is a major theme in the *Georgics*, and the story of Orpheus itself is part of a larger frame that exemplifies that order, the eternal cycle of death and rebirth, reflected in the loss and recovery of Aristaeus' bees. Aristaeus and Orpheus are complementary figures. The one is devoted to productive work and the continuity of the species upon which depends his glory as a herdsman-farmer (*pastor Aristaeus* [G.4.317-332]). The other is a poet, devoted to his emotional life and given over to his passions. Virgil's two figures, however, have one thing in common: both pay a penalty for yielding to passion. Aristaeus loses his bees after his amorous pursuit of Eurydice causes her death (453-459). Orpheus loses Eurydice when his love leads him to yield to *dementia* and *furor* (488, 495): he disobeys Proserpina's "law" (487) and makes the fateful backward glance. Virgil is sympathetic toward Orpheus but at the same time leaves it clear that Orpheus' passion is culpable and his suffering merited.

It is the presence of a stable, unbending world order that gives Virgil's Orpheus episode its tragic quality. To violate this order is to invite suffering. The consequences are almost automatic, inevitable. In conveying this sense of inevitability, Virgil is the heir of the great tragic poets of Greece.

Ovid's world is very different. There is no sure and stable divine order, or, if there is, its orderliness and objectivity are highly questionable. This world is full of capricious and arbitrary divine powers, easily aroused to love or to wrath, capable now of inflicting sudden and terrible punishments, now of bestowing unexpected, miraculous blessings. The gods' generosity appears in the tales of Iphis and of Pygmalion, which stand in close proximity to that of Orpheus.[14] In such a world human guilt and human responsibility for suffering are reduced, although they are not completely removed. There are still moral laws, and their violation brings punishment, as in the tales of the Cerastae, the Propoetides, Myrrha, Atalanta, which all follow shortly upon that of Orpheus and Eurydice.[15] Yet the suddenness with which lives are turned upside down and the fabulous or mysterious quality in the metamorphoses with which every episode necessarily concludes greatly weaken the firmness of this moral order.

Ovid's Orpheus episode, like Virgil's, is still a tale of human folly, but in a different way. Ovid replaces the heroic and tragic *humanitas* of Virgil with a humbler, less heroic *humanitas*. It is no less compassionate than Virgil's, but it operates on a smaller scale and in a lower key, and it makes greater concessions to the foibles and weaknesses and also to the needs of individual life.

Whereas Virgil's *Orpheus* concludes a poem in which the order and rhythms of nature are a major theme, Ovid sets his *Orpheus* into a context that virtually destroys Virgil's firm cosmic order, for he frames it by the miraculous tales of Iphis and Pygmalion. Correspondingly, the gods and the underworld in Ovid's narrative appear as far less stern or awesome. Finally, Ovid draws Orpheus himself in more human terms. He emphasizes not tragic *furor* but the strength of his love. He also gives his hero a fuller private life. Ovid's Orpheus does not merely reject women, as Virgil's figure does, but turns instead to homosexual love affairs (*Met.* 10.83–85). Hence Ovid breaks down the finality of

Virgil's tale, as is to be expected in his *carmen perpetuum*. The *Metamorphoses* allows the erotic life of Orpheus to continue, albeit on a path different from before.

The homosexual adventures of Ovid's Orpheus have a necessary structural function, as Otis and Simone Viarre have pointed out: they link his tale with the stories of Cyparissus and Hyacinthus that follow.[16] Yet they are also, possibly, an ironical comment on the absolute devotion of the Virgilian Orpheus to his Eurydice. Ovid's Orpheus is no exemplary figure. He makes his sacrifice for love, but he cannot be expected to resign himself to utter chastity. Ovid has here gone back beyond Virgil to a Hellenistic tradition represented by Phanocles' Ἔρωτες ἢ Καλοί. Phanocles used homosexuality to explain the reason for Orpheus' death.[17] The Bistonian women killed him

> οὕνεκα πρῶτος ἔδειξεν ἐνὶ Θρήκεσσιν ἔρωτας
> ἄρρενας, οὐδὲ πόθους ἤνεσε θηλυτέρων.

> because he was the first to show love among males in Thrace, and he praised not desire for females. (9–10)

(Compare Ovid's, *ille etiam Thracum populis fuit auctor amorem / in teneros transferre mares*, "To the peoples of Thrace he was the originator of transferring love to males of tender age" [*Met.* 10.83–84]). Ovid, however, shifts the emphasis of the homosexual theme from the causal sequence of excess and revenge to Orpheus' inner, emotional life, that is, the bitterness of his loss of Eurydice or some pledge to her.

> seu quod male cesserat illi
> sive fidem dederat.

> Either because it had gone badly with him, or else because he had given a pledge. (10.80–81)

Ovid hints at the affairs themselves only in a delicate and rather attractive metaphor: *citraque iuventam / aetatis breve ver et primos carpere flores*, "and while they are young plucking the brief spring of their age and the first blooms" (10.84–85). Ovid here modifies his Hellenistic source by separating the homosexuality from the Thracian women's vengeance and letting it stand simply as a development of Orpheus' personality after his experience of Eurydice's loss. He thereby introduces also a realistic note and a humanizing correction of Virgil. Indirectly he asks us to take Orpheus down from his tragic pedestal and *humanis concedere rebus*.

II ·

Ovid sounds his new note at the very beginning. Instead of Virgil's mysteriously doomed girl, *moritura puella* (*G.*4.458), Ovid introduces a new bride, *nupta . . . nova*, who meets her death as she rejoices among the companions of her now past girlhood.

> nam nupta per herbas
> dum nova naiadum turba comitata vagatur,
> occidit in talum serpentis dente recepto.

> For while the new bride wanders among the grasses accompanied by a band of Naiads; she meets her death by a serpent's tooth received into her heel. (*Met.* 10.8–10)

Despite the humorous twist in the last phrase, the mood is one of high pathos, asking our commiseration for the innocent victim. Norden has pointed out how closely the scene approximates to the situation of funeral epigrams with their pathetic contrast of joy and grief and the sudden transformation of the day of highest happiness into the day of black despair.[18] The contrast with the happy marriage of Iphis and Ianthe, which provides the narrative link between tales and between books, intensifies this pathos.

By omitting Aristaeus and thereby making Eurydice's death purely accidental, Ovid eliminates Virgil's complex moral scheme of crime and retribution. He also focuses attention more fully on Orpheus. His Eurydice remains a more shadowy figure than Virgil's.

> ipse cava solans aegrum testudine amorem
> te, dulcis coniunx, te solo in litore secum,
> te veniente die, te decedente canebat.
> Taenarias etiam fauces, alta ostia Ditis,
> et caligantem nigra formidine lucum
> ingressus manisque adiit regemque tremendum
> nesciaque humanis precibus mansuescere corda.

> He himself, consoling his saddened love with his hollow lyre, sang of you, sweet bride, of you upon the lonely shore, of you he sang when the day arrived and of you when the day departed. He entered even the jaws of Taenarum, the lofty portals of Dis, and the grove dim with dusky fear, and he approached the shades and their fear-

some king and the hearts that know not how to grow gentle to human prayers. (*G*.4.464–470)

quam satis ad superas postquam Rhodopeius auras
deflevit vates, ne non temptaret et umbras,
ad Styga Taenaria est ausus descendere porta
perque leves populos simulacraque functa sepulcro
Persephonen adiit inamoenaque regna tenentem
umbrarum dominum pulsisque ad carmina nervis
sic ait.

When the bard of Rhodope had sufficiently lamented over her to the winds above, lest he leave the shades too untried, he dared to descend to the Styx by the portal of Taenarum, and through the insubstantial peoples and the shades that had completed burial he approached Persephone and the lord who held the cheerless realm of ghosts. Striking the strings [of his lyre] for song, he speaks as follows. (*Met*. 10.11–17)

Ovid has dropped the elegiac tone and the extreme emotionality conveyed in Virgil's anaphoric repetition, four times, of *te*. Virgil's *solans aegrum testudine amorem*, "consoling his saddened love on the lyre" (*G*.4.464), becomes simpler and more immediately human: *quam satis . . . deflevit vates*, "had lamented over her sufficiently" (*Met*. 10.11–12). *Satis* suggests a human limit and measure lacking in the wild grief of Virgil's hero. By omitting the "pathetic fallacy" of the remote mountains' lament (*G*.4.461–463) and suggesting timidity and despair in *ne non temptaret et umbras*, "lest he leave the shades too untried," and in *est ausus*, "had the daring" (*Met*. 10.12–13), Ovid achieves this same lower and more human characterization.[19]

Ovid thereby presents Orpheus not merely as a heroic bard endowed with supernatural powers, but also as a single mortal, armed only with his love and his art. This polarity between the lone singer and the terrible powers of the underworld is, of course, given in the myth and suggested by Virgil too. Yet by developing the human side of Orpheus more fully than Virgil, Ovid makes the contrast especially pointed. A few lines later he opposes the personal pronoun *ego* to the full measure of Hades' terrors: *per ego haec loca plena timoris*, "I through these places full of fear" (*Met*. 10.29). And in the next lines he juxtaposes the name of Eurydice and the simple verb of entreaty, *oro*, against "huge Chaos and the silences of [Hades'] vast realm."

per Chaos hoc ingens vastique silentia regni,
Eurydices, oro . . . retexite fata.

In the name of this huge Chaos and the silences of the vast realm, re-
weave, I beg you, the fates of Eurydice. (*Met.* 10.30–31)

In his descent, Virgil's Orpheus witnesses all the grim power of
death. There is a strong evocation of Homer's underworld.

matres atque viri defunctaque corpora vita
magnanimum heroum, pueri innuptaeque puellae
impositique rogis iuvenes ante ora parentum.

Mothers and husbands and the bodies of great-souled heroes who
had done with life and boys and unmarried girls and youths placed
on the pyres before the eyes of their parents. (*G.*4.475–477)

The lines are a condensation of *Odyssey* 11.36–41. The Homeric echo not
only adds solemnity but also places this vision of death in an ancient
and venerable tradition. Hence it appears as a reflection of an objective, inexorable, timeless reality. Virgil found his lines sufficiently lofty
to include them in his epic treatment of another, more important
descent to the underworld (*G.*4.475–477 = *Aen.* 6.306–308). Ovid borrows one of Virgil's phrases but reduces the entire description to a
single line. Here mothers, heroes, boys, girls, youths are generalized to
far more neutral "peoples" and "shades": *perque leves populos simula-*
craque functa sepulcro (*Met.* 10.14). Ovid does, in fact, dwell on mortality,
but his description of death appears not as a part of the narrative
frame, but in the rhetoric of Orpheus' speech. By this displacement,
Ovid changes the heroic tone and the impersonality (relatively speaking) of Virgil's treatment of death to a mood of personal response and
rhetorical emotionality. He treats death not with a grim factuality, but
as part of an attempt to persuade. By presenting the universality of
death through the suffering participant's eyes, Ovid makes us perceive
it less as the manifestation of eternal laws than as the particular experience of a single man.

As Virgil's tone of lofty removal stresses the universality of death, so
his account of Orpheus' journey stresses the inexorability of Hades'
decrees. Three times he speaks of this inexorability: *regemque tre-*
mendum / nesciaque humanis precibus mansuescere corda, "The fearsome
king and hearts that know not how to become gentle to human
prayers" (*G.*4.469–470); *ignoscenda quidem, scirent si ignoscere Manes*,
"Things worthy of pardon, if indeed the Shades knew how to pardon"

(489); *immitis rupta tyranni / foedera terque fragor stagnis auditus Averni,* "The decrees of the harsh tyrant were broken, and three times a thunderous roar was heard over the swamps of Avernus" (492–493). As the last passage makes clear, Orpheus in Virgil has violated firmly fixed *foedera,* and there is no further recourse. He pays the price of his *furor;* and the threefold thunder over the Avernian lake, like the awesome thunder at the end of Sophocles' *Oedipus at Colonus,* seals his fate irremediably.[20]

Ovid has no equivalent to such verses. His world is characterized by fluidity and marvels rather than *foedera* and inexorable cosmic laws. The intractability of the gods plays only a minor role in Ovid's tale. Near the end of the episode, Orpheus laments that Erebus' gods are cruel (*esse deos Erebi crudeles questus* [*Met.* 10.76]), while Eurydice does not lament at all.

The inhabitants of the two underworlds illustrate analogous differences. Virgil's Furies are grim and horrible, enforcers of the poet's stern order. They may "be amazed" (*stupuere* [G.4.481]) at Orpheus' art, but they are still monstrous creatures, with their dark blue, snaky hair (482). Virgil strongly emphasizes their strangeness by in fact writing "entwined with snakes in hair" (*implexae crinibus anguis*), instead of the expected "hair entwined with snakes." In keeping with the more yielding quality of his underworld, Ovid forgoes any physical description of the Furies. When he does describe them, they are not merely "amazed," but they weep and wet their cheeks with tears, for the first time, as report has it (*Met.* 10.45–46). The picture of the awful goddesses with tears running down their cheeks might, if pressed, verge on the ridiculous,[21] and Ovid's self-conscious *fama est* shows his awareness of the strangeness of the scene. Yet Ovid has chosen this artificial picture to underline the emotional sympathy between the singer and the underworld.

To reinforce this same gentler and more fanciful tone, Ovid not only dampens the Furies' cheeks but also makes "the bloodless ghosts weep" (*exsangues flebant animae* [*Met.* 10.41]). Whereas Virgil had mentioned the amazement of only Cerberus and Ixion (G.4.481–484), Ovid adds Tantalus, Prometheus' vulture, the Danaids, Sisyphus (*Met.* 10.41–44). He pushes the image of Ixion *à l'outrance* by having the wheel not merely "stop" but "be struck dumb." We may compare Virgil's *Ixionii vento rota constitit orbis* (G.4.484) and Ovid's *stupuitque Ixionis orbis* (*Met.* 10.42). Through this and related modifications, Ovid transforms Virgil's stern and unbending underworld into a fanciful realm that shares the emotional coloring and erotic sympathies of the rest of Ovid's world. By becoming more fantastic, Ovid's Hades also becomes, paradoxically, more human.

Ovid's breaking down of Virgil's finality about death is especially marked in the case of Eurydice. In Virgil she dissolves into emptiness, like smoke into wind, and leaves Orpheus grasping empty shadows (G.4.499–502). Ovid takes over the detail of the winds (*nil nisi cedentes infelix adripit auras*, "unfortunate, he grasps only the yielding winds" [*Met.* 10.59]), but develops it less poignantly than Virgil and replaces the final *fugit diversa neque illum . . . / . . . praeterea vidit*, "she fled away, nor did she ever look upon him hereafter" (G.4.500–502), with the milder *revolutaque rursus eodem est*, "she turned back again to the same place" (*Met.* 10.63),[22] a phrase that prepares the way for the reunion of the couple in the next book.

Ovid also lessens the effect of Orpheus' grief by interposing an elaborate comparison with two obscure myths, one of a man turned to stone at the sight of Hercules with Cerberus, another of Olenus and Lethaea, turned to stone because of the latter's pride in her beauty (*Met.* 10.64–71).[23] The second tale is especially important for softening the harshness of inconsolable grief, for it places the union of lovers and nature's sympathy with them above the pride and folly that cause their doom.

> tuque, o confisa figurae
> infelix Lethaea tuae, iunctissima quondam
> pectora, nunc lapides, quos umida sustinet Ide.

> And you, O unhappy Lethaea, who trusted too much to your beauty, hearts once joined in closest union, [you are] now stones that damp Ida supports. (10.69–71)

Iunctissima pectora, "hearts most closely joined," turns our attention away from the tragic outcome of the lovers' error to the gentler pathos of their bond. The stones now resting on wet Ida solemnize that bond and immortalize it even in its sadness. This purely decorative addition also points ahead to the bittersweet reunion of Orpheus and Eurydice in the next book.

After the loss of Eurydice, Virgil's Orpheus wanders in the barren north "lamenting Eurydice snatched away and the cancelled gifts of Hades" (*raptam Eurydicen et inrita Ditis / dona querens* [G.4.519–520]). His death at the hands of the Ciconian matrons follows at once (G.4.520–522). Virgil's context suggests the continued passion and emotional violence of Orpheus: he fails to recognize the absoluteness of the *lex* (*G.4.487*) that he disobeyed, and thus he continues to lament his loss as a "gift canceled out" by cruel gods. Ovid borrows Virgil's expression *inrita dona* (*Met.* 10.52), but it occurs *before* Eurydice's loss, as part of the conditions of her return. Orpheus is not to look back, *aut inrita dona futura,* "or the gifts are to be canceled." Ovid's phrase foreshadows the outcome but does not, as Virgil's does, convey the hopelessness of interminable suffering.[24]

III ·

The corollary of Ovid's dissolution of Virgil's mixture of tragic loss and austere philosophical generality is a weaker, but more human Orpheus. The fact that Ovid relates Orpheus' speech in Hades whereas Virgil does not is symptomatic of such differences.[25] All the world loves a lover; and Ovid's Orpheus wins over the reader, as he wins over the gods, by a touching avowal of his utter subjection to love.[26] From the rhetorical elaboration and mythical paradigms of his prologue (*Met.* 10.17–22), Orpheus turns suddenly to the human pathos of Eurydice's premature death (*crescentesque abstulit annos,* "took away her increasing years" [24]) and his inability to overcome his grief: *posse pati volui, nec me temptasse negabo: / vicit Amor,* "I wished to be able to endure, nor will I deny that I tried: Love won" (25–26). These lines have been the most admired of the whole episode. Even Fränkel excepted them from his general condemnation.[27] Pavano says of them "The accent of sincerity finds again, sometimes unexpectedly, the secret pathos of our humanity."[28] The pathetic note is sounded in the immediately preceding *crescentes abstulit annos.* This phrase reinforces the pathos of the death of the "new bride" (8–9). It suggests also the young couple's loss of the happiness of their best years. We may compare the *concordes annos* of the aged Philemon and Baucis (8.708) and the expression *dulces concorditer exegit annos,* "passed their sweet years in harmony" (7.752), of Procris and Cephalus.

I have already mentioned the juxtaposition of Orpheus' "I" and the underworld's horrendous power in lines 29–30. Here, as Fränkel sensitively observes, "a very human voice, tender and melodious, makes itself heard over the horror and silence of Death's vast realm."[29] It is just this voice that Virgil suppresses, for he seeks to set Orpheus' *dementia* and *furor* into relief against the laws that he violates. Ovid's Orpheus goes on to make the infernal gods themselves his companions and fellow sufferers in love: *vos quoque iunxit amor,* "You too were joined by Love" (*Met.* 10.29). This short sentence reveals how different Ovid's gods are from Virgil's. The previous books have fully illustrated Orpheus' point, and the bard will himself sing of those amours later in the book (152ff).

Even the defiance of Orpheus at the end of his speech has a winning humanity.

> quodsi fata negant veniam pro coniuge, certum est
> nolle redire mihi: leto gaudete duorum.
>
> But if the fates refuse their pardon for my wife, it is my resolve to refuse to return: take joy in the death of two. (38–39)

This bravado in the face of the immutable laws of death is pathetic, but is also underlines his devotion and his lover's assumption that the display of his devotion can move even the shadowy hearts of the deities below. In a sense, Orpheus' assumptions are also the source of his victory. In this respect, as we shall see, he parallels Pygmalion. Assuming a world sensitive to love, he can speak with a confidence and a naive revelation of a lover's weakness that are virtually irresistible. He projects his own sensibility upon the gods. Acting on his imaginings, he proves them correct. In this respect Ovid's tale is exactly the opposite of Virgil's. He presents the triumph of imagination, emotionality, the interior life over external reality. Victorious as both a poet and a lover. Orpheus vindicates the two realms that for Ovid form the surest and finest basis for human happiness: love and art.

Amid the elaborate and artificial description of the underworld that follows Orpheus' speech (*Met.* 10.40–48), Ovid once more introduces a surprisingly poignant and unexpected detail. He actually permits us a glimpse of Eurydice in Hades: *umbras erat illa recentes / inter et incessit passu de vulnere tardo,* "she was among the newly come shades, and she walked with a step made slow from her wound" (*Met.* 10.48–49).[30] The concrete picture of Eurydice's underworld existence helps prepare for the ultimate union of the pair in book 11. Ovid, however, has borrowed a detail from another Virgilian source, the appearance of Dido before Aeneas: *inter quas Phoenissa recens a vulnere Dido,* "among whom was Phoenician Dido, fresh from her wound" (*Aen.* 6.450). The echo of this famous, highly charged scene gives an even greater, and more startling, emotionality to Ovid's narrative. He en-

riches his story with the evocations of the most tragic love story of
Roman literature.

Though Ovid closely follows Virgil in his account of Orpheus' actual
loss of Eurydice, he presents his turning around not as *furor* or *dementia*,
but as the solicitude of a lover or husband for the weakness of his
beloved.

> hic, *ne deficeret, metuens* avidusque videndi
> flexit *amans* oculos, et protinus illa relapsa est.

> He, afraid that she might fail and greedy of seeing her, in love turned
> back his eyes, and at once she slipped back. (*Met.* 10.56–57)

In Virgil it is Eurydice who stretches out her arms; in Ovid it is
Orpheus: *invalidasque tibi tendens, heu non tua, palmas,* "stretching forth
to you, alas no longer yours, hands without strength" (*G.*4.498);
bracchiaque intendens prendique et prendere certans, "and stretching forth
his arms, struggling to be held and to hold" (*Met.* 10.58). Ovid has
eliminated Eurydice's pathetic sigh (*heu non tua*) and made Orpheus
more energetic. Both poets have Orpheus reach for the empty air
(*G.*4.500–501, *Met.* 10.59), but here, as in the preceding detail, Ovid
gives our sympathies more directly and unambiguously to Orpheus.
He is *infelix* (*Met.* 10.59), a word that harks back to the foreboding at the
beginning of the tale (*nec felix attulit omen*, "nor did he bring a happy
omen" [*Met.* 10.5]).[31] In Virgil, on the other hand, Eurydice claims the
greater sympathy: it is she who is "unhappy" (*misera* [*G.*4.494]), the
victim of Orpheus' lack of self-control.

Ovid's sympathy for Orpheus is even more marked in his next lines.

> namque iterum moriens non est de coniuge quicquam
> questa suo (quid enim nisi se quereretur amatam?) . . .

> For dying yet again she made no complaint of her spouse (for what
> could she complain of save that she had been loved?). (*Met.* 10.60–61)

Virgil emphasized the bitterness of Eurydice's disappointment in
Orpheus' failure.

> illa "quis et me" inquit "miseram et te perdidit, Orpheu,
> quis tantus furor? en iterum crudelia retro
> fata vocant."

> "What madness has destroyed both me," she says, "and you too,
> Orpheus, so great a madness? Behold, the cruel fates call me back
> again." (*G*4.494–496)

Ovid has replaced bitterness with a womanly gentleness and sweetness. His Eurydice does not judge; she accepts. She understands, resignedly, that the very failure of her spouse is a proof, sadly, of his love. There is almost a tacit forgiveness, for the weakness of Orpheus is the pardonable weakness of love. The emphatic *amatam* (*Met.* 10.61), echoing *amans* a few lines before (57), stresses the fact that the bond between them, the bond between "lover" and "beloved," is still unbroken. It is still there to be fulfilled in the next book.

Ovid takes over from Virgil the final farewell:

> iamque vale: feror ingenti circumdata nocte
> invalidasque tibi tendens, heu non tua, palmas

> And now farewell: I am carried off surrounded by vast night, stretching forth to you, alas no longer yours, hands without strength. (*G*.4.497–498)

> supremumque vale, quod iam vix auribus ille
> acciperet, dixit revolutaque rursus eodem est

> And she spoke the final farewell, which he could now scarcely perceive with his ears, and was again turned back to the same place. (*Met.* 10.62–63)

In Virgil communication is utterly severed, and the next lines stress the finality of the separation (*G*.4.499–503). Ovid's Orpheus, however, can still hear the final farewell, though "scarcely" (*vix*). As I noted above, the intensity of grief is tempered by the literary allusions and the theme of *iunctissima pectora*, "hearts most closely joined," in *Met.* 10.65–71. It is only after these lines that Ovid repeats the Virgilian details of excluding Orpheus from Hades (*Met.* 10.72–73; cf. *G*.4.502–503).

In the account of Orpheus' mourning, Virgil moves farther into the realm of myth and fancy. They say (*perhibent*) that Orpheus lamented for seven consecutive months and that his plaint soothed tigers and moved oaks (*G*.4.507–510). Ovid, however, keeps his tale on the level of humanly comprehensible emotions. He reduces the period of mourning to seven days of fasting (*Met.* 10.73–74) and localizes this grief right by the banks of the Styx (74) rather than under the remote, gelid caves (or stars, reading *astris*) of the Strymon (*G*.4.508–509). The grief of Ovid's Orpheus is more tangible, more natural. We can understand more easily the short, intense agony that leaves one without desire to move or to eat than a strange journey to the mysterious north and seven months of lamentation.[32]

The general effect of Ovid's modifications of Virgil in the scene of *Met.* 10.50–75 is to transfer sympathy from Eurydice to Orpheus and in so doing to replace the Virgilian theme of passion violating cosmic order with the Ovidian theme of the pardonable weakness of human affection. What Otis observes of the Ceyx-Halcyon episode is (with an important reservation, to be made later) true here also: Ovid shows himself "the West's first champion of true, normal, even conjugal love."[33]

IV ·

What has been said of the Orpheus episode in book 10 applies also to its sequel in book 11. Here, however, the different genres and structures of the two poems involve a crucial difference. The episodic character of Ovid's narrative in itself breaks down the causal structure of the myth and with it the Virgilian presentation of Orpheus' fate as the condign punishment for his violence of passion. As the decorum of his didactic, nonerotic poem demands, Virgil is silent about Orpheus' homosexual loves. Since Ovid places an entire book between Orpheus' homosexuality and his death, there is no suggestion of a causal link between them. Indeed, as I noted above, he even suggests that these affairs result from the depth of his devotion to Eurydice (cf. *Met.* 10.80–81). Hence they are no obstacle to their reunion in the underworld. That reunion, in turn, cancels out the hero's aberrant amours and restores him, like Iphis and Pygmalion, to the number of normal, heterosexual lovers.

Virgil makes Orpheus' death appear as a kind of inverted fertility rite.

> spretae Ciconum quo munere matres
> inter sacra deum nocturnique orgia Bacchi
> discerptum latos iuvenem sparsere per agros.

> Scorned in this service, the Ciconian matrons tore him apart among the sacred rites of the gods and the revels of nighttime Bacchus and scattered the torn youth far and wide over the fields. (*G.*4.520–522)

His death exemplifies a certain poetic justice. Having refused to participate in nature's cycle of renewal and regeneration, he is "scattered over the fields" by "mothers" in an orgiastic ceremony. His death, then, stands against the background of the universal laws of nature to which he has refused obedience.[34]

Ovid eliminates entirely this sacral, ritual element and with it the cosmic and moral structure of Virgil's narrative. Following the Hellenistic version, he stresses instead the utter madness of the Ciconian women: *insanaque regnat Erinys*, "the crazed Fury rules" (*Met.* 11.14).[35] It is not the poet's body that is "scattered over the fields" (*sparsere per agros*, [G.4.522]), but the farm implements that the women use as weapons (*dispersa per agros* [*Met.* 11.35]). By echoing the Virgilian phrase in a different context, Ovid calls attention to the totally secular character of his story. These women are, in fact, themselves *sacrilegae* (*Met.* 11.41); and the civilizing art of this *vatis Apollinei*, "bard of Apollo" (*Met.* 11.8), opposes the insanity and wild chaos of his murderers. The details of stones turned aside by his song at times verge upon a grotesque blend of fantasy and bloodthirsty horror (cf. *Met.* 11.10–13, 39–40). Yet these details place the pathos of Orpheus' end above the justice of natural laws. This pathos reaches its logical climax in the Hellenistic motif of nature's lament for the dead poet (*Met.* 11.44–49).[36]

Toward the end of the episode, Ovid checks the gory exuberance of his narrative. He tones down the violence of the decapitation (cf. *marmorea caput a cervice revulsum*, "the head torn from the marble neck" [G.4.523]) and replaces the unassuaged and unassuageable grief of its cry, *Eurydicen . . . a miseram Eurydicen*, "Eurydice, ah, unhappy Eurydice" (G.4.525–527) with a more neutral *flebile nescio quid*, "something mournful" (*Met.* 11.52).[37] Some critics have seen here a rationalistic correction of Virgil,[38] others a comical parody.[39] Ovid perhaps felt the lament of a decapitated head as too much even for his fanciful world. A dying man may utter his wife's name as his last word, but not the dismembered head of a corpse.[40] There is another difference too. The three times repeated "Eurydice" of the Virgilian Orpheus stresses the irrevocable loss of the individual person, the hopeless destruction of the one-and-only love, as the name of the unique beloved echoes over the pitiless Hyperborean wasteland (G.4.517–518). Ovid reduces this supreme pathos of individual souls torn apart. His lovers are to meet again. Like Virgil's, his tale shades off into the miraculous, but the improbability in Ovid becomes increasingly kindlier. Given the fluidity of his world order, the fairy tale element can become as irrationally beneficent as maleficent.

The gods can also work miracles in Orpheus' favor: Apollo defends the severed head by turning to stone the serpent who would devour it (*Met.* 11.56–60). Ovid now moves fully into the realm of the grotesque.

hic ferus expositum peregrinis anguis harenis
os petit et sparsos stillanti rore capillos.

Here a savage snake attacks the head that had been thrust forth on foreign sands and [attacks] the hair drenched in the dripping spray. (*Met.* 11.56–57).

The snake sums up everthing that is marvelous, mysterious, and terrifying in this mythical world. Yet this exotic and fantastic detail is only the foil for the tender, human ending of his story, the reunion of Orpheus and Eurydice.

The horror of Orpheus' previous descent now gives way to recognition: *quae loca viderat ante / cuncta recognoscit,* "he recognizes all the places that he had seen before" (*Met.* 11.61–62). He seeks and finds Eurydice "in the fields of the blessed" (62). The fulfillment of his lover's devotion is signaled in the eagerness of his embrace: *cupidisque amplectitur ulnis,* "and with desirous arms embraces her" (63). These "desirous arms" mark him as still a lover (cf. 10.57ff.), and this ending is the triumph of his love.

Ovid has accomplished something of a tour de force. A pre-Virgilian version of the legend, used by Euripides in the *Alcestis* and by Hermesianax, made Orpheus successful in recovering Eurydice.[41] Ovid follows the Virgilian version: Orpheus fails. Yet even while following Virgil's version, Ovid manages to suggest Orpheus' success. The tragic backward look of Virgil's Orpheus (*victusque animi respexit* [G.4.491]) becomes now the fond glances of a happy pair: *Eurydicenque suam iam tutus respicit Orpheus* (*Met.* 11.66).[42] Eurydice is now "his" (*suam*), and he can "look back" at her without fear of loss (*tutus*).[43] Ovid ends his *Orpheus,* then, with the happy glances of lovers. Instead of tragic loss or epic monumentality, he concludes with a small, personal, intimate gesture.[44]

Yet the reunion of the two lovers has a less happy side. It vindicates the power of love, but it also shows us that love fulfilled only in a world beyond our own. Here Otis' view of Ovid as a poet of "normal" love needs qualification.[45] The happiness of such love has no place in the real world. In this respect the tale of Orpheus and Eurydice complements that of Iphis and Ianthe, even though the two stories are initially coupled as forming a contrast of happy with unhappy love (cf. *Met.*

10.1–8). In both episodes lovers are united, but only in a world of miracles.

V ·

Ovid's *Orpheus* exemplifies not only the victory of love but also, in a certain sense, the victory of art. It is both as poet and as lover that Orpheus wins over the deities in the underworld of book 10. Though the Ciconian women finally destroy him, the power of his song temporarily neutralizes their missiles, and his rhythms move the natural world to spontaneous sympathy for his fate (*Met.* 11.44–49).

In this theme the story of Orpheus closely parallels that of Pygmalion, which soon follows it (10.243ff.).[46] Both men abstain from intercourse with women. Both, through the magical power of their art, animate inert nature and break through the division between matter and spirit. Orpheus moves stones and trees and causes the laws of death to relax; Pygmalion sees the statue that he has created come to life. In intertwining the two myths, Ovid provides a metaphorical reflection of the creative and restorative power of his own art, its ability, as one critic has put it, "to introduce subtle transformations into the repertory of tradition, to breathe new life into the torpor of its players, and to resurrect the heritage of antiquity for the benfit of posterity"; and the poet also suggests "that of all human enterprises only the fine arts are capable of performing such miracles."[47]

It is one of the paradoxes of Ovid's style and Ovid's world view that he can humanize his mythical material through exaggerating the non-human, fantastic elements of his tales to the point of grotesqueness. This paradox is a corollary of that pointed out by Otis, that the fanciful, Alexandrian, erotic mythology contains a kind of humane seriousness and an ultimate symbolical truth—a truth, that is, to the constants of human nature—that Ovid could not find in the contemporary, historical, Augustan mythology. In human terms, Ovid finds the remote, fairy-tale myths "truer" and more "real" than the contemporary myths of Augustan ideology.[48]

The complexity of the *Metamorphoses* lies in no small part in this double-barreled attack on heroic seriousness. Ovid found a way of coupling together epic mythology and Augustan ideology and of standing both on their heads at the same time. The achievement was rendered possible by the devices of Callimachean narrative, especially discontinuity, erudite allusion and periphrasis, wit. As Robert Coleman has observed, Ovid had not only "brilliantly demonstrated how ἔπη τυτθά [modest verses] could be welded together to produce an un-heroic ἄεισμα διηνεκές [continuous song] but he had proved that epic themes of μέγα ψοφέουσαν ἀοιδήν [loudly echoing epic] can be effectively toppled not by rejecting them but by presenting them in mock-heroic tone within a context of capricious fable."[49]

Augustan morality and Augustan monumentality provided, as it were, a negative armature. Ovid's very opposition to Augustan ide-ology and to the Augustan epic that went with it could hold his poem, albeit in a negative way, close to the experience of his own times and could thus give it a freshness and immediacy that Callimachus could not attain. Something of the *Metamorphoses'* revolution against the heroic and the serious had its roots in Ovid's personal experience and doubtless spoke, if only indirectly, to his contemporaries.

For Callimachus the implications of the heroic style and the *mega biblion* did not extend beyond the aesthetic, purely literary realm. Out-side the study or the Library, the *mega biblion* was not a threat. For Ovid and his contemporaries style and ideology, poetry and politics, had again become intertwined. Since the *Aeneid,* the heroic style carried with it conceptions of commitment and sacrifice to a larger order that a more private outlook could not accept. Yet Ovid, though differing fundamentally in outlook, still shares with Virgil and Horace their peculiarly Roman ability to mold Greek mythology into the shape of historical experience and to discover a disturbing personal and social relevance in the umbratile learning of Alexandria.

It is in part because of this attempt to overturn the serious content and the stable, tragic world order of the heroic tradition that Ovid so often runs the risk of the grotesque. When Ovid transforms Virgil's austere tragic tale of Orpheus into the fantastic and rhetorically colored atmosphere of his own poem, he does not entirely escape that danger (cf. *Met.* 10.40–46, 11.15–43, 56–60). Yet that grotesqueness may be an essential part of Ovid's revolt against Augustan and heroic serious-ness. On the other hand, Ovid's presentation of a fluid, fabulous world can at times transform the harsh limitations of reality into some-thing responsive to man's emotional needs. Behind the lust and violence to which human lives are prone, he reveals a capacity for tenderness and devotion that can sometimes create their own reward.

Here the artist's imagination spins its own world of happy dreams and makes those dreams come true. Orpheus and Pygmalion reap the rewards of their artistic ability to transform unbending matter into the pliant warmth of their desires.

By dissolving the ordinary laws of reality, Ovid allows the weakness of the human condition to stand out all the more sharply. Ovid's heroes, unlike Virgil's, need not always resist or overcome emotion in obedience to laws of destiny. Those laws give way, and emotion exists for its own sake. Love's very defenselessness wins over the stern gods of the lower world, and ultimate reunion cancels out Orpheus' tragic failure. The bitterness of death as eternal separation is overridden by a vision of death as eternal union.

Ovid allies love and art as the major creative forces in a world of arbitrary powers. In Virgil's firmer and harder world order, love and art, though capable of miracles, are also potentially aberrant and destructive. For Virgil's Aristaeus, as for Virgil's Orpheus—as also for Virgil's Corydon and Gallus in the *Eclogues,* his Dido, Turnus, and Aeneas in the *Aeneid*—love clouds the mind and leads to death and loss.[50] Over against the refractory, potentially disruptive emotionality of the lover-poet-artist, Virgil sets the realm of productive work and the attitude of cooperation with the subservience to nature's laws: Aristaeus; the bees with their sexless life; Augustus, the conqueror and restorer of order, the giver of laws (*G.*1.499ff., 4.561–562). In Ovid's world love, not law, is the measure of existence. Art and love then fuse as means toward reaching truth and bringing happiness into human life.

In myths like those of Pygmalion and Orpheus, the poet—Ovid himself—finds his artistic life confirmed and its highest aspirations clarified: the creation of the possible out of the impossible, spirit out of matter, happy love out of tragic death. Yet all this exists, after all, only in imagination, in the unreal world of fable. If Ovid's dissolution of a firm and demanding cosmic order frees the individual and his emotional life, it also exposes him to the violence of those emotions and to the arbitrary, elemental forces, both divine and human, that are thus let loose in his world.

4

Virgil and Ovid on Orpheus
A Second Look

I · VIRGIL

The Fourth *Georgic* is one of those works that, once read, never ceases
to be part of your consciousness. It is also one of those works whose
internal relations change as you return to it at different stages of life. In
looking back at my study of some twenty years ago, I would particularly change my emphasis in one respect. I should pay more attention
to the mythical models behind Aristaeus' journey.[1] The recent books of
M. C. J. Putnam, Gary Miles, and Maurizio Bettini all show the importance of the Homeric parallels, especially Achilles' appeal to Thetis in
Iliad 1 and the Menelaus-Proteus encounter in *Odyssey* 4 (cf. G.4.319–334
and 387–452 respectively). Important too is the story of Theseus' dive into the depths of the seas in Bacchylides Ode 17 as a prototype for Aristaeus' plunge in *Georgics* 4.363–383.[2] The last parallel is also relevant to
the motif of initiatory passage in Aristaeus' journey, for this is clearly
in the background of the Bacchylides poem. Anne Burnett has recently
suggested that Theseus' dive carries associations of cosmic renewal
through immersion in the primordial matter of creation—an interpretation that is perhaps more appropriate for Virgil's text than for
Bacchylides.[3]

Many of these parallels have often been noted before, but the
ironies have not always received the attention that they deserve.
Achilles, first of all, is an improbable model for a minor agrarian divinity concerned with bees. Set beside the passion and resentment of the
epic hero, Aristaeus' complaint seems childishly petulant (cf. especially G.4.326–332). Achilles' intensity of emotion over the loss of Briseis
(as well as over the insult to his honor) would in fact be more appropriate to Orpheus than to Aristaeus. Is it relevant to recall that Achilles becomes responsible for the death of a beloved, and, on the other side,

that Aristaeus is himself a healer of plague (Apollonius, *Arg.* 2.516–527)? Characteristically, Virgil not only combines different sources but also uses them with multiple associations and ironies.

When Aristaeus reaches his mother, Cyrene, at the bottom of the sea, the Nereids around her are singing of "Vulcan's empty concern and Mars's wiles and sweet thefts" (*G.*4.345f.). The Nymphs' diversion is the story of the adultery of Mars and Venus (Ares and Aphrodite) sung by the bard Demodocus in book 8 of the *Odyssey*. Virgil has moved us rapidly from the *Iliad* to the *Odyssey*. But the content is as important as the generic association, for we soon learn of an attempted adultery whose consequences are far more serious than the frivolous loves of the gods. In this tale the offended husband's vengeance, unlike that of Homer's Hephaestus, has tragic rather than laughable consequences: "Orpheus rouses the anger of the Nymphs and he rages heavily over the wife who has been snatched away" (*rapta graviter pro coniuge saevit* [*G.*4.455f.]). This is obviously a far more serious emotional response than the Nereid's "empty concern" (*curam inanem*).[4]

The most important Odyssean echoes are not in the subaqueous divertissement of Cyrene and her company, but in her advice to Aristaeus and its sequel, his meeting with Proteus. Like Menelaus in *Odyssey* 4, Aristaeus has a challenging encounter with the Old Man of the Sea, from whom he must wrest the secrets of life and death.[5] Aristaeus also resembles Odysseus in seeking advice from a goddess (Cyrene, Circe) and then making a risky journey to consult a seer (Proteus, Teiresias). Both Menelaus and Odysseus follow the advice of a helpful and mysterious female divinity to secure the safety of the lives that are in their charge. But neither of the Homeric heroes is as gravely responsible as Aristaeus for the situation of suspended life that the consultation with a wise old man is to remedy. Menelaus and Odysseus suffer sailors' mishaps beyond their control; Aristaeus is guilty (however indirectly) of taking a human life. So, as it turns out, the Achillean model adumbrated at the beginning of the tale is the right one after all. Aristaeus combines the seriousness of Achilles' closeness to cosmic destruction with Odysseus and Menelaus' determination to survive amid forces beyond human control.

Like Achilles, Aristaeus also suffers from an initial moral blindness. Until Proteus tells him of Eurydice's death, he has no realization of what he has done, nor does he show any remorse or indeed any interest at all in her fate after this information.[6] Cyrene urges him to "put away the sad concerns from his mind" (*licet tristis animo deponere curas* [531]), but we cannot be sure whether these "concerns" are for his bees or for his guilt about Eurydice, and in any case they come in Cyrene's words, not his.

The parallels between Odysseus/Circe and Aristaeus/Cyrene deserve further scrutiny. In both cases the female advisor frames the quest to the wise old man; and in both cases the goddesses, rather than the wise old man himself, give the essential practical instructions for the immediate problem of survival. Teiresias' narrative, however, concerns the remote future, not the immediate past. Yet in both cases the prophet's words convey essential qualities in the questing hero's identity: travel and exploration for Odysseus, self-centered confidence and aggressive violence for Aristaeus. These multiple associations with remote mythical heroes also keep us distanced from Aristaeus. Orpheus' story, by contrast, is more "human" and, as I noted in chapter 2, told in a warmer, more passionate style and in a narrative form whose contemporaneity is more likely to engage the reader's sympathy.

The dialectical relation between Orpheus and Aristaeus, then, still seems to me, as it did in 1966, to hold the key to this close of the *Georgics*. On this point most recent interpreters agree, however much they differ in the division of sympathy between the two figures. William Anderson, for example, would keep a more even balance between them and would insist on Orpheus' guilt in the *furor* of the backward glance.[7] Putnam and C. G. Perkell, on the other hand, give more weight to the farmer's aggressive stance against nature, to Orpheus' suffering as a lover, and to his implicit association with the nightingale whose fledgelings the "harsh farmer" has plucked from the nest in the simile of *Georgics* 4.511–515.[8] Jasper Griffin points out the unpoetic nature of Aristaeus' bees. The absence of honey, usually associated with poetic inspiration, he suggests, keeps the two protagonists apart, with Aristaeus on the side of severe practicality, "impersonal and dispassionate."[9]

Virgil's nightingale simile, I believe (with Putnam and Perkell), shows where our sympathies belong. Anderson's attempt to explain away the farmer's "hardness" is not convincing. "When we place this ruthlessness, this destructiveness of individuals, this 'guilt' in the total context of creative purposefulness, the pathetic individuals must be regretfully rejected, even the passionately loving Orpheus, that singer of the most moving songs myth has ever imagined. The *'durus arator,'* the guilty but energetically purposive Aristaeus, should be our model."[10] Such a principle would apply, perhaps, to Aristaeus' sacrifice of the bulls, but not to the act that necessitates that sacrifice. The analogy between violating the nightingale's nest and Aristaeus' attempt to violate Eurydice breaks down. The farmer is presumably destroying the young birds to protect his seeds. Aristaeus' aggression against Eurydice is an act of wanton, selfish, lustful violence. It is the attempted rape of a married woman, hardly a necessary act of "creative purposiveness." As such, it incurs the "heavy wrath" of Orpheus for "a wife who has been carried off" (et rapta graviter pro coniuge saevit [456]). Each of the words in this line, along with the suggestive placement of graviter, "heavily," next to rapta, "snatched away" (but also "raped") carries a heavy charge.

The disjunction in Virgil's narrative between Aristaeus' difficult trial and the speedy conclusion leaves the moral issue unresolved. Proteus finishes his tale and leaps away into the sea. "But not Cyrene," Virgil continues, in an abrupt, eliptical phrase that has been much discussed (530). She then gives the instructions about appeasing the Nymphs (divinities associated with the marriage that Aristaeus has violated) and sacrificing the bullocks. The rapid leap to the ritual resolution deliberately elides the problem of Aristaeus' guilt and saves him from the necessity of an emotional response or moral acknowledgment. The sudden flight of the wise old man (three times solemnly called a vates or seer [387, 392, 450]) indicates that no easy moral solution is available to Aristaeus. Cyrene's quick intervention, then, underlines the farmer's practical grasp of what needs doing to keep life going. It too shunts aside questions of guilt or feelings of remorse and looks not to the past but to the future.[11] The fates are on Aristaeus' side (as they are on Aeneas' in his responsiblity for the deaths of Dido and Turnus, among others); but there is a hint that the wise seer is not wholly in agreement, for his phrase haudquaquam ob meritum in 455, implying that Orpheus' suffering are "undeserved," places the weight of moral judgment against Aristaeus.[12]

The contrast between epic and pastoral in Virgil's epilogue, discussed near the end of chapter 2, certainly deserves to be probed more deeply. Pastoral echoes, of course, abound in the Georgics, often with self-conscious reminiscence of the Eclogues (for example, G.1.76, 105; 2.19) and with an intentional contrast between pastoral ease and georgic labor. But in the Proteus episode, where Virgil is adapting and sometimes even closely translating book 4 of Homer's Odyssey, he creates an intergeneric dialogue between epic and pastoral as well as between epic and didactic poetry. In *Georgics* 4.432–436, for instance, Virgil expands to five lines a half-line in Homer comparing Proteus to a shepherd (*Od.* 4.413). But he also calls attention to this conflation of pastoral with epic in the lines immediately preceding, where he shifts from the gentler, pastoral associations of the noonday heat in *Georgics* 4.402 ("when the grass is thirsty and shade is now more pleasing to the herd") to a harsher view of the same moment in 427–428 ("the grass was parched, and the sun's rays were baking the hollowed rivers, with their dry jaws, into mud"). The pastoral content of a brief and familiar epic simile (Proteus as shepherd in Homer), in other words, is developed into a full-blown pastoral scene (*G.*4.432–436), but only after the epic associations of the *Odyssey* have converted a pastoral moment (402) into unpastoral violence (427f.).

This interplay of genres should also include the contrast between georgic and elegiac poetry suggested by G. B. Conte.[13] That contrast would in fact reach more deeply into the substance of the work if we pursue recent suggestions about the *laudes Galli* (praise of Gallus) that according to Servius were displaced by the present tale of Orpheus and Aristaeus. Howard Jacobson suggests that the Gallus section originally stood in close proximity to Orpheus's initial lament over Eurydice (that is, after line 466), which would then reflect the amatory themes of Gallus' amatory poetry while also expressing Virgil's personal sorrow over Gallus' death (we may think here of Milton's *Lycidas*).[14]

The recent studies by David Ross raise generic considerations of another kind. Farming requires man's right relation to nature. Agricultural poetry thus has close connections with scientific and cosmogonic poetry. Virgil takes pains to place his work in the tradition of poetry about the cosmic order, from Hesiod through the pre-Socratic dactylic poems of Empedocles and Parmenides and on to Lucretius. To this end he utilizes the scientific tradition of the four elements (so Ross argues) and has the song of one of Cyrene's Nymphs include "the loves of the gods, beginning from chaos" (*G.*4.347).[15] Orpheus is relevant to these themes not only as a participant in the process of death and regeneration, but also as the archetypal poet of sympathy with nature and of magical power over nature. In the Greek tradition he is included with Hesiod, Empedocles, and Parmenides as a singer of scientific lore. In the Sixth *Eclogue* the song of Silenus, which contains cosmogonic themes, is compared to the effect of Orpheus' music on trees and mountains (29f.). Aristaeus' binding of Proteus, who then tells a tale, has close parallels with the binding of Silenus, thus constrained to sing his song.

In an attractive essay of 1972, Adam Parry suggested that the Orpheus-Aristaeus episode was thematically as well as stylistically expressive of Virgil's conception of poetry. Both tales reflect the ability of song to incorporate grief into art and thereby to resolve the stark clash of life and death.[16] "Song in turn becomes the condition for the recreation of life."[17] Parry's optimistic view, however, overstates the association of Aristaeus' success with art. For Putnam the "dilemma of the artist" focuses on Orpheus, pulled between discipline and emotional intensity and, in the last lines of the book, between Virgil's own writing and Augustus' warlike fulminations.[18]

More pessimistic still, A. J. Boyle regards Orpheus's failure as a continuation of Gallus' defeat by Amor as he moves from *Eclogue* 6 to *Eclogue* 10. Augustus' "thundering" (*fulminat*) recalls the aggressive violence of Aristaeus in a post-Saturnian age as well as the poetic overreaching that Callimachus opposed in his dictum "Not for me to thunder, but for Zeus."[19] Boyle's point deserves to be taken even farther. Almost our last view of Orpheus in an active role is his "weeping to himself" as he "soothes tigers and leads oaks with his song" in the desolate northern landscape of Thrace, "beneath cold stars" (*G.*4.509f.). In the *Eclogues* the Orphic music of pastoral could make the forests follow and cause the "stiff oaks to move their tops" (*Ecl.* 3.46, 6.27-30); and we recall that Virgil quotes from the *Eclogues* in the last line of the poem. This detail also recalls the pastoral fantasy of stopping rivers and stupefying lynxes with song at the opening of *Eclogue* 8, perhaps Virgil's most spectacular instance of song's magical power over nature (*stupefactae carmine lynces* [8.3]). But in the *Georgics* we are far from pastoral gentleness or magic. The singer of the pastoral world is here reduced to frozen, impotent grief. His "soothing of tigers with song" in the Thracian wilderness is a waste of the civilizing power of song, a topos for other Augustan poets (for example, Horace in *Ars Poetica* 391-393). The nightingale, to whose melodious lament Orpheus' song is compared here in the *Georgics*, may "renew" her plaint (*lamentabile carmen / integrat*); but for Orpheus there is no renewal, no change from the austere concentration on barrenness, ice, and loss (*G.*4.516-520).

For Rilke it suffices that the voice survives (see *Sonnets to Orpheus* 1.26). The ancient poet, however, can never forget his place in a political world. Virgil's closing lines look beyond poetry to war.[20] Pastoral is indeed the vision of a poet who was "bold in his youth," *audax iuventa,* as Virgil here calls himself. The poet of the *Eclogues* was also bold in his innocence. Now Parthenope (Naples), flowers, leisure, and the unambitiousness of "unheroic idleness" are balanced by the Euphrates, thunder, war, and the "greatness" of one who gives laws and leads armies. The juxtaposition of "Caesar" and "Virgil" sets off the distance of the two realms that can never meet but, as Putnam says, "remain only slightly touched by each other's impressive but disparate powers."[21] The road to Olympus is hardly harmonious with the couch beneath the spreading beech tree. The *Eclogues,* of course, also know war. The ruler in these lines is making the world safe for the farmer by "giving laws," however remote "Euphrates" and "Olympus" may be.

In his closing lines, Virgil savors the achievement of the *Georgics* and the establishment of a stronger poetic identity. He is neither an idle pastoralist nor a suicidal elegiac but, among other things, a Pindaric bard who can celebrate great victories. As a *victor* himself, he can make a little thunder of his own (*G.*3.9). He would build a temple to his great ruler in his native Italian land (12ff.). He is also a learned didactic poet who can integrate complex myths and a variety of styles with a mastery that challenges his Hellenistic predecessors. The contrasts and analogies between georgic Virgil and martial Augustus, then, or between the hero of ruthless success and the hero of loss and feeling, aggressive activism and static self-indulgence, cannot be closed with a simple antithesis.

Recently the study of the Fourth *Georgic* has been enlarged by a shift from stylistics and aesthetics to mythical motifs and narrative patterns, thanks in part to structuralist analysis. In 1972 Marcel Detienne, studying myths of honey, stressed the association of bees with chastity and their hostility to an unchaste keeper. Virgil's Orpheus episode, he suggests, exploits the contrast between Aristaeus' excessive disregard of the marital bond in his desire for Eurydice on the one hand and Orpheus' excessive attachment to the marital bond in his *furor* and his inconsolable grief on the other. Virgil's myth, therefore, is not just a tale of passionate love and loss; its true subject is the "thwarting of a couple incapable of establishing a conjugal relation with 'the proper distance'" (*à bonne distance*).[22] Detienne makes an important contribution to the mythology of honey, but his analysis has only limited usefulness for Virgil's text. It begs too many questions about Virgil's sources and exaggerates the "honey-moon" aspect of Orpheus and Eurydice's union before Aristaeus' intrusion into their lives.

Since Detienne's study, J. Chomarat in 1974 and J. S. Campbell in 1982 have emphasized the initiatory motifs in the descents and trials of both male figures.[23] This approach lends further support to the breadth of Virgil's concerns in the episode. It is not just a pathetic tale but an encounter with the holy, a confrontation with the sources of life and death in their sacred dimension.

A fruitful development of this line of inquiry appeared in the chapter on "The Madness of Aristaeus" in Bettini's recent anthropologically oriented study. Beginning with a Proppian analysis of the motifs of the Aristaeus story, Bettini points out that the Orpheus episode has the structure of a fairy tale in reverse. It moves from success to failure, and also from a pattern of loss and regain to a pattern of loss and inertia (Orpheus' now futile song and his tears and death).[24] This inertia, on the level of plot, corresponds to the elegiac or "subjective" tone on the level of style. What Bettini adds to the earlier studies of the mythical parallels is a fuller consideration of the reversal of Aristaeus' usual role in Greek legends prior to Virgil. Whereas the pre-Virgilian Aristaeus is raised by Nymphs, has mantic powers, and seems to have a modest domestic and sexual life, Virgil's Aristaeus becomes hated by the Nymphs, is sexually aggressive, and lacks the knowledge either to understand or to remedy his bees' affliction.

Why this transformation of Aristaeus? Bettini suggests that Virgil is utilizing a notion of the transgressive character of the culture hero. The invention of the arts (the motif with which Virgil introduces the episode [G.4.315f.]) is an ambiguous activity and involves the founder in an ambiguous identity. He moves from justice to injustice, from chastity to licence, from knowledge to ignorance through a crime for which he must atone. Familiar examples are Prometheus and Odysseus. Indeed, for the Greeks in general, craft, *technê*, and related terms are perceived as highly ambiguous.[25]

These issues in one way or another stand at the center of the poem's ambivalence between marveling at nature and controlling or subduing nature, or, in the terms stated in chapter 2, between an Orphic and an Aristaean attitude. The violence that the farmer exerts upon nature has a tragic dimension, as the juxtaposition of Orpheus and Aristaeus implies. But nature is not entirely passive. It too reacts against the destruction of life through the Nymphs' wrath and the bees' failure to reproduce. Virgil recognizes that such violence as the farmer's against

the nightingale is a necessary condition for mortal life in a hard, im-
perfect world. This is a world from which Jupiter has banished the
Golden Age and given us, in its place, "grim toil" (*labor improbus*
[1.145f.]). It is no accident that Jupiter's suppression of the Golden Age
"so that man, by practising the uses [of things] might beat forth the
different arts little by little" (1.133f.) is evoked at the beginning of the
Aristaeus episode, where the poet asks the Muse, "What god beat
forth this art for us?" (4.315).[26] The answer, however, takes us not to
gods or back to the Golden Age, but to the essence of man and his
tragic mortality as that is defined in the following story in terms of
guilt, love, and death.

II · OVID

One of the hardest critical tasks for the modern reader is gauging the
tone of ancient rhetoric. Ovid's Orpheus episode presents particular
difficulties because Ovid is so skillful a rhetorician and so clever at
absorbing the literary tradition, sometimes for its seriousness and
dignity, sometimes for parody. The line between the cynical, parodistic
Ovid and the humanely sensitive Ovid will probably never be definitively drawn because both Ovids exist in the *Metamorphoses*.

As the preceding chapter has argued, parody of the Virgilian episode is all-pervasive in Ovid's version. But parody is a very general
term, and interpreters continue to differ on the major issues. Is Ovid
merely poking fun at the emotional extremes of Virgil's elegiac tone, or
is he reinterpreting the situation in order to explore areas of feeling and
modes of pathos different from anything in Virgil? The two positions
are not mutually exclusive, and I continue to believe that Ovid has his
own brand of seriousness and sympathy, mingled though it is with
irreverence. We can never be sure when Ovid will deflate the golden
balloons of epic grandeur and drop us with a bump. He clearly gives
us one such bump when he implies, early in his *Orpheus*, that the
grief-stricken poet may have "lamented [Eurydice] sufficiently in the
upper air" (*quam satis . . . deflevit vates* [*Met.* 10.11f.]).

Two recent studies illustrate how divergent can be interpretation of
this tale. For Adolf Primmer, writing in 1979, Ovid's own elegiac and
pathetic mood is meant to arouse our sympathies. Ovid, Primmer
argues, parades his scepticism about the mythical underworld; yet the
song of Orpheus in Hades becomes increasingly convincing as it
depicts the power of death and mortals' helplessness before it.

Omnia debemur vobis paulumque morati
serius aut citius sedem properamus ad unam.
tendimus hic omnes, haec est domus ultima, vosque
humani generis longissima regna tenetis.
haec quoque, cum iustos matura peregerit annos,
iuris erit vestri: pro munere poscimus usum.

To you [underworld gods] we belong in all respects, and with but little delay sooner or later we make haste to this one abode. Hither we all make our way; this is our final home, and you hold the longest sway over the race of mortals. She too, when she has completed her just years, will be under your sway: as a gift we ask her temporary loan. (10.32–37)[27]

Although Orpheus is close to victory, he ends on a despairing note.

Quod si fata negant veniam pro coniuge, certum est
nolle redire mihi: leto gaudete duorum.

But if the fates refuse favor in behalf of a wife, it is my decision not to return. Rejoice in a double death. (38f.)

The song of love, then, becomes a song of death – only to be redeemed, in fact, by love.

This Orpheus is not above using a famous ode of Horace on the inevitability of death: "We are all gathered to the same place; sooner or later (*serius ocius*) everyone's lot leaps forth from the urn" (*Odes* 2.3.25ff.). Yet Orpheus' point undercuts the logic of his claim, for (as Primmer argues), "if Orpheus concedes that even an earlier death for Eurydice corresponded to the law [of death], he cuts away the basis of his claim to her 'justly entitled years' in 36."[28] The logical contradiction reaches a climax in Orpheus' sudden willingness to abandon his whole project and to stay behind in the underworld: "Take joy in a double death" (*Met.* 10.39). For Primmer this shift marks a new appreciation of the irresistible power of death. Orpheus the rhetorician has become Orpheus the human being. Orpheus, then, shows us "no glorification of eternally surviving art, as in Monteverdi, no triumph of love, as in Gluck. . . . Amid all the smiling rejection of the mythical underworld love remains the highest life-force, and with it the still mightier reality of death."[29]

Though there is much to agree with here, the elusiveness of Ovid's tone remains. May not Orpheus' "anti-rhetoric" be the trump card of a master player at rhetoric? Is it not equally possible that Orpheus is deliberately recasting the standard topoi of consolation (accept death because it must come "sooner or later" anyway) for exactly the opposite meaning, namely to refuse death's power and to challenge the most intransigent laws of reality? His magical victory over just these laws, in fact, has been a part of the myth since at least Euripides (*Alc.* 962–1005). Orpheus' quasi-legalistic plea that he is only requesting Eurydice "on loan" (*Met.* 10.36, with the repetition of the term for legal rights in *iustos* and *iuris* in 36f.) is, of course, Ovid's humorous deflation of both Horace and Virgil. But we cannot be sure whether the joke is on us as readers or on the gods of the underworld as audience. Do we witness, through their eyes, a brilliant dramatic performance of myth's greatest, most persuasive poet?

Anderson's recent essay takes almost the diametrically opposite direction. He completely discredits Orpheus' rhetorical appeal, finds it a "tawdry" rehashing of poetic commonplaces: it "has plumbed the depths of bathos; it is utterly frigid." "In the Roman audience, it should have elicited smiles; Persephone should have burst into laughter." The closing lines that Primmer reads as despair are for Anderson "the trite baggage of expectable words about death." Even *Amor* in line 26, according to Anderson, has become "a chill abstract noun."[30]

If we return to the beginning of the episode, we can certainly find justification for Anderson's scepticism, not only in Orpheus' "sufficient" lamenting of Eurydice (*Met.* 10.10f.), noted above, but also in the dryness of his reasons for the descent.

> Causa viae est coniunx, in quam calcata venenum
> vipera diffudit crescentesque abstulit annos.

> My journey's reason is my wife, into whom a viper, trodden upon,
> poured forth its poison and took away the growing years. (23f.)

I continue to find these lines far below the tone of high seriousness. The indirect description of the death and particularly the relative phrase, "into whom," instead of "Eurydice," seems to me a deliberate reduction of Virgilian mood. Primmer, however, considers the lines expressive of "the greatest suffering of the greatest mythical singer." If we are unsatisfied by Orpheus' rhetoric, he claims, it is because the singer is so overcome by emotion that he has forgotten his persuasive skills.[31] This is not the place to resume a line-by-line analysis of Ovid's text. The divergence in critical response, I suggest, confirms my point in the preceding chapter, namely that Ovid employs a complex mixture of tones.

I would agree with Primmer that rhetorical topoi and even parody do not necessarily preclude Ovid's sensitivity to basic situations of human suffering. This mixture appears, for instance, in the contrast between the artificial periphrasis for Eurydice's death in line 23, discussed above, and the pathos of the second half of the sentence, "took away our growing years." But Ovid never lets us lapse into a comfortable sentimentality. Allusion to other poets lurks at nearly every point and keeps us alert to the text's sophisticated literariness. Phrases like "lamented sufficiently" and "into whom the viper poured its poison" remind us of the distance that this self-conscious literary style keeps between us and the events or characters.

A small but prominent (and much discussed) detail exemplifies this emotional distance. In contrast to the Virgilian Orpheus' fourfold *te*, "You, Eurydice," or the Virgilian Eurydice's final "Orpheus," Ovid's protagonists never address each other. In fact, Ovid keeps his Eurydice anonymous until *Metamorphoses* 10.31. Only at this point does her devoted husband give her a name: "Undo the [too] hastily woven fate of Eurydice" (*Eurydices, oro, properata retexite fata*). This suppression of her name is all the more striking as the story begins with the wedding-god, Hymenaeus, calling, in vain, to Orpheus (*et Orphea nequiquam voce vocatur* [*Met.* 10.3]). Does this opening motif prefigure the fact that in this telling of the myth the poignant Virgilian communications will be silent? The Ovidian Eurydice says nothing and even her final farewell is scarcely audible (*Met.* 10.60–63; cf. *G.*4.494). Later, Orpheus' head will not cry "Eurydice" in triple anaphora, as in Virgil, but only "something lamentable" (*flebile nescio quid* [*Met.* 11.52f.; cf. *G.* 4.526f.).

Deliberately correcting the extreme emotionality of the Virgilian Orpheus, Ovid has Eurydice begin as an unnamed "new bride" and end as "something tearful."[32] Even when Orpheus and Eurydice are reunited in Hades, they exchange only looks, not words (*Met.* 11.63–66). Is Ovid playing with surprise and anticlimax, first by reuniting the twice-separated pair and then by giving the most famous of all poets nothing to say at this great moment? For Anderson, Ovid's silencing of Eurydice in 10.60ff. simplifies "a grand human tragedy . . . into insipidity."[33] Certainly Ovid's Orpheus disappoints; but to assess the terms of that disappointment we have to turn to another controversial problem in the tenth book, the question of artistic failure.

III · ORPHEUS AND PYGMALION

Critics of Ovid increasingly appreciate the extent to which contiguous tales in the *Metamorphoses* provide an implicit commentary on one another.[34] In the case of Orpheus the assessment of his role as the paradigmatic poet depends in part on how we view his relation to the other great artist-lover of this section of the poem, Pygmalion, whose story Orpheus himself relates later in the book (*Met.* 10.243–297).

For Eleanor Leach, who stresses the motif of artists' failures, the Pygmalion story barely transcends its prurient Greek original, in which Pygmalion made love to the statue.[35] For Anderson, however, "Pygmalion's failure as an artist and his success as a human lover are Ovid's potent response to the myth of Orpheus."[36] Donald Lateiner regards Pygmalion as totally "triumphant" and as "the perfect artist."[37] To Leonard Barkan, Pygmalion unites "art and nature with a positive sense of human affirmation." Pygmalion's "belief in his art makes of shadow a very real substance."[38]

What is the critic to make of such differences of opinion among highly qualified interpreters? One obvious answer is that Ovid has deliberately made it hard for us to choose a single meaning. His use of the narrative frame creates multiple refractions (though not infinite possibilities) for each myth and lets us draw more than one possible conclusion or a single, simple moral.

Pygmalion belongs to a series of infatuated lovers, reaching from Narcissus in book 3 to Myrrha, who immediately follows his story, in book 10. But he also has a place in a series of contrasting paradigms of intense, steadfast love. At the end of the preceding book, the gods transform Iphis into a man so that "he" can marry his beloved, Ianthe. Here in book 10 the gods likewise heed the prayers of a faithful lover. Iphis, Pygmalion, and Orpheus (in the first part of his myth) are rewarded by the gods for the constancy of their love and their moral and emotional purity. Myrrha, like Pygmalion, conceives a desperate passion for the man who gave her life, but she is far from Pygmalion's piety.[39] Pygmalion takes advantage of a festival of the gods to bring his love to a happy conclusion (10.270–281). Myrrha invokes the gods, to be sure, but immediately rationalizes her guilty desire for her father by allegorizing Venus as an amoral force that sanctions incest (321–331). Soon after, with her nurse's connivance, she takes advantage of a religious festival that enjoins sexual purity. This is her opportunity to consummate her incestuous desires.

In contrast to Pygmalion, Orpheus exemplifies the failure of the artist insofar as his passion leads him to lose what his skill as a singer-poet has won. Yet this loss is attenuated by the reunion with Eurydice, somber though it may be, in the underworld (11.61–66). Pygmalion embodies artistic failure insofar as the metamorphosis of his beloved statue takes place not through art, but through the power of Venus. Yet it is his combination of love and art that calls Venus to the scene. His mimetic skill as sculptor has fashioned the object of beauty that inspires *amor* in the viewer (who in this case is also the artist) and leads him to seek the aid of the love-goddess on her feast day (10.270–276). Neither tale permits simple categorization into the black-and-white terms of the "success" or "failure" of the artist. By enclosing the story of Pygmalion within that of Orpheus, Ovid reflects on both the power and the limitations of art.

Pygmalion's transformation of hard ivory into the semblance of attractively yielding flesh reverses the tale of the Propoetides briefly mentioned just before (10.238–242). They refuse the goddess, profane love by becoming the first prostitutes, and are then changed "into hard stone, with but little difference from before" (*in rigidum parvo silicem discrimine versae* [242]). The sacredness of love in Pygmalion's story, on the other hand, enables him to give life to ivory. Instead of incurring Venus' anger, this transformer of matter through love calls Venus directly into his world. Like Orpheus' song in Hades, his work is inseparable from his love and is profoundly reverent toward love. His response to his own creation admittedly takes the rather silly form of offering jewels and flowers to a mere statue (260–269). Yet it also testifies to the power of art to excite love in a heart hitherto closed to it (243–246).

Orpheus, now a confirmed pederast, may be telling Pygmalion's story to make fun of the follies and excesses of heterosexual love. But if so, the tale conveys a meaning beyond the narrator's intentions (a point to which I shall return later). In disgust at the Propoetides, Pygmalion resolves to lead a life of celibacy. The beauty of his own art, however, leads him to break this vow. He overcomes his too hasty judgment of women and is rewarded by love. Orpheus follows the reverse pattern. He begins as a lover of women, resolves to love boys rather than women after his final loss of Eurydice, and is punished for the change. Where Orpheus lost a love, Pygmalion gains one.

The symmetry between the beginning and end of the Pygmalion episode suggests another harmony between art and love. Drawn by the "wonder" of the lifelike creation of his imagination (252f.), Pygmalion touches the ivory as if it were flesh. After Venus answers his prayer, he again places his hand on the form and tests it. But now life really does course through the veins. The verbal echo calls attention to the miracle.

> saepe manus operi *temptantes* admovet, an sit
> corpus, an illud ebur, nec adhuc ebur esse fatetur.

> Often he puts his hands on the work to *test* whether it is flesh or ivory, and even so he cannot admit that it is ivory. (254f.)

> dum stupet et dubie gaudet fallique veretur,
> rursus amans rursusque manu sua vota retractat:
> corpus erat: saliunt *temptatae* pollice venae.

> While he is dumbfounded and feels a joy not yet certain and fears to be deceived, in love again, again he touches with his hand the object of his prayers: it is indeed flesh, and the veins, *tested* by his hand, pulse with life. (287–289)

But the divine intervention only parallels the miracle of artistic creation: the goddess completes the work begun by the artist.

Despite the difference in outcome, the Pygmalion story is, in one sense, a characteristically Ovidian development of the Virgilian Orpheus. This is an artist whose work is intimately tied to his emotions and especially to his sufferings in love. Pygmalion is an Orphic artist in the sense that his art crosses the boundaries between his art and life. And, like Orpheus, he is not able fully to control the process.

Orpheus' art is richest in its power to lament lost love; Pygmalion's art has its fullest scope in effacing the distance between the imagined love-object and the tangible physical union that satisfies desire. Yet the ambivalence in the relation between the two tales remains, for without Venus' miraculous help, Pygmalion's ivory statue would be but another version of Orpheus' hopeless separation from his beloved. It would, in other words, again demonstrate the power of art only to stimulate desire, encourage fictional satisfactions, and project consummations in fantasy rather than in fact. Pygmalion's initial disbelief in the miracle reinforces this possibility of solipsism and self-delusion in the artistic experience: *stupet et dubie gaudet fallique veretur,* "he is dumbfounded and feels a joy not yet certain and is afraid of being deceived" (287).

As a self-reflective view of Ovid's own work, the Pygmalion episode acknowledges the power of art to arouse erotic fantasies as well as to explore the depths of eros. The poet can as easily spin a fantasy of erotic wish fulfillment as move us to tears with the loss of a devoted conjugal love. But Pygmalion is also the artist who (unlike Orpheus) remains faithful to his love. He is the artist whose work enables him, ultimately, to get beyond the sterility of empty desire with which Narcissus wastes away. Whereas Narcissus loses all corporeal substance in his hopeless fascination with his own form (3.486–510), Pygmalion can give corporeal form to his idealized love-object. Thus the miracle that his creation comes to life as a body that he can touch and hold (*corpus erat* [10.289]) is probably a conscious foil to the disappearance of Narcissus' body after it melts away in frustrated desire (3.486ff.): *nusquam corpus erat,* "nowhere was his body" (509).[40] Art offers the artist a way out of the self-enclosure of the erotic imagination. It enables him to project desire upon an Other that he can fashion as an object existing in the outside world. There are dangers here too. Without Venus' intervention the artist-lover would be lost in a self-absorbed, specular longing in place of real relation (cf. *stupet et dubie gaudet fallique veretur* [10.287], discussed above).

To this extent the Pygmalion episode offers a positive complement to Orpheus: Pygmalion is the artist who not only depicts objects worthy of love but himself remains reverent toward the divinity of love, that is, toward the erotic power that inspires his work of giving life to matter. He creates a form "that you would believe alive; and, if reverence did not stand in the way, you would believe that it wanted to move. To such a degree does art lie concealed in its own art" (250–252). On the other hand, Pygmalion's happy ending forms a potentially bitter and ironical commentary on the life story of its narrator. Whereas Orpheus eventually achieves reunion with Eurydice only in the form of a lifeless shade, Pygmalion embraces a voluptuous flesh-and-blood woman.

The Pygmalion story is not only a happy-ending counterpart to the Orpheus story; it also simplifies. The Orphic triangle love-art-death is reduced to art and love. The tragic overtones of the Orpheus tale thus dissolve into wish fulfillment, a sculptor's erotic daydream. Does the narrator, Orpheus/Ovid, through the framing device, make us see the daydream for what it is? If so, Pygmalion's story appears as pure indulgence – a heterosexual's indulgence. From the point of view of the narrator, now converted to homosexuality, it therefore deserves the scorn that its velleitarian "lived happily ever after" should arouse in more serious minds.

In Anderson's reading the homosexually biased Orpheus does not himself fully appreciate the meaning of the stories he tells. Orpheus now believes in the superiority of homosexual to heterosexual love, but his stories do not in fact bear out his argument. He begins his song with "the faults that nature gave in fullest abundance to the female mind" (10.243f.). In the sequel, however, a woman like Atalanta in fact shows better judgment than her beloved, Hippomenes, whose lack of restraint dooms them both to a bestial metamorphosis.[41] But if Ovid wishes us to see Orpheus as emotionally and poetically incompetent, as Anderson suggests, one would expect a more explicit indication of such a failing, especially as we are dealing with myth's most celebrated singer.

Assessing Ovid's aims here, as we have seen, is not easy. Ovid seems to be engaged in an ironizing deflation of his model; yet he takes one of Virgil's major innovations (Orpheus as poet-lover) and boldly carries it to a point far beyond where Virgil left it. Whereas Orpheus sings his songs ostensibly to express his disillusion with heterosexual love, his longer stories in fact illustrate the power of love, particularly love between a man and a woman: Pygmalion and his statue, Myrrha and Cinyras, Atalanta and Hippomenes, Venus and Adonis. There is even a climactic progression in the order of the songs, for the last one illustrates the power of love over the love-goddess herself.

By ending with an image of emptiness in Venus' transformation of the dead Adonis' blood into the "windflower," the anemone (10.738f.), Orpheus is perhaps also suggesting a sympathetic identification with his own loss of love, as he reached forth to grasp Eurydice and "seized nothing but the yielding breeze" (*nil nisi cedentes infelix adripit auras* [59]). So the anemone "offers but brief enjoyment, for those same winds that furnish its name also scatter it, as it cannot hold fast and because of its lightness falls to earth" (*brevis est tamen usus in illo; / namque male haerentem et nimia levitate caducum / excutiunt idem qui praestant nomina venti* [736–739])."Winds" is significantly the last word of the book and of Orpheus' song, its meaning underlined by the etymological play on anemone as "windflower" (Greek *anemos*, "wind," and Latin *ventus*).

The Pygmalion story, the first of Orpheus's longer tales, resembles Virgil's technique in the Orpheus-Aristaeus episode in that it utilizes the neoteric device of opposite tones for framing and enclosed narratives.[42] But when we reach the story of Venus and Adonis, we are in for a surprise. Orpheus/Ovid now has Venus tell a tale-within-a-tale-within-a-tale. Her story of Atalanta and Hippomenes is a monitory and etiological myth: lions harbor resentment against Venus because of the outcome of Hippomenes' love for Atalanta (10.522f.; cf. 702, 705f.). Like Orpheus at the beginning, she also seeks shade for her setting (555f.; cf. 90ff.). Is Ovid here trying to outdo Virgil in exploiting the resources of the embedded narrative? This dramatic device makes the narrator say both more and less than he knows. Such stories are hard to fix in final meanings; an apparently trivial transition or mistaken, exaggerated, or false premise by such a narrator may in fact be the point of departure for a deeper truth. The potential irony of the embedded narrative, however, gets a new twist when the love-goddess illustrates her own power in the first person (for example, 639, 647, 676–680).

Venus' embedded tale, like Orpheus' narrative, has a direction contrary to its main purpose, for it is ineffectual in preserving Adonis. Like the lovers she warns him against, she loses him to the wild. Here too, then, contrast and complementarity work together. If we look back to the main frame of Venus' story, we find a similar relation with Orpheus' framing situation. As we have observed, Orpheus' account of Venus' loss reflects his own emptiness in the attempted embrace of Eurydice. But his account of the goddess's sudden change from helpfulness to anger in telling Atalanta's story is also in keeping with *his* current suspicion of love and his negative view of the female mind. "Suddenly I changed to wrath," Venus says, as she describes how, thinking herself unappreciated, she engineers the events that transform the happily united Atalanta and Hippomenes into lions (682–685).

The interest in narratology over the past decade has helped us see how self-conscious Ovid is about the nature and limits of narrative.[43] Virgil recreates the myth in a contrastive setting that in fact harmonizes with the myth's underlying seriousness; Ovid places the myth in a deliberately jarring context (Orpheus' rejection of heterosexual love) that opens it to disparities, paradoxes, and surprises — effects characteristic of Ovid's poem as a whole.

Ovid wants us to recognize his reworking of the Virgilian model. He is unwilling to have his account stand as entirely independent of the earlier version. To this end he takes over Virgilian phrases verbatim, but he gives them a wholly different setting. Such, for instance, is the phrase *dispersa per agros*, "scattered over the fields," in *Met.* 11.35, transferred from the parts of Orpheus' body to the implements of the farmers whom the Thracian women have attacked (cf. *G.*4.522).[44] By having these women tear apart the oxen before falling upon Orpheus (*divulsere boves* [*Met.* 11.38]), Ovid reminds us of his skill in both dispersing and fusing different parts of the mythical tradition. In this case he combines Orpheus' end with Pentheus' death at the hands of the Maenads in Euripides' *Bacchae*, a myth to which Virgil had already alluded, albeit less directly ("the rites of nocturnal Bacchus" [*G.*4.521]). Ovid has already used such echoes from Euripidean tragedy at length in the story of Myrrha, where he closely models her confession to the nurse after Phaedra's confession of her incestuous desire for her "son" in the *Hippolytus* (*Met.* 10.391–430).

By such devices, Ovid indicates the self-conscious literariness of his narrative. This attention to the earlier narrative is a manifestation of what since Harold Bloom has come to be known as "anxiety of influence." Telling his tales within a long tradition, he is aware of his great Roman predecessor, but he also demonstrates that he has a fuller arsenal of literary weapons by which to surpass his model. He looks back to Virgil, but he also takes care to look beyond Virgil. He can contain his anxiety of influence, in other words, by placing the Virgilian version within the context of other literary versions of myths.

There are hints, however, that the anxiety is not always contained. What subject is more likely to arouse anxiety of influence than the myth of the poet par excellence? The silences of Ovid's Orpheus story are perhaps the most significant indication of such anxiety. In place of the Virgilian Orpheus' two most powerful utterances, Ovid puts— nothing.[45]

In my pre-Bloomian innocence of 1972 (chapter 3), I argued merely that Ovid consciously presents a different conception of the Orphic poet-lover and deliberately reduces the narrative to more human and more secular dimensions. Now, I would suggest that the indirect rhetorical question of Ovid's Eurydice, "What could she complain of except that she had been loved?" (*Met.* 10.61), is also at some level Ovid's question to himself: What can a post-Virgilian Eurydice say at this moment? In like manner the neutral "mournful something" (*flebile nescio quid*) of Ovid's dead Orpheus tacitly acknowledges the impossibility of competing with the Virgilian pathos on its own ground.

Instead, Ovid displaces the emotive effect of the anaphora to nature's lament over Orpheus himself: "You, Orpheus, did the birds in sadness lament, you the beasts and the rocks, over you wept the forests that had often followed your songs" (11.44ff.). But here he is still drawing on Virgil, albeit the Virgil of the *Eclogues*, with the pastoral convention of the "pathetic fallacy."[46]

In the light of these observations, the opening of the Ovidian Orpheus' song reveals the burden of following Virgil (*Met.* 10.148ff.). Orpheus begins with the familiar topos of invoking Jupiter (possibly echoing Virgil, *Ecl.* 3.60). But he combines this point with the equally traditional device of the *recusatio:* he will not claim the power to reach such high themes. "With plectrum more solemn I have sung of the Giants," he goes on, "and of the victorious thunderbolts scattered over the Phlegraean fields. Now I need a lighter lyre, and so let us sing of boys beloved by gods and of girls smitten with illicit flames of passion who received deserved punishment because of their lust" (*Met.* 10.150–154). Gigantomachy is a commonplace for the loftiest possible reaches of the epic tradition (cf. Horace, *Odes*, 2.12). But Ovid is contrasting the "heavier plectrum" of a previous poetic grandeur with a "lighter lyre" that sings only of love. May that contrast reflect the difference between the erotically colored, lighter narratives of the *Metamorphoses* and the traditional epic solemnity of Virgil's *Aeneid*? Ovid gives this contrast still another twist by deliberately echoing Virgil's own disavowal of grandiosity. Virgil follows up his Orpheus myth with a self-deprecating comparison between his own "ignoble leisure" and the martial glory of Octavian/Augustus who "thunders" and is "victorious" (*fulminat, victor* [G.4.561f.]). Ovid's verb, "I have sung," *cecini* (*Met.* 10.150) may recall the pastoral *cecini* of *Eclogue* 1, which Virgil quotes in the last line of the *Georgics*.

If Ovid is glancing at the invincible, Jove-like grandeur of the Virgilian Orpheus, he is also very much aware of his own subversion of Virgilian themes. He does indeed begin with Jupiter, but it is a very Ovidian Jupiter. This Olympian deity blazes not with victorious lightning but with the flames of love for Ganymede. Ironically, he resembles the girls "inflamed" with illicit passion whom Ovid has mentioned just before (*Met.* 10.153f.). Jupiter's celestial dignity (cf. *dignatur* [158]) continues to be compromised as he decides on a proper creature for his disguise in kidnapping Ganymede, and he finds that the only one "worthy" is the bird that bears his "lightning bolts" (157f.). The repeated *fulmina* (158 and 151) shows how far we have come fror the Giant-vanquishing cosmic ruler of the invocation. The last line of the tale shows Juno's reluctance to have Ganymede's services at th divine feasts (*invitaque Iovi nectar Iunone ministrat*, "against Juno's ʋ ill he serves nectar to Jupiter" [161]). Here again Ovid moves from the cosmic themes of gigantomachy to the domestic comedy characteristic of his gods. We seem to be back among the gods' amorous embarrassments of book 1 (cf. Juno and Io in 1.601ff.).

Ovid's Orpheus verges close to becoming a persona for Ovidian poetics, particularly for a poetics deeply conscious of the distance between the narrative of the *Metamorphoses* and its great predecessor. This function of Orpheus reappears in the reference to song that opens the long Myrrha episode.

> dira canam: procul hinc natae, procul este parentes,
> aut, mea si vestras mulcebant carmina mentes,
> desit in hac mihi parte fides, nec credite factum.
>
> Terrible the things I shall sing. Be far from here, daughters, far you too, parents; or if my songs will charm your minds, let me lack credence in this part of my tale, and do not believe the deed. (10.300–302)

Orpheus, the archetypal poet-enchanter, would now reverse the magical "charm" of his verses (cf. *mulcebunt carmina* [301]). Instead of asking for belief, as poets generally do, he asks for disbelief. Instead of a noble subject, he sings of "horrors" (*dira* [301]). Instead of summoning an audience, as he did in gathering the trees at the opening of his song (cf. 90ff.), he would distance an audience.

This passage again reminds us of Ovid's originality in remaking the Virgilian Orpheus. Virgil's Orpheus has a song that "soothes" or "charms" (*mulcentem tigris et agentem carmine quercus*, "charming tigers and drawing oaks by his song" [G.4.510]); but the *frisson* of horror in the "charm" of the Ovidian *carmina* is a wholly new touch (*mulcebant carmina mentes* [*Met.* 10.301]). One should not exaggerate these contrasts; but, when read against the grandiose Jupiter of Ovid's opening invocations, they show a narrator aware of the different tones in his work and in the work of the tradition on which he depends.

A Bloomian perspective, then, would supplement my remarks on Orpheus' invocation to the Muse in *Metamorphoses* 10.148 (*Musa parens*) with at least a trace of the anxiety of influence.[47] When Orpheus invokes the Muse as his parent, he is speaking the literal truth. Ovid's poetical "parent," however, is not a fostering mother, but a father against whom he must struggle, as Jupiter struggled against his father and against other threatening adversaries of an older order, like the Giants here in 150f. Yet for all the anxiety that entering the lists against Virgil must have occasioned, Ovid seems to have felt some measure of confidence, not only in rewriting Virgil's Orpheus episode and, soon after, Virgil's whole Aeneas epic, but also in ending his poem with a defiance of "Jupiter's anger" and with the certainty of his continuing poetic "life" (*vivam*) wherever Roman rule extends over the earth (15.871–879).

5

Dissonant Sympathy
Song, Orpheus, and the Golden Age in Seneca's Tragedies

I ·

Orpheus has a prominent place in the choral odes of Seneca's *Medea*, *Hercules Furens*, and *Hercules Oetaeus* (The last, even if not by Seneca, may be considered within the context of Senecan drama).[1] Outside the tragedies, Seneca has only a passing reference to Orpheus as the figure with whom poetry begins (*Ep.* 88.39). In the tragedies he treats Orpheus as a magical poet-savior and a civilizing hero. In contrast to Virgil and Ovid, to whose versions of the Orpheus myth he clearly alludes, he deliberately deemphasizes the brutal death at the hands of the Thracian Maenads.[2]

Seneca draws on the double focus of the myth in the earlier tradition. On the one hand, Orpheus is the consummate poet who knows the mysteries of nature and through his art stands in special sympathy to it. On the other hand, as a victim of love and the *furor* it may bring, he is also a tragic figure who through passion experiences loss, mourning, and death.[3] In this latter aspect the *Hercules Oetaeus* contrasts his end unfavorably with the future apotheosis of its hero (*H.O.* 1035); but, as we shall see, Seneca elsewhere takes a more favorable attitude to the poet-hero.

As a poet who moves animate and inanimate nature by the power of his song, Orpheus could well have exemplified for Seneca the ideal of art in harmony with nature, controlling inert matter by skill and intelligence as form controls matter (cf. *Ep.* 65.2ff). As one whom passionate love sends on a quest to the underworld to experience for a second time the loss of his beloved, he could also exemplify the knowledge of suffering that comes to every Senecan hero, from Phaedra's *fata cognosco domus*, "I recognize the fate of my house" (*Phd.* 698) to Thyestes' *agnosco fratrem*, "I recognize a brother" (*Thy.* 1006).[4]

In the songful laments in which the arch-poet involves the entire world of nature in his grief, he also embodies the extreme of that self-dramatization which, as T. S. Eliot noted, is central to the stance of the Senecan hero.[5] The sympathy that binds the individual to the universe in Stoic philosophy finds poetic expression in the tragic hero's reaching out to embrace all of nature. This latter is Seneca's most frequent rhetorical device in the tragedies, the reverberation of suffering in the movements of the sky or sea and its magnification in vast geographical hyperboles. The Senecan version of the "pathetic fallacy" (or perhaps we should say sympathetic fallacy) has its mythical roots in Orpheus. In a different mode, Virgil had suggestively sketched a poetics of "Orphic" participation in the *Eclogues*.[6] The *Georgics* and Ovid's *Metamorphoses* added their authority to the notion of an Orphic poetry that spanned the gap between the natural world and human emotions.[7]

Although the few occurrences of Orpheus and related themes do not justify speaking of an Orphic "heroism" in Senecan tragedy, there is certainly an Orphic voice. Himself a sufferer and traveler to Hades, Orpheus points to a poetic vision that mediates two extremes of human nature, the aspiration for a Golden Age realm of peace and beauty and the knowledge of the dark passions, disobedience to the gods, violations of nature's laws that bring suffering into human life. With his kindred spirit, Amphion, he serves as a foil, often momentary and pathetic, to the polluted world of the tragedies, a glimpse of an alternative to despair, hatred, and violence.

As a philosopher, Seneca has reservations about the wisdom of the poets. The "ancient quarrel between poetry and philosophy" finds some echoes in his work.[8] On the other hand he admits the poets' usefulness as teachers of moral wisdom (*Nat.* 6.2.2, *Ep.* 8.8ff.). He even translates a purple passage from Cleanthes on poetry as deepening ethical perception. "As our breath gives back a clearer sound when the trumpet pours it forth at last from its broad mouth after drawing it through the narrowness of its long channel, so the dense force of song makes our perception clearer" (*sic sensus nostros clariores carminis arta necessitas efficit* [*Ep.* 108.10]). Of all the ancient philosophers, the Stoics took the most kindly view of poetry.[9] Posidonius, from whom Seneca draws a great deal, regarded the arts in general as manifestations of the power of reason (*logos*) that gives man his distinctive place in the universe.[10]

II · *PHOENISSAE* AND *OEDIPUS*

In two of the Theban plays, *Oedipus* and *Phoenissae*, Seneca refers to the founder-poet Amphion whose song, like Orpheus', has power over brute matter. Like Orpheus too, Amphion is a civilizing hero: both Greek and Roman writers pair him with Orpheus as one who through music raises mankind from a primitive and savage condition.[11] In the *Phoenissae*, Jocasta invokes Amphion as a counterweight to Polynices, whose attempt to regain the throne would undo Amphion's work.

> poteris has Amphionis
> quassare moles? nulla quas struxit manus
> stridente tardum machina ducens onus,
> sed convocatus vocis et citharae sono
> per se ipse summas venit in turres lapis —
> haec saxa franges?

> Will you shake Amphion's buildings? Will you smash those blocks that no hand set in place, guiding the burden slow-moving on the groaning crane, but each stone, summoned by the sound of voice and lyre, came to its topmost tower? (*Pho.* 566–571)

The groaning of the machine contrasts with the magical music, ease with painful effort. But the passage as a whole develops the larger contrast between the civilizing art of song and the destructive savagery of war. As Jocasta concludes her plea some ten lines later, she calls Polynices' attack on these "dear walls" the sign of wildness, hardness, and savagery: *tam ferus durum geris / saevumque in iras pectus?* "So fierce, do you bear a hard heart, savage in anger?" (582f.).

If Amphion's song is a reminder of civilizing order in Thebes' past, the other figures of the play show a different side of Theban history. In the prologue, Oedipus, in despair, resolves to return to Cithaeron (12ff.), connected with the deaths of Actaeon and Pentheus, Zethus' fierce bull that dragged Dirce to death through the forest, and Ino's homicidal madness (13–25). Jocasta refers repeatedly to the disasters of the Theban house, especially to Pentheus' death (cf. 363ff., 646ff.). Seneca plays on this divided heritage of Thebes' past: the creative, songful moment of Amphion's effortless architecture and the savage forest, place of horrible bloodshed.

This contrast is even more marked in the *Oedipus* where Zethus and his "fierce bull" appear alongside the musical Amphion in the procession of Theban ancestors whom Teiresias and Manto summon up from Hades.

> dextra ferocem cornibus taurum premens,
> Zethus, manuque sustines laeva chelyn
> qui saxa dulci traxit Amphion sono . . .

> First from the ground Zethus comes forth, holding down the fierce bull with his right hand; and then Amphion, in his left hand bearing the lyre, he who drew the stones by his sweet sound. (*Oed.* 609–612)

Seneca pairs Zethus, figure of violent revenge through a beast's savagery, with Amphion, the man of peace. Niobe, Agave, the murdered Laius follow (613–623). Laius' ghost describes the monstrosity that Thebes now contains ("O savage—*effera*—house of Cadmus, delighting always in kindred slaughter" [626]). Oedipus, he charges, has committed a crime that even wild beasts (*feris* [639]) avoid. The pairing of Zethus and Amphion anticipates the ambiguous truth concealed beneath Oedipus' kingship: a murderous violence beneath the civilizing act of killing the Sphinx (cf. 640f.). Oedipus holds in himself the potential of both Zethus and Amphion.

In the *Hercules Furens* the hero, on the verge of his berserk fury, invokes "the founders of our city," beginning with "the forest caves of cruel Zethus" (*conditores urbis et silvestria / trucis antra Zethi* [915f.]). The absence of Amphion's music and the more elaborated setting of Zethus' revenge are appropriate to the moment. What Hercules calls up from Thebes' past is not the act of peaceful musical creation invoked by Jocasta in her attempt to forestall bloodshed in the *Phoenissae*, but murderous vengeance, which is his next thought: "Would that I could pour libation to the gods with the blood of a detested foe" (*H.F.* 902f.).

III · THE TWO HERCULES PLAYS[12]

In the *Hercules Furens* the figure of Amphion recurs, identified (as in the *Phoenissae*) with a fabled time of harmony and peace, a time resembling the Golden Age in the frequent and easy passage of gods among men. But now that happy time is long past, and Thebes is "oppressed by the foul yoke" of the tyrant Lycus (*H.F.* 267). Amphitryon laments:

quis satis Thebas fleat?
ferax deorum terra, quem dominum tremis?
e cuius arvis eque fecundo sinu
stricto iuventus orta cum ferro stetit
cuiusque muros natus Amphion Iove
struxit canoro saxa modulatu trahens,
in cuius urbem non semel divum parens
caelo relicto venit.

Who could bewail Thebes enough? Earth rich in gods, at what lord
do you tremble? From your fields and from your fertile bosom a band
of youths rose up and stood with their iron swords bared; and
Amphion, born of Jupiter, built your walls, drawing the stones with
his songful playing; and to your city not once only did the father of
the gods come, his heavens left behind. (258–265)

Once more the ambiguous history of Thebes contains both the
violence of the Spartoi and the songful creativeness of Amphion,
immediately juxtaposed. Hercules' return seems initially to have
restored the peaceful past of the city, along with its easy communication with the gods. But, as I have noted, he invokes at the end not
the songful Amphion but his vengeful brother, the "fierce Zethus" and
his "forest caves" (915f.).

After Hercules kills Lycus, he prays for the return of felicity in language that recalls Amphitryon's prayer earlier (926–937). But the prayer
is answered by darkness girding the midday sun (939ff.). His madness
plunges us back into the accursed past of Thebes (cf. 387–394) and into
the dark underworld that he has ostensibly escaped.[13]

The second choral ode invokes the arch-poet Orpheus, with whom
Hercules' descent to and return from Hades are compared (569–591). At
the simplest level, the chorus compares the hero of force with the hero
of art. Victory by brute strength introduces and concludes the mythical
paradigm (*fatum rumpe manu*, "break fate by force of hand" [566]; *vinci
viribus*, "defeat by strength," [591]). The chorus's point is that if
Orpheus could win by song, Hercules can win by might.

quae vinci potuit regia carmine,
haec vinci poterit regia viribus.

The palace that could be conquered by song will be able to be conquered by strength. (590f.)

The sequel shows how dangerous the victory by force really is. The violence that lies deep in Hercules' character is not unleashed with impunity. Physical force could defeat the monsters of Hades but not the monstrous within the hero's own soul (cf. 939 and 1063). Hercules will be defeated by an aspect of the underworld that his physical "strength" (*vires*) cannot subdue.[14]

Following the spirit of Ovid's version of the Orpheus legend, Seneca stresses the power of song to move the gods below (569–581).[15] He replaces the Virgilian "madness" (*furor*) with "true love," gives little blame to Orpheus, and in fact restricts his failure to the brief space of two lines:

> odit verus amor nec patitur moras;
> munus dum properat cernere, perdidit.

> True love loathes delays and cannot bear them; while he hastens to behold his gift, he loses it. (588f.)

Using the Euripidean technique of glossing one myth by another with multiple and sometimes dissonant resonances between them, Seneca suggests that a price must be paid for such a conquest and for such power, whether of art or of "strength." He is not merely warning us of "the impossibility of the situation," as has been suggested,[16] but rather developing the tragic dimension of the theme of catabasis, descent to the dark powers of death. Orpheus conquers death by song but through his "true love" loses his loved one; Hercules, like Orpheus, conquers death and also loses his loved ones, not because of love but because of his inner violence.[17] Orpheus' loss is due to a pardonable fault, Hercules' to tragic guilt, *scelus* (1034, 1300f., 1313), which he must acknowledge and expiate.[18]

Orpheus, like Hercules, violates the laws of the gods; but Seneca passes quickly over the transgression in order to stress the less serious flaw of the "true" lover's ardor: *oderit verus amor nec patitur moras: / munus dum properat cernere, perdidit* ("True love loathes and suffers not delays; while he hastens to behold his gift, he has lost it" [*H.F.* 588–589]). This sentiment closely follows the mood of the Ovidian version (see *Met.* 10.56–61). Like Ovid too, Seneca shifts from Proserpina as giver of the "law" of his return in Virgil (*G.* 4.487) to Pluto (*H.F.* 582). But whereas Ovid's tribunal consists of Pluto and Prosperpina as a married couple sharing the rule of Hades, Seneca more austerely makes Pluto alone issue the prohibition as the "judge of death" (*mortis arbiter* [*H. F.* 582]; cf. Ovid, *Met.* 10.15–16, 46–48).

Seneca develops the parallels between the two catabases, Orpheus's and Hercules', in the next chorus (834–837 recall 547ff.; 838ff. recall 556f.). This chorus too ends with a statement of Hercules' passage from Tartarus (889–892): "He returned when he had subdued to peace those below" (*pacatis redit inferis* [890]). The phrase recalls Orpheus' very different mode of "pacifying" the underworld powers.

> mulcet non solitis vocibus inferos
> et surdis resonat clarius in locis.

> He soothes those below with unaccustomed songs and echoes more clearly in those silent places. (575f.)

But Hercules' victory over Hades proves as illusory as his restoration of Golden Age "peace" in the prayer that precedes his fit of madness (*alta pax*, "deep peace" [929; cf. 882]).

The following ode (1054ff.) changes joy to universal grief (*lugeat aether*, "let the aether lament" [1054]); the renewal of cosmic harmony and fertility of 927ff., the logical result of the hero's defeat of death in all myths, is overturned (1054ff. verbally recall 927ff.). The ode ends with the personal, not the cosmic, results of that reversal. The chorus addresses the shades of Hercules' slaughtered children.

> ite ad Stygios, umbrae, portus,
> ite, innocuae, quas in primo
> limite vitae scelus oppressit
> patriusque furor; ite infaustum
> genus, o pueri, noti per iter
> triste laboris. ite, iratos
> visite reges.

> Go, you innocent shades, to the Stygian harbor, you whom your father's crime and rage crushed on life's first pathway. Go, children, a race accursed, along the grim voyage of a familiar toil, go and meet [Hades'] angered rulers. (1131–1137)

The "pacified underworld-dwellers" of Hercules' victory (*pacati inferi* [890]) are now the "angered rulers" of the underworld. The superiority of Herculean force to Orphic song is here revealed as fallacious (cf. 566, 590f.). Instead of rescuing his children from death, Hercules sends them down to Hades. Like Orpheus, but in a far more horrible and more culpable way, he destroys what he loves.

No hell is more terrifying than that of one's own inner darkness. This is the Hades that Hercules has not yet defeated. "Has my mind not yet shaken off those phantom-images of the lower world?" he asks himself (*an nondum exuit / simulacra mens inferna* [1144f.]).[19] In his initial readiness to search out and destroy the killers of his sons (1159–1173), he shows that he does not yet recognize his own infernal self, the monstrous double that is also "Hercules."

Orpheus' failure not only anticipates Hercules' but also implies another mode of overcoming the subterranean powers. Seneca, to be sure, does not create a fully developed poet-hero over against the hero of physical strength; the latter remains the prototype of Stoic heroism. Yet Hercules' suffering at the end of the play shifts the fulcrum of heroic achievement: physical force must be transmuted into spiritual insight and endurance.[20] In that process Orpheus does offer an alternative model of catabasis and conquest.

The *Hercules Oetaeus* devotes an entire chorus to Orpheus, where the topoi of the poet's power over nature and triumphant song in the underworld undergo turgid expansion (*H.O.* 1031–1130, especially 1036ff., 1061ff.). This Orpheus, like the Orpheus of Apollonius' *Argonautica* (1.494–515), is a scientist-poet who sings of the laws of the universe. He knows that the world will end in the universal conflagration taught by Stoic science (cf. *aeternum fieri nihi,* "nothing eternal comes into being" [*H.O.* 1035]). Hercules' end now proves Orpheus correct: his death will involve the world in universal chaos (1100ff.). This is the ultimate form of the topos of cosmic sympathy, the total destruction of the world in response to the death of the hero. The rhetorical possibilities, alas, do not escape the author's relentless pen (1131–1160, 1528ff.).

The descents of Hercules and Orpheus, however, are sharply contrasted. Hercules' underground journey is canceled out by his ascent to the stars (a point, once more, elaborated at length), where his *virtus* has its proper place (1564ff.).[21] His ultimate success in conquering death here contrasts with the poet's failure; it also disproves his teaching that "nothing is eternal" (1035), that death and chaos conquer all (1099, 1115; cf. 1946, *agnosco victum esse chaos,* "I recognize that chaos is overcome").

The lament of the whole world for Hercules eventually gets around to the Arcadians, whose mountains, Parthenius and Maenalus, echo with grief, after the manner of Virgil's Tenth *Eclogue* (*H.O.* 1883–1886; *Ecl.* 10.9–15). The gentle and songful aspect of this lamentation is short-lived. It soon gives way to the devastation that the building of Hercules' pyre wreaks on the natural world. Hercules' "whole sorrowing band laid hold of Oeta" so that "the beech tree loses its shade and lies there with its whole trunk cut down" (*huic fagus umbras perdit et toto iacet / succisa trunco* [*H.O.* 1619f.)].[22] As the desolation spreads, "even the holy oaks feel the hand that bristles with iron, and no grove benefited from its ancient glade" (1634–1636). Orpheus's song too brings violence, for Mount Athos breaks from its place and comes to Rhodope to hear the song, Centaurs and all (*Centauros obiter ferens* [1049]). On the whole, however, Orpheus, as is his wont, establishes a more peaceful harmony with the wild and brings a Golden Age peace in which woodland divinities and all the beasts, the wild and the tame, are joined together in the spell (1052–1060).

It would be mistaken to exaggerate the contrast between Hercules and Orpheus in its meaning for the *Oetaeus* as a whole, but their different relations to nature are an important element.[23] The violence always latent in Hercules finds its appropriate expression in the merciless machine of apotheosis. The cumulative repetitions and variations of the rhetoric are its proper expression. The incrusted language functions as a verbal bulldozer, smashing down the forest that came to sensate life at Orpheus' song: *advexit volucrem nemus / et silva residens venit*, "the grove brought its bird, and seated in its wood it came" [1043f.; cf. 1618–1641).

IV · MEDEA

Both Medea in her play and Atreus in the *Thyestes* are anti-Orpheus figures. Like Orpheus they place themselves at the center of the chords of sympathy that their artfulness creates between man and the world around him. But the energies that they thereby release, far from creating a new accord between man and nature, disrupt the peace of the world and of the soul.

Orpheus has a prominent place in the two central odes of the *Medea*. The first comes just after Creon's fatal acquiescence in Medea's request for one more day in Corinth (*Med.* 294f.). The ode (301–379) laments the violations of nature symbolized by man's conquest of the sea in the Argo's voyage. The chorus interprets the difficulty of the voyage as punishment for that violation (340ff.). Medea resembles Hercules in that she too harbors an inner violence that, like an elemental force of nature, is less amenable to rational control than the optimistic assumptions of progress in human history would suggest.

Jason has brought back from remote and barbarous Colchis something that remains untamed and untamable, something that remains in touch with its latent monstrosity (and *monstrum* is one of the key words of the play: 191, 473, 479, 675, 684).

Orpheus' song in the first ode, initially silenced by the numbing terror of the Symplegades, triumphs over the Siren and thus saves the voyage (341–360). And yet the victory proves hollow: the prize (*pretium*) is the Golden Fleece and Medea herself, "an evil worse than the sea" that they have subdued (360–363).[24] Now any ship can cross the sea; soon the whole world will disclose its secrets, and Thule will no longer mark the furthest limits of the earth (375–379).

Medea and the Argo's voyage crystallize the other side of man's power over nature: control brings the loss of innocence and lets loose nature's forces of vengeance. Medea herself embodies the two extremes of culture and nature. She is identified with both the dominated natural world and the magic arts that exercise dominion; she is both a victim of the violation of innocence and an agent of savage ferocity. Her homeland, at the extreme limit of civilization, contains the two poles of fantasied innocence and unimaginable monstrosity. In a way that bears comparison to the hero of the *Hercules Furens*, she both conquers *monstra* and is herself a *monstrum* (cf. 472f. and 479 with 191 and 674f.). She belongs to a world where the limits of nature are violated, but the Greek heroes must pay for violating those limits.[25]

The removal of boundaries in the Argo's triumph (364–372) is a victory of the heroic spirit, but there is an ominous note in the detail, *terminus omnis motus*, "every boundary-stone was taken away" (369). The exultant hyperbole of the Indian drinking the cold Araxes and the Persian drinking the rivers of northern Europe (373f.) anticipates the destructive confusion of the world order by Medea's vengeful magic (752–770).

Hippolytus' Golden Age speech of the *Phaedra* (to which we shall turn later) distinguishes two stages of marine events in the moral degeneration of mankind: first commerce and then the murderous violence that stains the water with blood (*Phd.* 530f. and 551f.). In his rabid misogyny he ends with Medea as the nadir of all female evil (*Phd.* 551–564). In the *Medea* the Argo not only ushers in the postlapsarian age of commerce (cf. *Med.* 301–308) but also fuses the two stages in the person of Medea herself, a "ware worthy of the first ship" (362) and a monstrous figure who has stained the sea with kindred blood and like Phaedra is associated with the violence of the sea.[26]

Shortly after the ode on the Argo's voyage, Medea's rage (*furor*) appears as a sealike "seething" of "waves" (*aestuatur, fluctus, exundat* [*Med.* 391f.]). She opened the play with the sea under the control of the gods: Minerva guides the Argo, and Neptune is the "harsh lord of the deep sea" (2-4). As she yields to her lust for revenge, the sea controlled by the Olympian patriarchs changes to the seething sea of her hatred and anger (cf. 408-414, 765f., 939-943) and to the sea overwhelmed by her magic spells that "confound the ether's law" (*lege confusa aetheris* [757]) and disrupt the whole Olympian world order (752-770). In the pervasive Senecan (and Stoic) correspondence of microcosm and macrocosm, the world order will be as disturbed as the order in the soul; it will be as confused inwardly by her vehemence of passion (cf. 166f.) as by her magic spells that wreak havoc on the face of nature (752ff.). Indeed the subjection of nature by the supernatural power of her magic is simultaneously the symbolic projection of her violent emotions and the expression of a world order thrown into chaos. As Medea displays the last of her magical powers and soars away from the scene of her terrible vengeance on the serpent-drawn chariot (1023-1025), Jason, in the words that close the play, depicts the moral chaos that now afflicts the universe.

> per alta vade spatia sublimi aetheris;
> testare nullos esse, qua veheris, deos.
>
> Go then through the lofty tracts in the celestial air; bear witness that where you soar there are no gods. (1026f.)[27]

We may contrast the very different image of the world order at the opening of the play (for example, 1-5, 57).

The second ode (579-669) is sung after Medea has found out Jason's vulnerable spot, his love for his children (549f.). The ode begins by comparing her wrath to the violence of fire, wind, storms, and other disturbances of nature (579-594). It goes on to describe the vengeance that the sea exacted from the Argonauts. The conqueror of the sea is now in danger of his life (595f.), and "the lord of the deep," invoked early in the play as a mainstay of the Olympian order (4 and 57), now "rages" in fury at the subjection of his domain (*furit vinci dominus profundi regna secunda*, "the lord of the deep sea rages that the second realm is conquered" [597f.]). The pilot Tiphys and Orpheus, who emerged victorious over the sea in the previous ode (346ff.), are the first victims. The Argo's voyage meant the end of the Golden Age; and that loss of innocence is reenacted in microcosm as we move from the magical spell of Orpheus' music to his violent death.

> ille vocali genitus Camena,
> cuius ad chordas modulante plectro
> restitit torrens, siluere venti,
> cum suo cantu volucris relicto
> adfuit tota comitante silva,
> Thracios sparsus iacuit per agros,
> at caput tristi fluitavit Hebro:
> contigit notam Styga Tartarumque,
>   non rediturus.

Born of the songful Muse, he at whose notes the rushing stream stood still as he touched the strings, he at whom the winds grew silent when the bird, leaving its own song, attended with all the woods following—he lay scattered among the Thracian fields, and his head was carried down the gloomy Hebrus. He reached the Styx that he already knew and Tartarus, never to return.

Here Orpheus' divine origins and his power to involve nature in his art and his feelings are of no avail. His song's previous victory over the underworld (only barely hinted), like his victory over the Siren in the previous ode, is canceled by his death: this time Orpheus will not return (633). The death of other Argonauts in the immediate sequel (634ff.) portends the end of the heroic age as well.

Orpheus' song could silence the winds (*siluere venti* [627]). The "swelling winds" of the ode's first line were an image of Medea's dangerous anger (*tumidi venti* [579]). As the last instance of the sea's vengeance the chorus lists the death of Pelias.

> ustus accenso Pelias aeneo
> arsit angustas vagus inter undas.
> iam satis, divi, mare vindicastis:
>   parcite iusso.

Burned in the heated bronze [cauldron], Pelias blazed, a wanderer amid narrow waves. Enough vengeance, gods, have you exacted for the sea. Spare the one who was commanded [to the deed]. (666–669)

Pelias' death, however, far from appeasing the vengeful magic of Medea, is another confirmation of its power. The Argo's great conquest of the open sea is symbolically reversed in the "narrow waters" (*angustas undas* [667]) of Medea's cauldron. Compared to the violence of

wind, water, and fire (579), she exercises her power with equal viru-
lence in the realm of culture. The figurative fire of passion within may
be just as deadly as the literal fire outside.

The previous ode, we recall, opened with the risks of sea travel and
the demise of the Golden Age through man's violation of nature
(301ff.). But the "audacity" of sea travel (*audax* [301]) soon appeared as
the skillful "daring" of Tiphys (*ausus* [318]); and Orpheus' music defeated the Siren, symbol of the sea's mystery and danger (355–360). That
ode concluded with the optimism of limitless exploration (375–379), in
contrast to 301–308. At the end of the second ode, those journeys beyond "farthest Thule" (379) end in the deadly narrowness of the small
vessel. The initiator of the Argo's heroic enterprise, he who "commanded" it (*iussit* [665; cf. 669]), is reduced to impotence before a
woman's power. The expansive conquest of the world by male heroic
ambition is here checked by the small but powerful constriction of
female guile. "A wanderer among the narrow waters" (668) evokes the
image of the newborn child emerging from the waters of birth (compare Lucretius' description of the infant "thrown up like a sailor from
the cruel wave . . . on to the shores of light" [5.222–225]). We recall too
that Medea's cauldron was to effect a rebirth for Pelias. But the image
of the narrow waters also recalls the other, more elemental realm
where the female is all-powerful. It is precisely through her power as
a mother, through the power of the womb that bore Jason his sons, that
Medea attains her fullest triumph and her most effective revenge (cf.
1012).[28]

The Nurse's horrified account immediately after this ode confirms
Medea's potency. Her power to charm nature by black magic invites
comparison with Orpheus' white magic. Both use "songs" (*cantus
carmina* [229, 356, 358; 684, 688]). The stupefaction produced by
Orpheus' "song" is now an effect of Medea's "spell."

> carmine audito stupet
> tumidumque nodis corpus aggestis plicat
> cogitque in orbes.

> Hearing her song, the serpent stops still and folds its swollen body
> into heaps of knots and forces it into coiling circles. (688–690)

Although Medea's *carmina* (688) or *cantus* (684, 699, 704, 760, 779, etc.)
may share with Orpheus' the power over beasts, they have the
opposite effect: they bring not Golden Age nonaggression but the

rebirth of noxious monsters, particularly the dangerous serpents that are generally absent from such scenes. When Orpheus sings in the *Hercules Oetaeus*, "the serpent flees its lair, forgetful of its venom" (*H.O.* 1059f.; cf. Virgil, *Ecl.* 4.24f.). When Medea exerts her power over the lower world (*Med.* 740ff.), she releases rather than calms nature's violence. Like Orpheus, she acts out of desperate love (*saevo amore* [850; cf. 743]); whereas Orpheus tames the beasts, however, she lets loose her bestial savagery, like a tiger, and cannot "rein in" her anger or her passion (826-865, 866f.). She is identified with the natural phenomena that she would control, particularly fire, but also water. *Torrens*, "rushing stream," for example, describes both her wrath in 584 and the snake she calls forth in 694. Orpheus, savior of the ship from the Siren's song, is a civilizing hero; but Medea's power over nature reflects the ambiguous mixture of regret and admiration felt toward civilization in this play.

As the Argo's voyage brings the loss of Golden Age innocence, its success demands a just retribution from the violators of nature (301ff.). Yet the exploration of uncharted lands at the end of the first ode does not appear in an entirely unfavorable light: it is the laudable and optimistic extension of man's conquest of the unknown (364-379).[29] The fascination with exploring the unknown limits of the earth in this passage corresponds to the play's fascination with the uncharted depths of Medea's passion. In such a passage we can glimpse the "autobiography of the work,"[30] not necessarily the personal motives of Seneca the man but a symbolic reflection of the genesis of an idea and a style, the fascination with pushing language into the uncharted regions of experience and making it reveal the hidden darkness of a passion that would destroy the creations of its own life-giving energy.

Medea's victory over Jason not only undoes the explorations of the Argo and reverses the heroic deed of capturing the Golden Fleece; as a symbolical restoration of her virginity, it also cancels out the violation of her body. At her moment of triumph she cries out:

> iam iam recepi sceptra germanum patrem
> spoliumque Colchi pecudis auratae tenent;
> rediere regna, rapta virginitas redit.

> Now, now have I regained scepter, brother, father; and the Colchians hold the spoils of the golden ram. My kingdom has returned; my virginity, wrested from me, has returned. (982-984)[31]

Yet in the paradoxes that surround her every action, she regains purity by "crime" (*scelus* [986, 994]); she renews her virginity by taking vengeance as a mother (cf. 1000f., 1008, 1012f.). The glimpse of a pre-Argonautic purity and the Orphic vision of a Golden Age of universal peace only set off the "hard" primitivism of her regression to brutality and the cruelty of pitiless vengeance.[32]

V · *THYESTES*

Like Medea, Atreus in the *Thyestes* is a character whose insatiable drive for vengeance (cf. *Thy.* 1052–1068) sets him at the farthest remove from the inward contentment of the Stoic sage. He is an anti-Orphic figure in two respects. In place of the cosmic sympathy that distinguishes the man who lives in harmony with nature stand the hyperbolic reversals of natural processes that his ghastly crime provokes. In place of the Golden Age pacification of nature by Orphic music (cf. *Med.* 625–629) stands the dangerous luxury of a rich urban palace.

The trembling of the grove at his horrid rite (*Thy.* 696) is the dark opposite of Orpheus' charming of trees and forests. It is accompanied by the shaking of the ground and the palace (696–698) and by other sinister prodigies summed up in the collective term *monstra*, "monstrosities" (703). As the horrors increase, the sun darkens over the whole world (776ff., 789ff.). Other celestial disturbances threaten a return to chaos and dark night (cf. 804ff., 813ff., 827ff., 830ff.).[33] On a slightly more modest scale, Atreus would himself hold back the stars and dispel the darkness in order to show the full extent of his revenge (892–897). Yet all the accumulated artistry of his elaborate vengeance contrasts with the spontaneous refusal of the wine to touch his victim's lips; the movements of the earth and the sudden darkness also run counter to his desire for the consummate revenge (985–995).

The cosmic sympathy of these supernatural events, for all their horror, are on the victim's side. Whereas Atreus loses touch with reality in the quasi-divine transports of his exultant success (885f., 911f.), Thyestes, though tricked and besotted with the wine of his gruesome feast, has an instinctive feeling of distress (942ff.). His anxieties, soon to increase to the spontaneous inhibitions of 985ff.—'My hands refuse to obey . . . ; the wine flees from my lips'—are a small remnant of his harmony with himself and with nature. Amid the macabre horrors of this nightmarish world, that instinctive revulsion is the only thing to survive.

The second part of the *Thyestes'* Orphic theme is the pastoral-sylvan peace of nature that serves as an objective correlative for a mind at rest. The motif appears in the contrast between the sylvan exile of Thyestes and the luxurious palace in which and by which Atreus entraps him. The choral ode on the desirability of rule over oneself rather than over far-flung empires (348ff.) immediately precedes Thyestes' instinctive retreat back to the forest.

> repete silvestres fugas
> saltusque densos potius et mixtam feris
> similemque vitam.
>
> Rather seek again your woodland exile and the thick-grown glades and a life mingled with the wild beasts and resembling theirs. (412–414)

But the disastrous effects of not following these good instincts are foreshadowed by his praise of "meals free from care, lying on the earth" and "not nourishing a full belly by the tributes of [subject] races" (*securas dapes / humi iacentem* [450f.]; *nec ventrem improbum / alimus tributo gentium* [46of.]). Atreus lures him to a meal of just the opposite kind. The palace where it is offered encloses its own forest (649ff.), the setting for the ghastly sacrificial murders of Thyestes' sons (682ff.).

Thyestes' forest-life and refusal of the artifical forests of splendid palaces (464f.) are canceled out by the elaborate imagery that compares Atreus to a hunter (491–503) or to a lion or tiger raging in the forests (707ff., 732ff.). Instead of living a simple life like the beasts (413f.), Thyestes is hunted like a beast (491ff.) by an unspeakable foe who is himself "wild" (*ferus* [721]) or "raging" (*saevit* [737]). In his ultimate vengeance, Atreus goes beyond the outrage of giving his victims' bodies to wild beasts to tear (*feris lanianda* [747]; cf. 1032f.). He thereby surpasses the savagery of the remotest barbarian (1047ff.). Thyestes would have found more humanity in his wild forest; the ruler of a regal palace outdoes savage nature in his cruelty. This inversion reflects the internal corruption of power that Silver Age writers are fond of describing. In the *Octavia*, for example, the urban center holds a ruder, more bestial savagery than the rudest barbarian land (973–983; also 636ff., 918–923).[34]

In the *Thyestes* the very intelligence that makes Atreus the consummate artificer of vengeance places him as far out of harmony with nature as it is possible to be. He totally perverts man's noblest means for living in accord with nature. The hyperbolic reversals of the celestial order at the completion of his crime measure the extent of the perversion.

The two sides of the moral inversions, destruction of harmony with the cosmos and loss of a quasi-sylvan peace and simplicity, meet in the fourth choral ode, sung between the murder of Thyestes' sons and the ghastly banquet. After describing the preternatural darkness, the chorus evokes a momentary image of rustic life.

> stupet ad subitae tempora cenae
> nondum fessis bubus arator.

> The plowman, his oxen not yet tired, is amazed at the hour of the
> suddenly approaching meal. (800f.)

Seneca draws on Horace's Second *Epode* but brilliantly adapts the Horatian image to his own purposes.[35] The remote celestial events are tied to the concrete details of the simple farmer's daily round. Agriculture contrasts with Atreus' wild "hunting." The plowman embodies the kind of simple virtue that Thyestes might have enjoyed had he remained in his forest retreat. His *cena*, "banquet," (800) is very different. "Evil crimes do not enter lowly huts," Thyestes had moralized to his son, "and safe food is received on a narrow table" (451f.).[36] The plowman and his "tired oxen" anchor the action for a moment in real things and in a normal productive life, against which we can measure Thyestes' loss. For a moment it creates a middle ground, rare in the tragedies, between outrageous savagery and a mythical, unattainable Golden Age.

VI · *PHAEDRA*

A lost Golden Age is even more central to the *Phaedra*. Seneca adapts Euripides' pointed contrast between the forests of the virginal Hippolytus and the sea associated with Phaedra's sexuality and her ominous Cretan past.[37] Hippolytus' opening song extolling the forests and the mountains of Attica where he hunts (1–84) is sharply juxtaposed to Phaedra's opening invocation to Crete, mistress of the sea, and the sea imagery of her passion (*Phd.* 85ff.; cf. 103). The sinful love of Pasiphae for the bull that fathered the monstrous Minotaur presents a different view of the forest in Phaedra's eyes: *peccare noster novit in silvis amor,* "our love [Pasiphae's and Phaedra's] knew how to sin in forests" (114).

Like Thyestes, Hippolytus loses this forest-world of a simpler life. The Nurse, pleading on Phaedra's behalf, would show him his sylvan celibacy as something rude, harsh, savage (461ff.). Phaedra would accompany him to the woods and share his hunting (234ff., 613ff.). Her accusations, which take place in the interior spaces of the palace, whose enclosed quality is heavily underlined (860–863), reverse the meaning of his sylvan pursuits in Theseus' eyes (922ff.). At the end her wish to follow him to the woods changes to a wish to follow him to Hades (1179–1191; cf. 241). Under the impact of her passion, the landscape of Hippolytus' velleitarian retreat changes to a nightmare landscape of castration (1099), dismemberment, and bloody death (1080ff.).

In his removal from urban life and in the manner of his death, "bloodying the fields far and wide" (1093), Hippolytus resembles the figure of Orpheus.[38] But in his case the Orphic sympathy between man and nature through song is lacking. On closer examination his aspirations toward Golden Age innocence appear torn by contradictions.

Rather than leading a life of philosophic serenity characterized by the "gentle leisure" praised in the Thyestes (lene otium [Thy. 394]; cf. dulcis quies, "sweet calm" [395]; quies [469]), Hippolytus follows the strenuous exertions of the hunt. Rather than pastoral peace in the midst of easeful song in a soft idyllic landscape, he engages in a bloody sport amid rugged mountains and solitary woods (cf. Phd. 1–8, 48–65, 77–80).[39]

When the Nurse, speaking on Phaedra's behalf, urges him to enjoy life and leave the savage woods for the joys of Venus (446ff.). Hippolytus runs through the familiar topoi of Golden Age simplicity (473ff.). As in the Thyestes, there is little middle ground between "luxury" (449f.) and rudeness, vice and primitive harshness. Hippolytus, however, defines his Golden Age in largely negative terms. He makes no mention of song or music. In fact in the erotically colored counterworld of love's triumph in the chorus's first ode, the god of song puts away his lyre under the influence of Amor (296–299).

Hippolytus' image of the Golden Age is deformed by the violence in his own character. He would banish sacrifice, imagining a time when "no abundant flow of blood washes over the holy altars" (non cruor largus pias / inundat aras [498f.]). Yet his elimination of bloodshed makes an exception of hunting, which he excuses as the "only form of crafty deceit" that Golden Age man "knows how to devise" (callidas tantum feris / struxisse fraudes novit [502f.]). Seneca's reader would recognize at once that something is wrong; fear, trickery, craftiness have no place in the Golden Age and are conspicuously removed from the most famous Golden Age of Latin literature, Virgil's Fourth *Eclogue* (cf. *Ecl.* 4.14, 22, 24, 31). Hippolytus' lines also replace the civilized practice of sacrifice with the ruder occupation of the hunt.[40] His prelapsarian ideal forest dweller "possesses the empty countryside and wanders unharmed and harmless (*innocuus*) beneath the open sky" (*rure vacuo potitur et aperto aethere / innocuus errat* [Phd. 501f.]). This picture strikingly contradicts the universal fear that his hunting and his goddess inspire in the animal kingdom, including the beasts in "the empty fields" of the "wandering Sarmatian" (*vacuisque vagus Sarmata campis* [71]). He is (literally) lyrical in praise of the terror that his huntress-goddess brings to wild creatures everywhere (54–72). He deplores the loss of the Golden Age when warfare and its weapons bring "bloodshed" (*cruor*) that "pours forth and stains every land, and the sea grows red" (*hinc terras cruor / infecit omnes fusus et rubuit mare* [551f.]). But his opening song ended with his exultation at the bloodied muzzles of his hunting dogs (*tum rostra canes / sanguine multo rubicunda gerunt*, "then do the dogs bear their muzzles red with much blood" [77f.]).

The latent violence in Hippolytus' forest-world makes its full appearance in the climactic situation that eventually costs him his life. In his abhorrence at Phaedra's declaration of her love, he vehemently pulls back her head (note the savage gesture of *crine contorto*, "twisting her hair" [707]) to expose her throat in a gesture of sacrifical killing. "O goddess who bears the bow," he prays, "never has blood been given more justly to your altars" (*iustior numquam focis / datus tuis est sanguis, arquitenens dea* [708f.]). We recall his praise of that murderous and terror-inspiring bow in his first song (54ff.). The Golden Age hunter (itself a contradiction in terms) who would forbid the shedding of animal blood in sacrifice 499f.) has no hesitation about bloodshed in the hunt or about the homicidal slaughter of a human sacrifice. Righteous purity and sacrilegious outrage are strangely mingled.

Extreme devotion to the hunt, delight in all its gory details, from the cutting out of the entrails to the blood smeared over the dogs' snouts (48–52, 74–80), are part of the psychic adjustments that this figure has had to make in order to repress his sexuality. His wild hatred of women is the necessary complement to the murderous hunting. The Golden Age that Hippolytus imagines is in fact an image of his own character and its unresolved tensions: a quasi-pastoral sylvan peace that licenses the sadistic practices of his way of hunting. His extreme vehemence in defending his neurotic substitution of Diana's bow for that of *Amor* (56ff. and 275ff.; cf. 709), of killing for loving, is a necessary mechanism of a self-mutilation soon to become literal.

His opening image of spring breezes "soothing the meadows with dew-bearing winds" (*rorifera mulcens aura* [10]) prepares us for a Golden Age landscape of idyllic tranquillity. But he soon is scrutinizing the "dewy earth" for tracks of the prey he will hunt (42). Near the end of the play, the dew on Hippolytus' mountains recurs as the "spray" of the sea-monster that destroys him (*summum cacumen rorat expulso sale*, "it bedews the highest peak with the salt sea that it drives forth" [1027]). His dogs, instead of tracking the wounded quarry, will follow the bloody trail of their now physically mutilated master, his limbs scattered over the fields (1106–1108). The idyllic landscape of his hunt is thus transformed into its underlying reality, the appropriate landscape of his soul. This was the potential there from the beginning in his version of the Golden Age.

Phaedra attacks this world at its psychological roots. Hippolytus would replace his lost Amazon mother with his goddess of the wild and the hunt to whom a human (female) sacrifice could be offered (708f.). Both mother figures, Diana and the Amazon, stand in a problematical relation to marriage, sexuality, and civilization. Hippolytus' Amazon mother met violent death at his father's hand (cf. 226f., 578f., 1166f.), is far removed from civilized life (904–908), and vacillates between the extremes of sexual abstinence and promiscuity (cf. 908f.).[41] In replacing this ambiguous mother of his lost childhood with another strenuous female of the wild and of hunting, his goddess Diana, he is only reenacting the ambivalence that attaches to the first, "real" mother. The ostensible Golden Age world that Hippolytus sketches as the background of his way of life can only perpetuate, not reconcile, the contradictions of his personality. When Phaedra finds sex appeal in his heritage from his mother and his "Scythian hardness" (658–660), she becomes a prey to her own impossible fantasies. When Hippolytus creates a forest world as the autonomous landscape of a life of untroubled, desexualized purity, he too is living in unreality.

The challenge to this world image comes in the very different world of the chorus's first ode: this forest-world is in fact permeated by sex. Love defeats song in these forests. Because of love Apollo puts away his lyre to herd Admetus' cattle (296–298). Because of love the wild beasts (which Hippolytus regards only as passive victims of his or Diana's arrows) fight savage battles (339–353). This forest "groans with the savage roaring" of these sexually motivated combats (*cum movit Amor,* /

tum silva gemit murmure saevo, "When Love moves them, then does the forest groan with the savage sound" [349f.]).

Traditionally the naiads who inhabit these woods flee the embraces of lustful Pans and Satyrs. Horace's Faunus is a "lover of Nymphs who run away" (*Faune Nympharum fugientum amator* [*Odes* 3.18.1]). In Hippolytus' forest, as a later chorus sings, these denizens of the woods are shameless and forward creatures, *Naides improbae* (*Phd.* 780), "lascivious goddesses of the groves" (*lascivae nemorum deae* [783]). They lie in wait for good-looking young men and take the initiative in wooing the Pans that wander on the mountains (*Panas . . . montivagos petunt,* "they seek out the mountain-wandering Pans" [784]). To complete the picture of a forest-world that clashes drastically with Hippolytus', Diana herself appears as not immune to love but full of passionate desire for Endymion—or Hippolytus (786–794). These choral passages reveal Hippolytus' Golden Age world as a fragile mental construct, soon to be overthrown by exactly what it excludes.

Hippolytus gives an initial appearance of an "Orphic" heroism of simplicity, inner peace, harmony with nature. But the initially idyllic-looking forest-world of his opening lines soon reveals itself as a place of bloodthirsty slaughter, not musical serenity or philosophical leisure (*otium*). The sexual forces that he refuses to acknowledge rebound upon him. The destructive rather than the creative power of love and of nature triumphs. Love subdues not only the songful Apollo in his pastoral setting (296–298) but also the Stoic hero of physical endurance, Hercules, who has exchanged club and lion skin for the Eastern apparel and exotic emeralds of a Lydian temptress (317ff.).

VII · CONCLUSION

Senecan tragedy creates a world of its own, a world defined negatively, in part, against the topoi of pastoral peace and musical calm that symbolize a potential harmony between man and nature. Throughout the plays that vision takes concrete poetic form in the figure of Orpheus and the related figure of Amphion, remote personages whose music charms nature, renders it useful to human purposes, and can sometimes even defeat death. More frequently, however, this songful accord is effaced by the violence that makes man a bestial victim of his own passions (*Hercules Furens, Phaedra*), or else it is overwhelmed by an anti-Orpheus whose magical control of nature images the abyss of insatiable hatred or vengefulness (*Thyestes, Medea*). This is the dark underside of Orphic harmony with nature; this kind of cosmic sympathy dramatizes the depths of evil in the human soul.

Some recent critics describe Senecan tragedy as "baroque" or "mannerist."[42] The usefulness of the term lies perhaps in a certain suggestive vagueness. One component of Senecan "mannerism," I would venture, lies in this shifting movement between a philosophical ideal of harmony with nature, tranquillity, freedom from passion, and the rhetorical elaboration of grotesque and uncanny horrors, the plunge into a realm of surreal nightmare shapes.

The shifting between horror and clarity, nightmare and idyll, visions of purity and visions of corruption, are rapid and disturbing and keep us always a little off balance.[43] The geographical hyperboles, with their implicit breadth of view over the whole world, may suddenly give way to the interiorized, visceral knowledge of the soul's hidden terrors as the poet takes us with him into the Stygian depths of evil. Thyestes' opening vista of his native land as he moves from the sylvan simplicity of his exile to Atreus' palace (*Thy.* 404-414) is the pathetic foil to his enclosure in the bloody chambers of Atreus' feast and the terrible crime enclosed now in his own flesh.

> volvuntur intus viscera et clusum nefas
> sine exitu luctatur et quaerit fugam.

> My entrails heave within me, and the crime, shut within, wrestles, with no way out, and searches for escape. (1041f.)

Or, as in the *Oedipus*, images of light and confidence suddenly shift their opposite: Creon's "chariot of bright day" in the "pure ether" (*Oed.* 219f.) or "twin peak of snowy Parnassus" (227) change to the abrupt chill of terror in the physiological sensations of fear: *torpor insedit per artus, frigidus sanguis coit,* "numbness seeps throughout the limbs; blood, made cold, congeals" (224). In the *Thyestes*, once more, Atreus' striding to the stars and the limits of the heavens in the exultation of revenge (*Thy.* 885-888, 911f.; cf. 992f.) is immediately undercut by the concentrated images of fullness, weight, and heaviness in the imprisoning inner space of the palace and the body, of interior organs, of a stomach stuffed with a poisonous food that it can neither reject nor assimilate.[44] Reduction to the mangled flesh and the primary processes of ingestion and digestion block the openings to sky and forest and join victim and agent in a common horror. The perspective is decentered, asymmetrical. Exaggeration takes the place of balance;

deliberate distortion replaces the traditional "classical" values of proportion, grace, stability of images or of emotion. Seneca exploits the "subjective," "empathetic" inwardness of Virgil's lucid and expansive geography and fresh delight in nature.

A recurrent element in this deliberate imbalance is the vacillation between the conventional Golden Age world of idealized simplicity— well established by a long tradition in Latin poetry from Catullus 64 and Lucretius on through Virgil, Tibullus, and Ovid—and the "visceral" sensations that exploit our fundamental horror at the violation of the boundaries of our physical being.[45] In the *Oedipus* for example Seneca shifts the emphasis from Sophocles' themes of divine knowledge and Delphic prophecy to a penetration between the skin as we probe the palpitating flesh for polluted entrails, hidden monstrosities, embryonic deformities of nature (*Oed.* 353ff.).[46] This scene, like the groaning of Thyestes' horribly burdened intestines, could serve as an emblem for the peculiar tonality of the tragic experience in Seneca: entrapment amid the nightmarish forms of a subterranean darkness whose imprisoning power is ultimately the darkness that each of us keeps closed within. In the *Oedipus'* imagery of handling and scrutinizing these concealed deformities, we have also another depiction of the autobiography of the work, a tactile experience that is a model of the work's total effect and perhaps of the imaginative genesis that impelled it into being.

6

Orpheus in Rilke
The Hidden Roots of Being

I ·

The most important poetic realization of the myth of Orpheus in the literature of the twentieth century occurs in the work of Rainer Maria Rilke. Rilke's Orpheus bears traces of the archaic shamanistic figure who crosses between the living and the dead. He is also a magician, a wonder-worker in words, transfiguring external reality by sounds. The first of the *Sonnets to Orpheus* describes his power over nature; the last speaks of his magic (*Zauberkraft* [*Sonnets* 2.29]). Rilke himself practices the incantatory power of Orphic song-music in the untranslatable rhythms of *Sonnets* 1.6.

> Kundiger böge die Zweige der Weiden
> wer die Wurzeln der Weiden erfuhr.

> More knowing would he bend the willows' branches
> who has experienced the willows' roots.[1]

But the Rilkean Orpheus does not embody merely the magic of consummate verbal skill. At a profounder level, he is the poet who touches the extremes of life and death and overcomes the threat of nothingness by transforming the physical world into pure Being: "Gesang ist Dasein" (*Sonnets* 1.3). The task of the poet, as Rilke put it in his famous letter to the Polish translator of his *Duino Elegies*, is to transform the visible, phenomenal world into an "invisible" spiritual intensity, fullness, and meaningfulness.[2] This process takes many forms. In the *Duino Elegies* it informs a movement from despair at being heard by the angels in the first *Elegy* to the power to "speak" of the things in this world in the Ninth.

Sind wir vielleicht *hier,* um zu sagen: Haus,
Brücke, Brunnen, Tor, Krug, Obstbaum, Fenster,—
höchstens: Säule, Turm . . . aber zu *sagen,* verstehs,
oh zu sagen *so,* wie selber die Dinge niemals
innig meinten zu sein.

Are we, perhaps, here just for saying: House,
Bridge, Fountain, Gate, Jug, Olive tree, Window,—
possibly: Pillar, Tower? . . . but for saying, remember,
oh, for such saying as never the things themselves
hoped so intensely to be.[3]

(9.32–36)

This empowered "saying," like Hölderlin's "poetically living" (*Dichterisch lebt man auf dieser Erde*), irradiates the transient surface of daily life with a sense of permanence and beauty. But for Rilke this transformation takes place in the face of the destruction, violence, and disintegration of civilized values after World War I. Rilke's poetry, as Heidegger suggests, is "work of the heart (*Herzwerk*); it consists in what Heidegger calls "an unconcealing of Being," and it takes place "in a barren time" (*in dürftiger Zeit*).[4]

This attempt to encompass the world's totality in the inner space of the heart belongs firmly in the Orphic tradition: the poet's song resonates in sympathy with all of nature. Song at its highest is "praising," and Orpheus is the poet of pure praise.

Rühmen, das ists! Ein zum Rühmen Bestellter,
ging er hervor wie das Erz aus des Steins
Schweigen.

Praising, that's it! One appointed to praising,
he came like the ore forth from the stone's
Silence.

(*Sonnets* 1.7.1–3)

But song is also the fragile voice of a mere mortal, a puff of air in the wind, "a breath for nothing" (1.3.13f.). "To sing in truth" is to summon up the Orphic magic in darkness, over the abyss of nothingness. At the end of part 1 of the *Sonnets,* the darkness takes the form of the raucous cries of the enraged Maenads who drown out the song and murder the poet. Yet the final sound is affirmative: Orpheus' harmonies and magic still linger among us (*Sonnets* 1.26).

II ·

Rilke's *Orpheus. Eurydike. Hermes,* composed in 1904, is modern poetry's richest lyrical retelling of the classical myth as a single sustained narrative. Following Virgil and Ovid, Rilke dwells on the failure of Orpheus. But he shifts its meaning from Orpheus himself to Eurydice. The "new virginity" of the Maiden wedded to Death symbolizes an inward, subjective dimension of existence. This lies on the other side of life; and the poet, with all the intrusive energy and power of his art, is unable to reach, perhaps unable even fully to comprehend it. Some have read this failure as a statement about the limitations of poetry. For Paul de Man, for instance, it is an "allegory of figuration" in which the language of poetry is unable to recuperate "presence," the fullness of being that is here identified with Eurydice.[5] Such an approach, however, is both too narrow and too negative.

Rilke's refocusing of the myth on the subjective side of experience, on the potential delusiveness and illusoriness of the realm of "shades" and shadows, is certainly one of the main departures from classical poetry. The classical poet does not doubt his ability to convey the actuality of the journey. Rilke's shifting light, ambiguous images, unstable point of view (especially in his last stanza) express a more hesitant relation between language and reality. In changing the focus from Orpheus to Eurydice, Rilke also moves from exterior to interior realms and thereby depicts the otherness, the unreachableness, of death and the dead.

What interests the Latin poet is a scene in which the presence of death only intensifies the violent emotionality of the still living lover, Orpheus. For Ovid, even more than for Virgil, the myth is the occasion for developing the rhetoric of love (or, rather, of man's professions of love) and pushing to a new level the achievement of Catullus and the elegists in conveying erotic emotion. What interests Rilke, on the contrary, is not love or the emotional interaction of human lovers but the privacy and autonomy of Eurydice as a being who is now given over to the otherness of death, a being who thus stands outside human sexuality and male sexual possessiveness.

> Sie war schon nicht mehr diese blonde Frau,
> die in des Dichters Liedern manchmal anklang,
> nicht mehr des breiten Bettes Duft und Eiland
> und jenes Mannes Eigentum nicht mehr.

> She was no longer this blond woman,
> who often echoed in the poet's songs,
> no longer the broad bed's scent and island,
> that man's possession no longer.
>
> (*Orpheus. Eurydike. Hermes*, stanza 8)

Rilke's shift of perspective from exteriority to interiority, from relation to enclosure, parallels his shift from a male to a female point of view. Love is conceived of in terms less of passion and act than of a calm grace and a state of being. For this reason too, Rilke inverts the classical view of love and insists on the great perfection of the woman's love by comparison with the man's, the theme of a famous letter from Duino and a celebrated passage in the *Notebooks of Malte Laurids Brigge*.[6] In this latter passage, in fact, he even describes the woman's love in terms very similar to the enclosed and perfected inwardness of his Eurydice.

> Entschlossen und schicksalslos wie eine Ewige, steht sie neben ihm, der sich verwandelt. Immer übertrifft die Liebende den Geliebten, weil das Leben grösser ist als das Schicksal.

> Resolute and free of destiny, like one eternal, she stands near him who changes. The woman who loves always surpasses the man she loves, because life is greater than destiny.[7]

For Virgil and Ovid, as for classical art in general from Odysseus's descent to Hades in *Odyssey* 11 to the Attic grave reliefs of the fourth century B.C. and onward to *Aeneid* 6 and even to Dante's *Inferno*, the situation of death is itself a means to render more expressively the preciousness of life, its sufferings and its pleasures and the passions they inspire.

For Rilke, however, death is the other side of life, complementary rather than contradictory. His setting at the beginning of the poem is a landscape of passage between worlds, a "mine of souls" that shifts between animate and inanimate, between "veins" of rock and veins of blood.

> Das war der Seelen wunderliches Bergwerk.
> Wie stille Silbererze gingen sie
> als Adern durch sein Dunkel. Zwischen Wurzeln
> entsprang das Blut, das fortgeht zu den Menschen,
> und schwer wie Porphyr sah es aus im Dunkel.
> Sonst war nichts Rotes.

That was the so unfathomed mine of souls.
And they, like silent veins of silver ore,
were winding through its darkness. Between roots
welled up the blood that flows on to mankind,
like blocks of heavy porphyry in the darkness.
Else there was nothing red.

(*Orpheus. Eurydike. Hermes*, stanza 1)

The destabilizing of familiar boundaries between states of being continues in the fusion of nubile virginity, pregnancy, and death in Eurydice herself. She is both freshly virginal and expectantly pregnant. Her enclosure in the fullness of her death resembles the fulfillment of a pregnant woman (*Sie war in sich, wie Eine hoher Hoffnung* [stanza 6]); yet the "fullness" of this fruit is of both "sweetness and darkness."

Und ihr Gestorbensein
erfüllte sie wie Fülle.
Wie eine Frucht von Süssigkeit und Dunkel.

(stanza 6)

The heavy fruitfulness of her new condition is also "a new maidenhood" in which she is untouchable, her sex "like a flower closed toward evening."

Sie war in einem neuen Mädchentum
und unberührbar; ihr Geschlecht war zu
wie eine junge Blume gegen Abend.

(stanza 7)

These conjunctions are not only part of a mythical *coincidentia oppositorum*; they are also the sign of the mystery of death, viewed as acceptant fulfillment, another state of our being, in which pregnancy and virginity can coexist. Eurydice is both beyond sexuality and in a new, nonpossessive form of sexuality. Her death is a calm acquiescence in nature's gentle generosity, breadth, and suprapersonal unity.

The following stanzas separate her from the marriage bed where she was "that man's possession" and frees her to become "unloosened," "unbound" (*aufgelöst*) like long hair, or "given forth" (*hingegeben* [stanza 9]) in hundredfold abundance, like rain. Death is a process of becoming part of nature, as is implied by the plant imagery with which this section concludes, "she was already root" (*sie war schon*

Wurzel [stanza 10]). Rilke completes his radical decentering of the classical versions by replacing the heroic-tragic mode of death as inconsolable individual loss with death as metamorphosis, part of a suprapersonal process. In the classical myth death wrings from the poet-singer the lament of total, ultimate loss. For Rilke's Orpheus death belongs to a perspective beyond the personal and beyond what the poet, rooted in the emotions of his life only, is able to understand.

Fascinated by the Romantic theme of death-and-the-maiden, Rilke finds in Eurydice's virginity-in-death something analogous to the virginity of the romance heroine: it symbolizes the integrity of the self. But this is a self beyond the selfhood of narrow individualism; it is a self that has found peace in the mystery and privacy of union with its hidden other side in death. It will not be reborn into the dichotomies and possessiveness of the upper world. So read, this Eurydice embodies something of Rilke's own ambivalences toward sexual experience and privacy, his own pull between relation and his beloved solitude.[8]

Through the inversions and paradoxes surrounding his Eurydice, Rilke is able to give a new richness of characterization to each of the three actors in his drama. At the same time he etches their individual movements against a strange, unreal background. Like Cocteau in his film version, he exploits the dreaminess of the setting, the instability of the material world, and the fluidity between animate and inanimate. His mythical frame permits him to omit the names and thereby to create a suggestive generality. His characters are *der Mann, der Gott*. The absence of direct address, except for the momentous syllable "who" at the end of the penultimate stanza, confers a richly muffled indirectness on events.

Rilke's direct inspiration was a sculpted relief, the celebrated three-figure relief in the Naples Archeological Museum. His periods between the three names in his title is the printed text's way of conveying that sculptural quality. But Rilke also seeks to render poetically the relief's ebb and flow of contact and separation. As in the relief, a few details stand out boldly: the impatient gesture of Orpheus in his blue cloak; the traveling hood of Hermes that shades the godlike radiance of his eyes; the long shroud that enfolds Eurydice. All these details gain a tragic dimension from the immateriality of the surroundings, the substanceless forests that wait on life's other side (*wesenlose Wälder* [stanza 2]). The anti-world of Eurydice's fertility-in-death is a grief-world, *eine Welt aus Klage* (stanza 5). Its existence as a separate realm of existence is marked by the repetition of the phrase, "the so-much beloved," *die so-Geliebte*, at the beginning and end of the fourth stanza.

The chiaroscuro of light and shade around Orpheus, as we see him at the end, seems at first to define him in a human landscape: he waits "as on the strip of meadow-path" (stanza 12). But this human-looking setting immediately becomes irrelevant, for it is now the point of Eurydice's disappearance. The hopeful, if precarious, landscape of the opening scene, "between meadows, soft and full of patience" (stanza 2), held out the possibility of a union of solid, mortal bodies after the preceding "mine of souls," "immaterial forests," and "bridges over void." In the last stanza, Orpheus stands at the edge of a foreign world that shuts him out. He is only "someone" in another's fading, distant vision.

> Fern aber, dunkel vor dem klaren Ausgang,
> stand irgend jemand, dessen Angesicht
> nicht zu erkennen war. Er stand und sah,
> wie auf dem Streifen eines Wiesenpfades
> mit trauervollem Blick der Gott der Botschaft
> sich schweigend wandte, der Gestalt zu folgen,
> die schon zurückging dieses selben Weges,
> den Schritt beschränkt von langen Leichenbändern,
> unsicher, sanft und ohne Ungeduld.
>
> But in the distance, dark in the bright exit,
> someone or other stood, whose countenance
> was indistinguishable. Stood and saw
> how, on a strip of pathway between meadows,
> with sorrow in his look, the god of message
> turned silently to go behind the figure
> already going back by that same pathway,
> its paces circumscribed by lengthy shroudings,
> uncertain, gentle, and without impatience.
>
> (Stanza 12)

As point of view here changes from Orpheus to Eurydice, so too the initiative moves from Orpheus to Hermes and then to Eurydice. The god turns "to follow" the "figure" who has already "gone back on that same pathway." Thus the decisive act lies not with Orpheus or even with Hermes, but with a mysterious yet fulfilled Eurydice, "uncertain, gentle, and without impatience." The electrifying *sie*, "*her*" (stanza 4,

Rilke's emphasis), at her first appearance halfway through the poem, as we now understand, was a subtle projection of Orpheus' own involvement. As "she" fades into her darkness of being-in-death, Orpheus is frozen into the pose of helpless onlooker: "He stood and saw" (stanza 12). Eurydice is only "the figure," muffled and constrained by the robes of death.

Rilke's flow of narrative from Orpheus to Hermes to Eurydice is a response to the rhyth.. '- movement of the classical relief, where the flowing lines of the drapery and the position of the hands and arms lead us gracefully from one figure to the other. But Rilke has recreated this movement in a wholly new way, setting the materiality of the sculpture off against the elusiveness and ghostliness of his setting. What in the classical work (both literary and sculptural) was sharp, plastic outline here becomes an evanescent play of elusive subjectivities. Yet Rilke has caught the tone of quiet pathos in the original, its mood of ambiguous waiting and hesitation; but (to use a Rilkean metaphor) he plays its music on very different instruments and with very different effects.

III ·

The *Sonnets to Orpheus* are not a random collection of poems. Rilke composed them, as he tells us, in a single rush of inspiration sustained over a period of some three weeks. "They came up and entrusted themselves to me," he wrote, "the most enigmatic dictation I have ever held through and achieved. The whole first part was written down in a single breathless act of obedience, between the 2nd and the 5th of February [1922], without one word being doubtful or having to be changed."[9]

Whatever the actual circumstances of writing, Rilke's conception of the unitary genesis of these works ("a single breathless act of obedience") at once poses the problem of defining this text. The *Sonnets* are both multiple and unitary; they are fifty-five separate poems, each one complete in itself, and also compose a unified *Sonnet*-book. They may therefore be viewed on both a paradigmatic and a syntagmatic axis, both as symbol and as narrative. Each sonnet is a separate interpretation and realization of the meaning of Orpheus; yet the succession of individual sonnets also follows a quasi-narrative development or syntagmatic progression.

The mythic base of the poems in the legend of Orpheus is particularly important for the dynamic interplay of these two axes or directions in the work. The complex, alternating rhythm of the two books of *Sonnets* is that of the myth of Orpheus himself, a structure of discontinuities, of alternating gain and loss, of figures surfacing in virtual epiphany and then submerging again in darkness and mysterious concealment.

These poems also have a double relation to the Orphic tradition. They both derive from it and modify it for all subsequent literature. They are unintelligible without some knowledge of the myth of Orpheus; yet they transcend that myth and rebuild it into their own structure of meanings. One could legitimately read these *Sonnets* as part of an open-ended poem whose text is all the poems ever written, or ever to be written, about Orpheus. A full analysis of such a "text" could never be complete; and even an integration of the *Sonnets* into existing literature would require, at the least, a lengthy volume. Here I can only sketch some possibilities.

The *Sonnets* draw on two interlocking aspects of the Orphic tradition. First, Orpheus is a creator of music, song, poetry, a mythical embodiment of the magic of words. In him poetry has power not only to move and persuade, but also to cross the familiar boundaries between man and nature, between spirit and matter. Orpheus is the magical singer who moves the beasts and trees to the accompaniment of his song and his lyre. On the other hand, Orpheus is also the central character in a mythic narrative concerned with art, love, and death.

In *Orpheus. Eurydike. Hermes*, written nearly two decades before the *Sonnets to Orpheus*, Rilke had recounted the myth, in more or less sequential narrative. The poem was concerned principally with the theme of artistic failure, the impenetrability of death, and by extension with the failure of both love and art in attaining and communicating the fundamental otherness of reality. The *Sonnets*, though more difficult, are also more optimistic. They return to the fundamental theme of the myth as treated by Virgil and Ovid, the relation between love, art, and death. They refocus this basic Orphic triangle, however, on a series of interrelated issues having to do with change and permanence.

Orpheus' power of song embodies the power of language to impose form on the formless through naming and classification. In him song—poetry—can also view and hold the fleeting moment in stable cohesion and fixity. In speaking that which cannot be contained in the abstractive structure of words, Rilke's Orphic voice seeks to open our excessively conceptualized world to hidden or excluded aspects, especially the knowledge of death, the "subjective" side of the phenomenal world, the validity of nonrational understanding and experience. Through language he will make language able to render what is really antithetical, or at least resistant, to language, namely the elusiveness of our sensuous experiences in endless variety, endless flux. "Orpheus" is that potential surfacing of being in the world of change, that coming together, ever unreconciled, of the transient and the eternal in art.

Rilke sometimes phrases this paradoxical essence of Orpheus in terms of a tension between "monument" and "metamorphosis." These words recur again and again in the *Sonnets*. They, and related antitheses, denote two contrasting possibilities in poetry. On the one hand the poet seeks to capture and monumentalize the timeless. On the other hand he seeks to convey the flowing, passing moment in all of its transient beauty, relinquishing any permanent hold on it. Already for Virgil and Ovid, Orpheus is both the suffering poet-lover who himself experiences loss and death and the artist whose songs are victorious over brute matter and death.

Even as early as the fifth century B.C., Orpheus served as a symbol for the persuasive power of poetry over death. But Rilke abandons that one-dimensional meaning of the Orpheus myth for a more complex vision. His Orpheus is a symbol of process rather than fixity, a locus where irreconcilable, and therefore tragic, oppositions meet. The power of language that he symbolizes is not merely language as magical persuasion but language reaching toward transcendence while yet not denying its ground in the time, death, and suffering of language users, mortals.

"Eurydice" is the young girl, Vera Knoop, a dancer who died at the age of nineteen. A prefatory inscription dedicates the *Sonnets* as "written as a monument for Vera Ouckama Knoop." This dedication is itself part of the "text" and part of the tensions that that text delineates, for even in asserting itself as a "monument" the collection strives against the temptation to monumentalize.

So viewed, the problem of the "text" has another level. The poetic text, like Orpheus, is both permanent and changing, both flow and crystal. It exists, in one sense, out of time, as achieved form. But it has another kind of existence only as each of us, as readers or listeners, realizes it and recreates it in the moment-by-moment, syllable-by-syllable sequence of its unfolding on our lips and in our minds. It is this paradox for which Rilke himself finds an image in "the ringing glass, which shivers even as it rings" (*ein klingendes Glas, das sich im*

Klang schon zerschlug [*Sonnets* 2.13.8]). In the next line, however, this "being" in the moment of death-and-transcendence of the glass-shattering note has as its opposite and also as its necessary prerequisite that we "know the condition of nonbeing / the infinite ground of your deep vibration, / that you may fulfill it this single time":

> Sei – und wisse zugleich des Nicht-Seins Bedingung,
> den unendlichen Grund deiner innigen Schwingung,
> dass du sie völlig vollziehst dieses einzige Mal.
>
> (2.13.9–11)

"This single time," *dieses einzige Mal:* almost the same collocation occurs for Orpheus himself in *Sonnets* 1.5: *Ein für alle Male / ists Orpheus wenn es singt,* "Once and for all it's Orpheus when there's singing." Orpheus spans eternity and the moment. He is once, unique, but also forever. The phrase *wenn es singt,* like the *klingendes Glas* (note the present, continuative participle) defines Orpheus as process. But once seen as process, he also escapes definition. Thus the *Sonnets* that evoke and create him are always establishing "the condition of their nonbeing" (2.13.9) at the same time as they create their "infinite ground" in the timeless.

Orpheus, as I suggested above, has both a paradigmatic and a syntagmatic function in the *Sonnet*-book; he is a symbol for a view or an aim of poetry throughout the book and also has a narrative role in a plot of sorts, a progression in the *Sonnets* toward or away from his "Eurydice." Rilke has reconceived the meaning of the myth, however, so that the separation and reunion of Orpheus and Eurydice refer not so much to personal relationships as to the definition and symbolical recreation of the power of poetry to convey truth. Orpheus the poet is defined by Eurydice in a double relation to reality: losing and regaining the beautiful young beloved who is the helpless victim of death, he is a poet of both joy and grief. Celebration and lamentation, the knowledge of both beauty and pain are but the two poles of the unitary function of poetry. In Rilke's view all life has death as its ever-present other side, and the poet has his "roots" in both realms.[10] It is in this sense that Rilke reinterprets the meaning of Orpheus' descent to the underworld and return (cf. *Sonnets* 1.6). Orpheus, on the one hand, is "one appointed to praising," one for whom "everything turns to vineyard, to grape, ripened in the sensual South"; on the other hand he is also "one of the staying messengers / who still holds far into the doors of the dead / bowls with fruits worthy of praise" (*Sonnets* 1.7).

"Orpheus" for Rilke means this accessibility of both realms, death and life, to poetry. He thereby helps to make "visible" the hidden permanence that the changeful phenomena of life acquire as they are filtered through and transformed by the spiritual energy of our consciousness. Rilke himself describes the process as follows:

> Hence it is important not only not to run down and degrade every-thing earthly, but just because of its temporariness, which it shares with us, we ought to grasp and transform these phenomena and these things in a most loving understanding. Transform? Yes; for our task is so deeply and so passionately to impress upon ourselves this provisional and perishable earth, that its essential being will arise again "invisible" in us. *We are the bees of the invisible. We frantically plunder the visible of its honey, to accumulate it in the great golden hive of the invisible.* The "Elegies" show us at this work, the work of these continual conversions of the beloved visible and tangible into the invisible vibration and animation of our [own] nature, which intro-duces new frequencies into the vibration-spheres of the universe.[11]

For the *Sonnets*, as for the *Elegies*, the poet's "work" consists in "transformation"; and here its center is Orpheus, the poet in whom the "invisible" life of spirit becomes "visible" in tangible human experience. Only insofar as the *Sonnet*-book realizes this aim of "trans-formation," does Orpheus exist. The *Sonnets* not only address Orpheus as the patron and symbol of inspired poetry but also create their own "Orpheus." The achieved corpus of the *Sonnet*-book is the "visible" manifestation of the Orphic voice; yet, since "Orpheus" comes into being only at each individual moment of song (cf. *Sonnets* 1.5 and 2.13), the act of "transformation" that evokes him is always in process. As the last lines of the *Sonnet*-book imply, the book, even as it recreates and realizes its "Orpheus," also seeks to evade its status as fixed form, as "monument."

To describe this crossing of monument and metamorphosis, Rilke uses the term *Figur*, "figure." An important and recurrent word in his poetry, "figure" embraces both the remote constellations of stars and the warm, vital rhythms of the dance. It has affinities with both the loneliness of Orpheus in failure and his social, associative magical power over trees and beasts. It includes the abstractness of pure form on the one hand and the concrete plasticity of art forms on the other, whether the dance or the statue.[12] It implies both the ordering power of the imagining, artistic mind and the possible unreality of pure imagination, "mere" images. "Figure" is both the crystallization of being in art and the evanescent shapes of momentary events, like the shifting patterns of the dance. Dance, in fact, is one of Rilke's favorite images for the two sides of "figure," for it partakes both of the temporariness of matter in flux and the ordering power of art.

In "The Ball," written some fifteen years before the *Sonnets,* playful movement has a dancelike effect that conveys the double meaning of "figure." The ball in play displays both the ordering power of aesthetic pattern and the momentary, unstable quality of a brief, felicitous configuration of phenomena. It holds a shape and then dissolves into something else. At the end of this poem, the ball seems to order the players, free and capricious above them in its movement.

> und sich neigt
> und einhält und den Spielenden von oben
> auf einmal eine neue Stelle zeigt,
> sie ordnend wie zu einer Tanzfigur,
> um dann, erwartet und erwünscht von allen,
> rasch, einfach, kunstlos, ganz Natur,
> dem Becher hoher Hände zuzufallen.

> It bends and pauses and suddenly, from above, shows to the players a new place, ordering them as if in a dance-figure; and then, awaiting and wished for by all, quick, simple, artless, entirely Nature, will fall into the goblet of high hands. ("Der Ball," 11–17)[13]

The human mind has always delighted in fashioning recognizable shapes from raw nature and giving them names. Rilke explores this idea in *Sonnets* 1.11, where he asks whether there is a constellation called "The Rider" or "The Horseman." Yet the task of bridging the space between star and earth, man and beast, by mental images may be too great for language. Finally, horse and rider go separate ways to "meadow" and "table," and they are "without names": "Namenlos schon trennt sie Tisch und Weide" (line 11). The constellation (*Sternbild,* "star-image") may, after all, be merely "picture," a mental image. If so, we are forced to accept the otherness of a nature that refuses assimilation to human thought processes and is as alien to us as the "nameless" stars.[14]

Rilke raises this possiblity, only to reject it.

> Auch die sternische Verbindung trügt.
> Doch uns freue eine Weile nun,
> der Figur zu glauben. Das genügt.

Even the starry union is deceptive.
But let us now be glad a while
to believe the figure. That's enough.
                    (1.11.12–14)

Here the full ambiguity of the figure becomes explicit. The "union" that enables us to connect the separate stars into a humanly meaningful "star-picture" (*Sternbild*) depends on the capacity of language to "deceive." Yet "for a while" we can take some joy in the coherence of an imaginatively connected universe, even if we have to find or make the pattern. Yet the closing *Das genügt* indicates how elusive is this capturing of presence in the lyre's song.

When Rilke returns to the "dance-figure" in the next-to-last of the *Sonnets*, he associates it with the transient childhood of Vera-Eurydice, whose attempt to perform the dance in "perfect celebration" is a reaching toward Orpheus, but also only "a hope" and an "attempt."

O come and go. You, still half a child,
fill out the dance-figure for a moment
to the pure constellation of one of those
dances in which we fleetingly transcend

dumbly ordering Nature.
·   ·   ·   ·   ·   ·   ·   ·   ·   ·   ·   ·   ·   ·
For this you *tried* the lovely steps and *hoped*
one day towards the perfect celebration
to turn the pace and countenance of your friend.
                    (2.28.1–4, 12–14)[15]

IV ·

The first and last two *Sonnets* of part 1 form a particularly clear and important instance of the dialectical process that the book both describes and enacts. *Sonnets* 1.1 and 1.2 are linked by the word *and*, which begins the second poem (*Und fast ein Mädchen wars und ging hervor / aus diesem einigen Glück von Sang und Leier,* "And almost a girl it was and issued forth / from this concordant joy of song and lyre" (1.2.1f.). The conjunction links her emergence from the poet's song with the thronging together of the animals who push "out of the clear released wood from lair and nesting place" in the first poem (1.1.5f.). The closing pair of poems of the first part are each addressed to a "Thou," *Dich aber, Du aber* (1.25.1 and 1.26.1), meaning Eurydice-Vera and Orpheus respectively. This pairing of singing poet and dying maiden at each end of the part is also significant for the unity of the work as a whole text. It marks that tension between the transcendence of art, embodied in the figure of Orpheus, and the sadness of loss and death, associated with the girl.

The first poem opens the *Sonnet*-book with an image of Orpheus' song in its reaching toward transcendence, order, control of nature by man and implicitly of matter by form. Orpheus is alive and present, "singing." All else is silent.

> Da stieg ein Baum. O reine Übersteigung!
> O Orpheus singt! O hoher Baum im Ohr!
> Und alles schwieg. Doch selbst in der Verschweigung
> ging neuer Anfang, Wink und Wandlung vor.
>
> There rose a tree. O pure transcendency!
> O Orpheus singing! O tall tree in the ear!
> And all was silent. Yet even in the silence
> new beginning, beckoning, change went on.
>
> (1.1.1–4)

Yet Orpheus' song is less a manipulative control over nature than a fluidity of passage between man and nature. The tree of transcendence climbing toward the heavens is, typologically, the cosmic tree of *axis mundi*, which symbolizes the unity and coherence of the world.[16] But it grows also "in the ear." The song is the source of ever-new beginnings, not a frozen monument, static in eternity. As the present tense of *singt* implies, the song is process (*ists Orpheus wenn es singt*, as *Sonnets* 1.5 puts it). Thus it is also part of change, invitation, metamorphosis, *Wink und Wandlung*, the last words of the first stanza, closely linked by the alliteration.

The power of Orpheus' presence is clear from the first word, *Da*. The effect of Orphic song, in its transcendent aspect, has the suddenness of a divine epiphany. The word points: the tree is *there* (*Da stieg ein Baum*), almost out of time, as if *stieg*, the preterite, were like the Greek aorist. Repeated in the second half of the line, this "climbing," or climbedness, is qualified as *reine*, "pure" (*stieg. . . . O reine Übersteigung*). We see the effects of Orpheus before we hear his song. But suddenly with his song that tree, free and pure, is infused with inwardness, with the privacy of the "hearing" of the listener, *im Ohr*, "in the ear." The repeated interjection, *O*, three times, stresses the quality of epiphany. Continued in the *o*-sounds of *hoher . . . Ohr,* it becomes the silence that surrounds the apparition of the holy in the next line (*und alles schweigt*). But, as I have noted, it is a silence that "invites" the ebb and flow of life and of the senses, beginnings and changes.

If the first stanza draws up the myth of Orpheus to present the power of poetry to transcend, the second draws upon the figure of Orpheus as magician and enchanter.

> Tiere aus Stille drangen aus dem klaren
> gelösten Wald von Lager und Genist:
> und da ergab sich, dass sie nicht aus List
> und nicht aus Angst in sich so leise waren,
> sondern aus Hören.

> Creatures of stillness thronged out of the clear
> released wood from lair and nesting-place;
> and it turned out that not from cunning and not
> from fear were they so hushed within themselves,
> but from harkening.

> (1.1.5–9)

Orpheus' power over the animals, which lures them out of the dark forest of inchoate desire (*aus dunkelstem Verlangen* [line 12]) is part of the impelling, incantatory power of song, suggested in the verb *drangen* in line 5.

This hypnotic force of song, one of the recurrent attributes of Orpheus as archetypal poet in the myth, is closely associated with the power of poetry to bring order out of chaos, to impose form on the formless. Sound and hearing especially convey this significance of Orpheus. The mysterious, almost religious silence of transcendence in the first stanza gives way to the voice that brings the forest creatures from their "stillness" (*Tiere aus Stille* [line 5]), transfiguring their sylvan dwelling place too, now "clear" and "released" (*klaren/gelösten Wald* [lines 5f.]), as if it has been called forth from pure potentiality into existence through form and art. The sound and the hearing through which this change is effected function both literally and metaphorically: they are narrative elements in the mythic event recounted in the poem, Orpheus' power over wild creatures; but they also reflect the "listening" of the readers as they let the poem weave its spell around them. The poem creates that "silence" of calm and attentive patience in which outside concerns are "stilled" so that the readers/listeners can truly "hear."

Functioning as invocation, this initial sonnet not only introduces Orpheus as a symbol of the various aspects of the power of poetry but also itself casts the spell of calm and receptivity through which Orpheus' song exists. By one of the key paradoxes of the poem, that attentive silence not only makes the hearing possible but also summons Orpheus and his song into reality.

This inner stillness leads not only the animals of the myth, but also, by implication, the human hearers of the poem. It brings them from the "craft" and "anxiety" that mark (and mar) our lives to a state of receptive "hushedness" (cf. *leise* [line 8]). "Hearing," in this pregnant sense, is the culmination as well as the beginning. The careful sentence structure makes this clear: there is a climactic progression (or priamel), "not from cunning . . . and not from anxiety . . . , but from hearing" (*nicht aus . . . nicht aus . . . sondern aus . . . .*). The special quality of that "hearing" (*Hören* [line 9]) is depicted not only through enjambement, but also through the juxtaposition with another type of sound in the same line: *sondern aus Hören. Brüllen, Schrei, Geröhr.* This disordered cry of animal violence (which in the last sonnet of part 1 will finally overcome the poet, temporarily) is here introduced to show the power of the sound that originates from his realm. Just as the inward mood of cunning and fear yields to peace and stillness in the previous stanza, so here the diminution of the bestial roar is internal, spiritual: it "seemed small in their hearts."

The long "where" clause of the next sentence [lines 10–13] moves from the aural to the visual. The architectural metaphor, in which the poet replaces the dim, formless forest, "a covert out of darkest longing" (*ein Unterschlupf aus dunklestem Verlangem* [line 12]) with a "temple," draws upon an ancient association of Orpheus with the power to civilize. The power of poetry is a civilizing power. In ancient literature, Orpheus often appears as a culture hero, inventor of the arts, founder of religion. In one legend, particularly relevant to Rilke's architectural imagery here, he is paired with Amphion, whose lyre compelled the stones to move of their own accord and take their place in the city wall of Thebes.[17]

This externally visible triumph of form over the formless, however, remains subordinate to its inward, private effect. The poet "creates" (*schufst* [line 14]), but his "temple" is "a temple in their hearing" (*Tempel im Gehör*). The sonnet reaffirms the sensory limit of its own auditory form, the "hearing" of the poet's voice in the inner ear of the receptive listener. Thus *Gehör* not only answers and supersedes the animal "roaring" with which it rhymes (*Geröhr* [line 9]), but also in sound and meaning pulls together the entire poem. *Im Gehör* echoes *im Ohr* of line 2, thus reminding us that this temple of art as form and order, like the tree of art as transcendence, is metaphorical and inward. *Gehör* also echoes *Hören* of line 9, the point where animal cunning, fear, and roaring are transmuted into quietness and attentive listening, disordered into ordered sound.

The last line, *da schufst du ihnen Tempel im Gehör,* also recalls the first, with its repetition of *da*. *Da* carries over to the end of the idea of epiphany, the sudden manifestation of a hidden, mysterious, quasi-divine power: the ordered geometric form of the temple emerges from the forest's "darkest longing" (line 12). Now, however, the remote climbing of the tree in "pure transcendency" becomes present, active, and personal: "You built. . . ." More important, Orpheus, the mythic singer named in the third person in line 2 (*O Orpheus singt*) is now a *du*, which implies somewhere an *ich*. The creative energies of the poet have become incorporated—in the literal sense of the word—into a human poet who can be addressed in the second person. Through the *du* of the speaker, the presence of Orpheus becomes concrete and tangible. The readers participate in that presence, as they have participated in the gradually unfolding power of Orpheus as the poem moves from verse to verse. As a form of invocation, the poem not only describes but virtually enacts its subject: the *effect* of Orpheus' magic, the "pure transcendency" of his song, gives way to the personal presence in which the magic is possible.

The second sonnet deepens the tensions between death and art focused by the Orpheus myth. It introduces the "girl," Rilke's "Eurydice," and along with her the feelings of loss and powerlessness. With Eurydice too comes first-person statement, the poet's "I," as he wonders at her death and at the poetic power that might overcome it. The hearing and shaping of the first poem now yield to the maiden's sleep. In the dialectic that runs throughout these poems, the creative energy of form overcoming the formless in the first sonnet is replaced by the reluctance of the pure potentiality of the world to awaken to realization. This "Eurydice's" sleep reabsorbs the otherness of the world back into subjectivity. Trees, symbol of the transcendence of Orphic art in *Sonnets* 1.1 are here left suspended in a sentence without a verb (lines 6–8), while the physical elements of nature, "distances" and "meadows," hover between spirit and matter, feeling and external reality, through the adjectives that modify them: *"feelable* distances," *"felt* meadows" (*fühlbare Ferne, die gefühlte Wiese* [line 7]).

The power of Orpheus to cross the boundaries between different conditions of existence (spirit and matter, sentient and inanimate, human and bestial) here enlarges to span wakefulness and sleep, life and death. The maiden's sleep incorporates the world into the hesitant life-as-potentiality that she, like Michelangelo's Night, symbolizes. *Sie schlief die Welt*, "She slept the world," in line 9, harks back to *Und schlief in mir* in line 5. The speaker's first-person relation to the sleeping maiden (*"my* ear" [line 4]); "slept in *me"* [line 5], "wondering that befell *myself"* [line 8]) is now universalized through Orpheus, for he is invoked as the god of the power of song in the next lines.

> Singender Gott, wie hast
> du sie vollendet, dass sie nicht begehrte,
> erst wach zu sein? Sieh, sie erstand und schlief.
>
> Wo ist ihr Tod? O, wirst du dies Motiv
> erfinden noch, eh sich dein Lied verzehrte?–
> Wo sinkt sie hin aus mir? . . . Ein Mädchen fast . . .
>
> You singing god, how
> did you so perfect her that she did not crave
> first to be awake? See, she arose and slept.
>
> Where is her death? O will you yet invent
> this theme before your song consumes itself?–
> Whither is she sinking out of me? . . . A girl almost . . .
>
> (1.2.9–14)

Orpheus' song does not awaken Eurydice-Vera to life, but to contentment with death, so that "she did not crave first to be awake." She "arises" (*erstand*) only to sleep (*sie erstand und schlief* [line 11]). Even her death is elusive, a creation of the poet's song, which itself is part of the process of coming to be and passing away, in danger of "consuming itself." The poet's "invention" (*erfinden* [line 13]) is not the clarification of the unformed into firm classic shapes, like the "temple" in the dark forests of the first sonnet, but is itself contingent, uncertain, transient. Hence its object, the maiden, sinks back into that fluid inner world of death and sleep, the realm of feeling, grief, inertia, which refuses to push through into the crystallized forms of art. Orpheus' power here is to accept rather than to overcome death and change.

When the poet returns to first-person reference in his last line, therefore, it is to show the maiden slipping away, back into that realm of inchoate shapes: *Wo sinkt sie hin aus mir? . . . Ein Mädchen fast . . .* (line 14). The circularity marked by the repetition of line 1 (*Und fast ein Mädchen wars und ging hervor*) suggests the circularity, the self-enclosedness, of this maiden in her death. Instead of "issuing forth" (*ging hervor*), she fades away. The three dots before and after "a girl almost" creates an almost visual representation of her evanescence and elusiveness. She is not unlike that other Eurydice of Rilke's earlier poem, *Orpheus. Eurydike. Hermes.* At Orpheus' fatal backward glance, that Eurydice is fused back into a nonindividualized oneness with the earth and the rhythms of nature.

> She was already loosened like long hair,
> and given far and wide like fallen rain,
> and dealt out like a manifold supply.
>
> She was already root.
> (Stanzas 9–10)[18]

By shifting the focus in the longer poem from Orpheus to Eurydice, Rilke turned the significance of Orpheus from the power of art to overcome death to the problem of art and poetic language to cross the barriers between self and other, between subjective and objective reality.[19] In like manner the shift from Orpheus to the Maiden in *Sonnets* 1.1 and 1.2 transforms the symbolic meaning of Orpheus from classical and aesthetic order to the poet's precarious place between reality and dream, actuality and potentiality, the timeless and the transient. These latter qualities of resistance to the eternal, crystalline, "wakeful" forms of art center upon Eurydice, the "girl almost." She is elusive but not passive, mysteriously united with the world in the sleep to which she clings (*sie schlief die Welt* [1.2.9]), as is the Eurydice of the earlier poem in her "new virginity" of death.

The girl here serves as a mysterious anima figure for the poet; she is what comes forth from Orpheus' song as the proof and result of his musical power. She is, therefore, associated with the process of creative metamorphosis that lies at the heart of the divine poet's ability to elicit art from his "wonder" at the world. Her sleep contains everything that the poet wonders at in nature. Yet it also marks the elusive, inchoate quality of the vision. The poet's song hovers between life and death, but also between dream and presence, vague intuition and full realization in the "concordant joy of song and lyre" ("aus diesem einigen Glück von Sang und Leier" [1.2.2.]).

The poet of the *Sonnets* appears in the first person only in the second sonnet. His "I" is called into being only at the point where the Orphic power of transcendent forms (the "temple" of *Sonnets* 1.1) acknowledges and receives its complementary side, its place in the flowing, changing, death-bound world of the Maiden, herself the Bride of Death. The girl is the hidden life of that changeful realm where sensations and emotions have not yet coalesced into objectified forms. She is the hidden but necessary side of Orpheus himself. But not even this inward grasp of reality is a stable acquisition of either the first-person poet (that is, Rilke himself) or the poet Orpheus. The latter's song is itself in danger of wasting away before it can form and hold in "invention" the maiden's death; and the Maiden, in the last line, is "sinking away" from the speaker.

The third sonnet brings these two sides of the Orphic poet together. From their interaction, song itself emerges as transience, fragility, the elusive passing of a puff of wind.

> In Wahrheit singen, ist ein andrer Hauch.
> Ein Hauch um nichts. Ein Wehn im Gott. Ein Wind.

> Real singing is a different breath.
> A breath for nothing. A wafting in the god. A wind.
>
> (1.3.13–14)

The "god" of the last line is the achieved reconciliation of change and permanence that constitutes Being. The opposition man/god in the poem's opening stanza follows from the complementary relation of Orpheus and Eurydice in *Sonnets* 1.1 and 1.2. The god can hold these antithetical states of reality in balance, but that is precisely what defines him as god, a state of being beyond the reach of human capability.

> A god can do it. But how, tell me, shall
> a man follow him through the narrow lyre?
> His mind is cleavage. At the crossing of two
> heartways stands no temple for Apollo.

> Song, as you teach it, is not desire,
> not suing for something yet in the end attained;

song is existence. Easy for the god.
But when do we *exist*?

(1.3.1–8)

In this perspective of unattainable Being, the "concordant joy of song and lyre" in 1.2.2 becomes the "narrow lyre" in 1.3.2. The "temple" of Orphic poetry-as-order in *Sonnets* 1.1 is now negated by the contradiction between being and flux that mortal song cannot contain. The classical images of the temple and Apollo, ancient god of music, purity, and aesthetic order, have no place at the heart's crossings, the contradictions that constitute the Orpheus of the *Sonnets*.

In this slow progression toward the definition of Rilke's Orphic voice the fifth sonnet, as I observed earlier, has an important role. The speaker's voice is now strong and assured in the two imperatives that open the poem.

Errichtet keinen Denkstein. Lasst die Rose
nur jedes Jahr zu seinen Gunsten blühn.

Set up no stone to his memory.
Just let the rose bloom each year for his sake.

(1.5.1–2)

These negative injunctions against monumentalizing juxtapose the rose's fragile annual bloom to the massive gravestone. As Orpheus comes into "being," he incorporates metamorphosis.

Denn Orpheus ists. Seine Metamorphose
in dem und dem. Wir sollen uns nicht mühn

um andre Namen. Ein für alle Male
ists Orpheus, wenn es singt. Er kommt und geht.
Ists nicht schon viel, wenn er die Rosenschale
um ein paar Tage manchmal übersteht?

For it is Orpheus. His metamorphosis
into this and that. We should not trouble

about other names. Once and for all
it's Orpheus when there's singing. He comes and goes.
Is it not much already if at times
he overstays for a few days the bowl of roses?

(1.5.3–8)

The "bowl of roses," like the rose of line 1, symbolizes the transient beauty that poetry seeks to grasp even as it passes. Orpheus can "over stay" (*übersteht* [line 8]) their swift blooming, but only "for a few days": he refuses to be defined in spans of time longer than the measurable rhythms of daily life.

These mortal rhythms find expression in the word-rhythm. His "metamorphosis into this and that," *in dem und dem*, in line 4 is echoed syntactically and rhythmically in *Er kommt und geht*, "He comes and goes," in line 5. In both cases the monosyllables joined by "and" express that metamorphic participation in the changing and ephemeral variety of life that constitutes part of Orpheus' Being (*Denn Orpheus ists* [line 3]: *Ein für alle Male / ists Orpheus, wenn es singt* [lines 5f.]).

The progression of the *Sonnets* continuously refines and qualifies the "pure transcendency" (*reine Übersteigung*) of *Sonnets* 1.1. Transcendence is expressed by compounds of *über*, like *Übersteigung* in the very first line of the *Sonnets*. The acceptance of the limited "overstaying" (*übersteht*) of 1.5.8, the last word of the second stanza, stands in tension with *übertrifft*, "transcends," and *überschreitet*, "oversteps," in lines 11 and 14, the last words of the third and fourth stanzas respectively.

> O wie er schwinden muss, dass ihrs begrifft!
> Und wenn ihm selbst auch bangte, dass er schwände.
> Indem sein Wort das Hiersein übertrifft,
>
> ist er schon dort, wohin ihrs nicht begleitet.
> Der Leier Gitter zwängt ihm nicht die Hände.
> Und er gehorcht, indem er überschreitet.
>
> O how he has to vanish, for you to grasp it!
> Though he himself take fright at vanishing.
> Even while his word transcends the being-here,
> he's there already where you do not follow.
> The lyre's lattice does not snare his hands.
> And he obeys, while yet he oversteps.
>
> (1.5.9–14)

The sequence of the three stanzaic endings, *übersteht, übertrifft, überschreitet*, contains the kernel of the contradictions that the poem seeks to present.

In the third stanza this "transcending of being-here" (*Hiersein*) in Orpheus' word (*Indem sein Wort das Hiersein übertrifft* [line 11]) follows upon his own terror at "vanishing" and hangs poised in an incomplete sentence enjambed with the next stanza. "Overstepping" of the last line (*indem er überschreitet*) is also in a subordinate clause (introduced by the same conjunction, in fact, as in line 11, *indem . . . übertrifft*). It is in itself ambiguous, for it suggests both the possibility of crossing the mortal limits of *Sonnets* 1.3 and the potential danger of "overstepping" those limits. Orpheus' "overstepping," however, is an act of "obedience" rather than an arrogant assertion of power. Hence the penultimate line stresses his harmonious, nonviolating relationship with his lyre: *Der Leier Gitter zwängt ihm nicht die Hände.* We recall the god's "narrow lyre" in 1.3.2, impassable for man. Orpheus' lyre, unlike Apollo's, signifies the possibility of crossing between opposites, of mediating the world's ultimate contradiction between life and death, permanence and passage, the memorial stone and the blooming rose (line 1).

The negative command of the first two lines implies a reader who needs to be dissuaded from the natural human urge to overcome death and change by the erecting of monuments. Four lines then explain Orpheus' paradoxical being-in-change and in song (lines 2–5). "We" in line 4 momentarily includes the reader in the poet's wisdom and understanding, the willingness to relinquish static definitions and the false crystallization that they might imply: "We should not trouble about other names" (lines 4f.). The closing two lines of the second stanza, however, "Is it not much already . . . ," (lines 7–8) imply the reader's reluctance or inability to be content with Orpheus' (and Rilke's) easy converse with change. The next line hammers in the addressee's anticipated difficulty in "grasping": "O how he has to vanish for you to grasp it!" (line 9). The ensuing clarification of the paradox of Orpheus includes the reader (*ihrs* [line 12]), but again as one who is unable to comprehend fully: "Even while his word transcends the being-here, / he's there already where you do not follow." Thus the mysterious "transcending" of Orpheus is not only defined but dramatically recreated through the rhetorical device of an addressee who is unable to follow. As the closing verses return to third-person description, they leave Orpheus in the absolute realm of his difficult nature, whose essence is paradox: "And he obeys, while yet he oversteps." Orpheus both inhabits the transient sense-world and reaches toward the permanence of art. He spans and joins living and dead.

By opening the next sonnet (1.6) with a question, Rilke acknowledges the difficulty of grasping this mediatory function of Orpheus.

"Does he belong here?" he asks (*Ist er ein hiesiger* (line 1). He definitively answers that question with a strong assertion of the place of his
"wide nature" between realms.

> Does he belong here? No, out of both
> realms his wide nature grew.
> More knowing would he bend the willows' branches
> who has experienced the willows' roots.

> (1.6.1–4)

Orpheus' spanning of the breathlike transience of poetry (cf. 1.3.14)
and the "pure transcendency" of the climbing tree (*Sonnets* 1.1) finds a
deepened expression now in the lovely pairing of "the magic of earthsmoke and rue" and "the clearest relation."

> Und der Zauber von Erdrauch und Raute
> sei ihm so wahr wie der klarste Bezug.

> and may the magic of earthsmoke and rue
> be to him as true as the clearest relation.

> (1.6.10–11)

Here the classical motif of Orpheus' magic includes both the wispy
incense of line 10 and the power of sympathetic fusion with all of
existence, where man crosses the barriers between subjective and
objective forms of experience. This latter power of Orphic song
appears in the image of Orpheus as the "conjurer" (*der Beschwörende*)
who "under the eyelid's mildness / mix(es) their appearance into
everything seen" (lines 7f.). "Their" probably refers to "the dead" of
line 6. The language of magic also reminds us of the incantatory power
of song that virtually transpires in the sound pattern of lines 3–4.

> Kundiger böge die Zweige der Weiden,
> wer die Wurzeln der Weiden erfuhr.

·   In the classical myth of Orpheus, his magic is the magic of language
to persuade, to carry us along with its flow and movement in rhythmic
responsion to the poet's song, as the wild beasts and even the trees
move in harmony with Orpheus' music.[20] That power enabled
Orpheus to persuade even the gods of the underworld and bring
Eurydice back from the dead. Here both parts of this myth, the incantatory magic of inspired poetry and the power of song to overcome
death, have a new meaning. The assured power of song in the classical

version now becomes the paradoxical place of the poet at the point of crossing between change and permanence, between the realms of death and life. His mysterious knowledge spans both the visible ("the willow's branches," "everything seen") and the invisible ("the willows' roots," "the dead"). Hence his "magic" embraces both "earthsmoke" (with its suggestion of what belongs to the hidden realms of earth) and "the clearest relation."

V ·

To continue with the poem-by-poem elucidation of this complex work would require a much fuller discussion than is possible within the limits of this chapter. One feature of the *Sonnets*, however, deserves further consideration, namely the pairing of Orpheus and "Eurydice" to frame the complementing of monument and transcience so essential to Rilke's conception of poetry. This pairing, already noted in the first two of the *Sonnets*, concludes both parts 1 and 2 of the whole. By establishing this complementarity of Orpheus and Eurydice at the significant junctures of this collection, Rilke implies a new meaning for his "Eurydice." She is not the poet's passionately beloved, as in the earlier *Orpheus. Eurydike. Hermes*, but only his "friend" (cf. 2.28.14). She is herself a dancer and therefore also an artist in touch with a transcendent "music": "Then, from the high achievers / music fell into her altered heart" (1.25.7f.). She thus symbolizes a part of Orpheus himself, not that part which transcends and orders nature's rude, unformed impulses, but those deep springs of his knowledge that extend down into the realm of the dead in a mysterious unity with all being. Rilke thus fuses the classical significance of Orpheus as the symbol of the magical ordering power of language with the mystical meaning of Orpheus as a figure endowed with a vision of the ultimate unity of life and death, able to cross between these two poles of existence.[21] This aspect of Orpheus is important in the religious sect of the ancient Orpheus and is developed in the Christian imagery of Orpheus. It is part of the religious dimension of Orpheus and recognized by Rilke as such.

The penultimate poem of part 1 associates Eurydice-Vera with the fragility of passing youth and beauty. The images are of flowers, play, dance, flowing. (1.25):

But you now, you whom I knew like a flower whose name
I don't know, I will *once* more remember and show you
to them, you who were taken away,
beautiful playmate of the invincible cry.

Dancer first, who suddenly, with body full of lingering,
paused, as though her youngness were being cast in bronze;
mourning and listening—. Then, from the high achievers
music fell into her altered heart.

Sickness was near. Already overcome by the shadows,
her blood pulsed more darkly, yet, as if fleetingly
suspect, it thrust forth into its natural spring.

Again and again, interrupted by darkness and downfall,
it gleamed of the earth. Until after terrible throbbing
it entered the hopelessly open portal.

(*Sonnets* 1.25)

Read mythically, this sonnet presents the girl as a Persephone
figure, subject to the changes of the year, an embodiment of the shifting seasonal rhythms that bring spring out of winter "darkness," only
to enter the darkness again in the next year, "Again and again, interrupted by darkness and downfall" (line 12). Read as moment in a con-
tinuous narrative from poem to poem, the sonnet is (among other
things) part of an upswing to Orpheus, also addressed as *Du*, in the
next poem, *Du aber, Göttlicher* (1.26.1). Not knowing the name of the
flower whom the girl resembles is tantamount to a refusal to monumentalize. She is like the rose of *Sonnets* 1.5, where also "we should not
trouble / about other names" (1.5.4f.). Here, however, the poet's relation to his "Eurydice" is more intimate: he uses "I," not "we." The
simile of casting her body in bronze alludes to the permanence of
monuments. But this simile describes the most transient, elusive part
of this "Eurydice," her art of creating ever passing, ever disappearing
"figures" with her tentative body. These "figures," as we have seen,
suggest an art not only of images, but of mutable, ever-vanishing
shapes. They may form distant "star-images" for a moment, as in *Sonnets* 1.11, but they pass quickly to the less stable constellations of
human feeling, bound up with our mortality, in *Sonnets* 1.12.

Hail to the spirit that can unite us;
for we do truly live in figures.

And with little steps the clocks go on
alongside our essential day.

(1.12.1–4)

The counterpart to *Sonnets* 1.25 in the second part, namely 2.28, stresses the momentary duration of these figures. Now explicitly associated with the figures of the stars, symbols of eternity and infinity, they indicate the paradox of art, which both is immersed in and transcends the caducous realm of the senses.

O come and go. You, still half a child,
fill out the dance-figure for a moment
to the pure constellation of one of those
dances in which we fleetingly transcend

dumbly ordering Nature.

(2.28.1–5)

The "almost child," viewed as being in the process of growth and in passage ("come and go") will nevertheless "complete" a figure in the changing patterns of the dance. The "completion" of that temporary, shifting figure on earth, however, can reach toward the fulfillment of the "pure star-image" in the heavens. Both the theme and the language hark back to the still dreaming, unawakened child of *Sonnets* 1.2 and to the "lie" of humanizing the stars by language in *Sonnets* 1.11, giving them the names of constellations.

How, then, do we "fleetingly transcend dumbly ordering Nature" in such a dance? A possible answer lies in Orpheus' song. Unlike nature, it allows the silent "figure" of the constellation to express meaning through the verbal music of poetry. Dance, song, music, poetry are all manifestations of the power to shape those "figures" by which we transmute the changeful matter of the life around us into the "permanent" forms of imagination, spirit, thought, just as we trace permanent "figures" in the flecks of starlight to which we give names and coherent shapes. The young dancer, fully immersed in growth and change, completes her figure for only a moment; but in that second we transcend, through her, the physical limits of nature.[22]

The paradox of fleeting transcendence takes another form in *Sonnets* 1.25, where the dancer's pause marks the state of process, as though her young, hesitant body were being cast in bronze.

Tänzerin erst, die plötzlich, den Körper voll Zögern,
anhielt, als göss man ihr Jungsein in Erz;
trauernd und lauschend—.

Dancer first, who suddenly, with body full of lingering,
paused, as though her youngness were being cast in bronze;
mourning and listening—.

(1.25.5–7)

The monumentalizing bronze statue, however, like the sculpted dancers of Degas, remains in tension with the momentariness and tentativeness of the subject,[23] the brief, "sudden" pause in which she is caught, the pose of "mourning and listening," and, in the next stanza, the "sickness," "shadows," and mortal pulsing of her "darkened" blood, which all forebode her death (lines 9–11). What the bronze would fix is not her participation in a transcendent world of eternal forms but the passing moment of her "being-young" (*Jungsein* [line 6]). The casting of the bronze itself is expressed in a verb that evokes one of the *Sonnets'* most persistent images for the mutability of the world, namely flow and liquidity (*göss*, "cast," from *giessen*, "pour").[24]

Du aber Göttlicher, "But you, divine one," of the next poem, 1.26, is the foil to the *Dich aber* of the mortal, springlike beauty of the doomed Vera-Eurydice in 1.25. Over against the Maiden wedded to death, involved in change and time like a nameless flower (1.25.1f), stands the other side of the Orphic theme, the power of song to direct and subdue the formless passions embodied in the Maenads, the raw animal energy coursing through nature.

Du aber, Göttlicher, du, bis zuletzt noch Ertöner,
da ihn der Schwarm der verschmähten Mänaden befiel,
hast ihr Geschrei übertönt mit Ordnung, du Schöner,
aus den Zerstörenden stieg dein erbauendes Spiel.

But you, divine one, you, till the end still sounding,
when beset by the swarm of disdained maenads,
you outsounded their cries with order, beautiful one,
from among the destroyers arose your upbuilding music.

(1.26.1–4)

Orpheus, "the resounder," is triumphant even in his demise. The "climbing" of his "upbuilding music" (literally, "upbuilding play") out of "the destroyers" in the last line of the stanza recalls the first sonnet's climb toward the tree of transcendence and the "building" of his temple in the dark forest (1.1.1 and 4). Likewise, his ability there to calm animal fear and cunning and to still "bellow, cry, and roar" (1.1.7–10) parallels his song's victory of "order" and "beauty" (*mit Ordnung, du Schöner* [line 3]) here over the Maenads' wild cries.

Rilke here renews one of the most important themes of the classical myth of Orpheus, the power of language, art, and mind to overcome brute nature. In Ovid's influential version the sheer power of song can temporarily keep at bay the raging Maenads' missiles.

> Another's missile was a stone, which, even as it was thrown, in the very air was conquered by the harmonious song of voice and lyre and like a suppliant asking pardon for such deeds of furious violence fell before his feet. But the raging attack grew. All measure fled away, and the maddened Fury reigned. Even so all the weapons would have been softened by his song, but the huge shouting and the Phrygian flute with the raucous horn and the drums and the breast-beating and the Bacchic howls drowned out the lyre's music. Only then did the rocks grow red with the blood of a singer no longer heard. . . . And as then, for the first time, he spoke in vain and moved nothing with his voice, the impious women killed him; and through his mouth, by Jupiter, that voice, heard by the rocks and understood by the sense of wild beasts, departed as he breathed his life out into the winds (*Met.* 11.10–19, 39–43)

In Ovid, as in Rilke, the poet finally succumbs. Rilke conveys this vulnerability of the poet through a shift from the symmetrically placed caesuras of the first stanza to the uneven, excited rhythms of the second.

> Keine war da, dass sie Haupt dir und Leier zerstör,
> Wie sie auch rangen und rasten; und alle die scharfen
> Steine, die sie nach deinem Herzen warfen,
> wurden zu Sanftem an dir und begabt mit Gehör—.
>
> None of them there could destroy your head or your lyre,
> however they wrestled and raged; and all the sharp
> stones they flung at your heart
> turned soft on touching you and gifted with hearing.
>
> (1.26.5–8)

The assonance of *rangen und rasten,* "wrestled and raged," and the contiguous rhyming of the words of physical violence, *scharfen* and *warfen,* "sharp" and "flung," underline the wildness against which Orpheus has to struggle.

The Maenads' triumph, however, is only temporary. Tempered by the more symmetrically balanced line at the beginning of the third stanza, their victory wavers before the persistent lingering of that song in wild nature ("in lions and rocks / and in the trees and birds" [lines 10f.]). Song still lingers, vibrant and alive, in the stanza's concluding "singing still," *singst du noch jetzt.*

> Schliesslich zerschlugen sie dich, von der Rache gehetzt,
> während dein Klang noch in Löwen und Felsen verweilte
> und in den Bäumen und Vögeln. Dort singst du noch jetzt.

> In the end they battered and broke you, harried by vengeance,
> the while your resonance lingered in lions and rocks
> and in the trees and birds. There you are singing still.
>
> (1.26.9–11)

The last stanza achieves a balance between Orpheus' fragility and power.

> O du verlorener Gott! Du unendliche Spur!
> Nur weil dich reissend zulezt die Feindschaft verteilte,
> sind wir die Hörenden jetzt und ein Mund der Natur.

> O you lost god! You unending trace!
> Only because at last enmity rent and scattered you
> are we now the hearers and a mouth of Nature.
>
> (1.26.12–14)

"Divine" in line 1, Orpheus is now "a lost god," (compare *du aber, Göttlicher* in line 1 with *O du verlorener Gott* in line 12). He is only "an unending trace," something to be endlessly searched for, tracked down, discovered, and rediscovered. His existence, then, is not that of the static monument but of process, of the flowing life of nature. Only insofar as we participate in his triumphant, but vulnerable song are we both hearers and poets ("hearers," "mouth"), both active and passive recipients/celebrators of nature's life and beauty. The movement from "thou" to "we" (*du, wir*) in these last lines conveys that special intimacy between the poet's death and the living song that is his abiding gift to "us," even "now" (*jetzt*).

This notion of art as both the receiver and the celebrant of nature's generosity has a close parallel in *Sonnets* 2.15, where the generous "fountain mouth" is also the "marble mask," symbol of art, through which the vital waters of life flow inexhaustibly.

> O Brunnen-Mund, du gebender, du Mund,
> der unerschöpflich Eines, Reines, spricht, –
> du, vor des Wassers fliessendem Gesicht,
> marmorne Maske.

> O fountain-mouth, o giving, o mouth that speaks
> exhaustlessly one single, one pure thing, –
> before the water's flowing face,
> you marble mask.
>
> (2.15.1–4)

Active and passive interchange here too, for this "mouth" is also "the marble ear" in which nature always speaks, "an ear of earth's"; and its intimate converse with nature would be interrupted by a pitcher placed between.

> the marble ear in which you always speak.

> An ear of earth's. So that she's only talking
> with herself. If a pitcher slips between,
> it seems to her that you are interrupting.
>
> (2.15.11–14)

In the Christ-like paradox of *Sonnets* 1.26, Orpheus' being-in-death, like the breaking glass whose song is its shattering (*Sonnets* 2.13), creates a new bond, through the power of hearing and singing, between man and nature. The "enmity" that "scattered" him (*die Feindschaft verteilte*) leads ultimately, through the magic of art, to a new participation (cf. *Teil*, "share," *teilnehmen*, "participate") between man and the world around him.

Part 2, like part 1, ends with "Eurydice" and Orpheus paired in two successive poems, *Sonnets* 2.28 and 2.29. The two figures still stand in a relation of both contrast and complementarity. Eurydice-Vera embodies the momentary, fleeting, inarticulate realm of pure immanence in her "coming and going," her childlike immaturity, and her nonvocal, shifting art of "dance-figures."

> O komm und geh. Du, fast noch Kind, ergänze
> für einen Augenblick die Tanzfigur
> zum reinen Sternbild eines jener Tänze,
> darin wir die dumpf ordnende Natur

vergänglich übertreffen.

O come and go. You, still half a child,
fill out the dance-figure for a moment
to the pure constellation of one of those
dances in which we fleetingly transcend

dumbly ordering Nature.

(2.28.1–5)

Orpheus, on the other hand, is still the poet of transcendence here,
associated, initially, with the vast silences of space and the night sky
rather than with the earth.

Stiller Freund der vielen Fernen, fühle,

wie dein Atem noch den Raum vermehrt.

Silent friend of many distances,
feel how your breath is still increasing space.

(2.29.1–2)

Here, at the end of the *Sonnet*-book, however, complementarity
prevails over contrast, and the interpenetration of the two figures
defines the totality of Rilke's Orphic vision. Thus "Eurydice's"
ephemeral "dance-figures" reach toward the "purity" of Orphic art.
Mutability and permanence join in the paradox of "fleetingly transcend / dumbly ordering Nature" (*vergänglich übertreffen* [2.28.4–5]). The
stellar distances of the constellations, the remote "figures" in the sky
that elsewhere symbolize the unattainability of the "pure relation" (cf.
Sonnets 1.11 and 2.20), can now be bridged on both sides. Vera-
Eurydice's "dance-figure" reaches to the "constellation" (*Sternbild*
[2.28.2–3]), while Orpheus in *Sonnets* 2.29 has a new kinship to earth as
well as sky.

In *Sonnets* 2.28, Orpheus is the more remote figure, but it is now
only through Eurydice that we experience the magic of his song. The
frail girl, who at the beginning issued forth from the poet's lyre only to
fall asleep in the private, inner space of the speaker's ear (*Sonnets* 1.2),
now rouses in response to Orphic song.

Denn sie regte

sich völlig hörend nur, da Orpheus sang.
Du warst noch die von damals her Bewegte
und leicht befremdet, wenn ein Baum sich lang

besann, mit dir nach dem Gehör zu gehn.
Du wusstest noch die Stelle, wo die Leier
sich tönend hob—; die unerhörte Mitte.

For she roused
to full hearing only when Orpheus sang.
You were the one still moved from that earlier time
and a little surprised if a tree took long to consider

whether to go along with you by ear.
You still knew the place where the lyre
lifted sounding—: the unheard-of center

(2.28.5–11)

The "tree" of line 8 recalls both the tree of transcendence of *Sonnets* 1.1 and the power of Orphic art to bring order to the formlessness of nature. For this power of song, however, it is Eurydice, not Orpheus, who holds the foreground, reversing the relationship of *Sonnets* 1.1 and 1.2. Nature herself, though dumb, has her own quality of "order," (*dumpf ordnende Natur* [line 4]). No longer the hesitant, unrealized, evanescent figure of the end of part 1 (especially *Sonnets* 1.25), "Eurydice" here can establish a new connection with Orpheus, the "friend" whose "pace and countenance" she hopes one day to "turn."

Für sie versuchtest du die schönen Schritte
und hofftest, einmal zu der heilen Feier
des Freundes Gang und Antlitz hinzudrehn.

For this you tried the lovely steps and hoped
one day towards the perfect celebration
to turn the pace and countenance of your friend.

(2.28.12–14)

"Celebration" sounds the note of achieving permanence in the midst of our changeful sense-world (cf. *Sonnets* 1.7 and 1.19). Eurydice's figural art of dance ("the lovely steps") thus comes to share something of Orpheus' transcendent "celebration" through poetry. But ambiguity remains. Although "friend" in the last line suggests a possible reunion of Orpheus and Eurydice, "steps" and "turning" also recall their final separation in Orpheus' failure to lead her forth from Hades. Thus here, as everywhere in these poems, loss and regain, death and life, mourning and "celebration" remain commingled.

The next sonnet, however, ending the book, takes up "friend" and thus keeps alive the possibility of intimacy and connection. The "friend" is also more present because he is now addressed directly in the second person.

> Stiller Freund der vielen Fernen, fühle,
> wie dein Atem noch den Raum vermehrt.
> Im Gebälk der finstern Glockenstühle
> lass dich läuten.

> Silent friend of many distances,
> feel how your breath is still increasing space.
> Among the beams of the dark belfries let
> yourself ring out.
>
> (2.29.1–4)

Orpheus is both close and distant, both accessible and mysterious. His "stillness" or "silence" (*stiller*) recalls the atmosphere of calm that he brings to brute nature in *Sonnets* 1.1 (*leise* [line 8]) and his ability to "soften" the enraged Maenads' cries in *Sonnets* 1.26 (*zu Sanftem an dir und begabt mit Gehör* [line 8]). We have reached Vera-Eurydice's "unheard of center" where the poet, "magic power at your senses' crossroad," can occupy both earthly and celestial space, both metamorphosis and permanence, both "consuming" and "strength."

> Das, was an dir zehrt,
>
> wird ein Starkes über dieser Nahrung.
> Geh in der Verwandlung aus und ein.
> Was ist deine leidendste Erfahrung?
> Ist dir Trinken bitter, werde Wein.

> What feeds on you
>
> will grow strong upon this nourishment.
> Be conversant with transformation.
> From what experience have you suffered most?
> Is drinking bitter to you, turn to wine.
>
> (2.29.4–8)

The last line cited here associates the mystery of the Orphic paradox with that of the Christian. It also recalls the resolution of the transient and the "unending" in the "praising" that constitutes Orpheus' communion between living and dead in *Sonnets* 1.7.

Rühmen, das ists! Ein zum Rühmen Bestellter,
ging er hervor wie das Erz aus des Steins
Schweigen. Sein Herz, o vergängliche Kelter
eines den Menschen unendlichen Weins.

Praising, that's it! One appointed to praising,
he came like the ore forth from the stone's
silence. His heart, o ephemeral press
of a wine that for men is unending.

(1.7.1–4)

The metamorphosis of the "bitter" into the sweet drink of wine in 2.29.8 (*Ist dir Trinken bitter, werde Wein*) not only has the poet enact the miracle of Orphic/Christian transmutation of "becoming" to "being" but also leads into that interpenetration of flow and permanence, movement and stillness that ends the poem and the *Sonnet*-book.

Und wenn dich das Irdische vergass,
zu der stillen Erde sag: Ich rinne.
Zu dem raschen Wasser sprich: Ich bin.

And if the earthly has forgotten you,
say to the still earth: I flow.
To the rapid water speak: I am.

(2.29.12–14)

Earlier, in *Sonnets* 1.3, the poet allowed no meeting of contradictions (*An der Kreuzung zweier / Herzwege steht kein Tempel für Apollo*, "At the crossing of two / heartways stands no temple for Apollo"). Now in the "senses' crossroad" the poet becomes one with his "magic power" (*Zauberkraft* [2.29.10]). The double effect of both rhyme and assonance in the last lines (*Sinne, Sinn . . . rinne, bin*) creates a sense of union and wholeness at the level of sound, as if the poem were both imitating and creating the word-magic that it describes, enacting its own incantatory power as it describes the epiphany of that power.

Both thematically and formally the last stanza is the culminating point of the *Sonnet*-book, the realization of the Orphic interpenetration of self and other, speech and silence, passivity and energy, metamorphosis and permanence. The "stillness" that was an attribute of Orpheus in line 1 (*stiller Freund*) is now an attribute of the earth (*stillen Erde* [line 13]). We have not merely become the "mouth" of nature, as in the last poem of part 1 (*sind wir die Hörenden jetzt und ein Mund der*

Natur [1.26.14]), but the poet now speaks to nature in an *ich-du* relation.

Here again the form of address is crucially expressive. In the alternating "I" and "Thou" of these lines, the present and the distant poet rejoin. By quoting Orpheus' first-person statement as part of his own injunction to Orpheus, Rilke finally breaks through the barrier between mythic and contemporary time. He achieves, finally, a fusion with Orpheus. This identification of the "real" poet of the *Sonnets* with the mythical poet whom they address and recreate is suggested in Rilke's note to this last poem: "To a friend of Vera." This "friend" is not only the "friend" whom she addresses in the last line of her poem, *Sonnets* 2.28, and not only Orpheus, the "friend of many distances" in *Sonnets* 2.29, but Rilke himself. Thus the *Sonnets* work through and beyond Orpheus' death at the end of part 1 to a symbolical, Christ-like rebirth and recreation of Orpheus in the triumphant "I am" at the end of part 2.

These words belong as much to Rilke as to Orpheus. "I" and "thou" at this point have become almost inextricable. At the same time the half-rhyme, *Ich rinne, ich bin*, in these last two verses is a final validation of the paradoxical union-in-contraries in Rilke's "Orphic" vision: the interpenetration of the eternal forms of art and the ever-shifting sense-impressions of a mutably beautiful world. "Flowing" and "being," *Ich rinne* and *Ich bin*, come together as the projection of an "I" that is both person and persona, both individual and universal. In the device of command and reply and in the almost-rhyme of *rinne, bin*, movement and being, metamorphosis and eternity, draw near with an infinite nearness without ever actually being able to meet. This, perhaps, is the final message that these poems convey about the relation between language and reality:

> Zwischen den Sternen, wie weit; und doch, um wievieles noch weiter,
> was man am Hiesigen lernt.
> . . . .
> Alles ist weit—, und nirgends schliesst sich der Kreis.

> Between the stars, how far; and yet, by how much still farther,
> what we learn from the here and now.
> . . . .
> Everything is far—, and nowhere does the circle close.
>
> (2.20.1–2, 9)

7

Orpheus from Antiquity to Today
Retrospect and Prospect

Few, alas, are the lovers of poetry these days who read Virgil's *Georgics*. Yet the entire tradition of Western poetry has been profoundly influenced by the Orpheus-Eurydice episode that ends the poem. Indeed, had Virgil written nothing else, these two hundred verses alone would have assured his poetic immortality. Virgil's contribution is not just the beauty of his language and rhythms. So far as we can tell, he also radically reconceived the meaning of the myth.

Before Virgil, as I have shown in chapter 1, Orpheus embodies the power of music over animate and inanimate nature, its civilizing power, and, as an extension of its healing spell, its ability to reach across the divide between life and death and even restore the dead to life.[1] For Euripides and Horace, writing half a millennium apart, the motif "Not even Orpheus' songful magic could reverse death" has become a rhetorical topos of consolation literature. Virgil, however, makes Orpheus a great lover and a tragic lover. The same force that enables him to descend to the underworld and regain Eurydice also causes him to lose her for a second time.

How much of the story of the descent, the impulsive and fatal backward glance, and the poet's wasting away in grief did Virgil find in earlier writers? Despite several excellent recent studies, we still do not know for certain. If we read through the ancient references to Orpheus, we are struck at once by how small a role Eurydice (or her equivalent) plays. Orpheus' success in leading forth souls from Hades is already a commonplace for Isocrates in the fourth century B.C. (*Busiris* 8). According to Hellenistic sources, Aeschylus, in his lost play, *The Bassaridae*, told how Orpheus descended to Hades "because of his wife";[2] and this motive for the underworld journey is certainly in the

background of Euripides' *Alcestis* of 438 B.C. The earliest explicit
reference to Orpheus' attempt to rescue an individual woman, however, is the controversial account of the myth in Plato's *Symposium* (see
below). The earliest unambiguous account of a successful Orpheus in
our preserved texts occurs in Hermesianax's *Leontion* of the third century B.C.[3]

We do not know how much importance Aeschylus gave to rescuing
the wife. The main concern of his play, however, seems to have been
the religious rather than the emotional life of Orpheus, his conversion
from worshiping Dionysus to worshiping Apollo, as a result of which
the Bassarid women, followers of Dionysus, tear him apart. It is quite
possible that the wife, and Orpheus' love for her, did not interest the
dramatist. Hermesianax's Orpheus, in any case, braves the terrors of
Hades to bring back a woman. She is described only as "the Thracian
Agriope" (or Argiope). Hermesianax does not say that she is his wife
or even a beloved. The backward glance is entirely absent. There is no
term of endearment or other indication of emotional engagement.
Instead, Hermesianax stresses Orpheus' courage amid the dangers of
the descent. This emphasis may be a deliberate reply to Plato's charge
that Orpheus (unlike Alcestis) was too cowardly to die in the place of
his beloved.[4] The gods, therefore, says Plato, gave him only a phantom
Eurydice, a *phasma*, not a real woman (*Symposium* 179D). Plato's
version, however, implies a successful rescue of the wife in the mythical tradition, for the passage reads most naturally as a deliberate,
slightly perverse revision of a familiar tale.

In having the speaker, Phaedrus, thus refashion the established
myth to prove the superiority of homosexual to heterosexual love,
Plato is also drawing upon other myths of cloud images. The seventh-
century lyric poet Stesichorus had told how the gods gave Paris a
cloud-Helen instead of the real one, and Euripides used this version in
his *Helen* a generation before Plato. He had also written a play about
Protesilaus, who won his dead bride, Laodamia, back from Hades for
a single day.[5] The *Alcestis* draws on such myths too, particularly in the
closing scene, where Admetus cautiously warns Heracles, who is
leading the veiled Alcestis back from the dead, that this might be a
"phantom of those below" (*phasma nerterôn* [line 1127]).

The first solid reference in Greek literature to Orpheus's second loss
of Eurydice because "he forgot the commands about her" occurs in a
collection of stories by a late Hellenistic writer, Conon.[6] Conon, however, is contemporary with Virgil and, for all we know, may have

borrowed this motif from Virgil rather than the other way around. Just as Virgil made a major innovation in the myth in combining the stories of Orpheus and Aristaeus, so he may have originated the story of the impulsive backward look.

It is salutary to remember how relatively sparse are the references to Orpheus in archaic and classical Greek literature: none in Homer, Sophocles, Herodotus, Thucydides, or Xenophon; one each in the extant work of Aeschylus, Aristophanes, and Demosthenes; none in Theocritus (which is rather surprising) or Callimachus. The story told in Aeschylus' lost *Bassaridae*—the tale not of the lover or husband but of the religious teacher and magical singer who abandons Dionysus for Apollo and is then torn apart by Thracian Maenads—is also the commonly illustrated version of the myth on Greek vases of the fifth and fourth centuries.

Writers from classical times through the Roman Empire pay particular attention to Orpheus' role as a religious teacher. He is joined to Hesiod, Empedocles, and Parmenides or regarded as the earliest of the philosophers. He inaugurates mysteries, initiation ceremonies, purificatory rites, and holy festivals like the Thesmophoria. He teaches the Greeks their myths about the gods, gives oracles, and founds temples.[7]

In a celebrated passage, Diodorus Siculus says that he "acted in a way resembling Dionysus" when the latter brought back his mother Semele from Hades (4.25.4). This passage is widely interpreted as evidence for Orpheus' catabasis (descent to the underworld) and thus as part of the mystery religion of Orphism. R. J. Clark conveniently distinguishes between descents in a "fertility tradition" and those in a "wisdom tradition."[8] In the fertility tradition the descent restores a lost vitality to the earth, renewing a failed vegetative life, as in the myth of Kore (Persephone) told in the Homeric *Hymn to Demeter*. In the wisdom tradition the descent does not necessarily result in a victory of life over death but provides the underworld traveler with knowledge about the afterlife, what the *Odyssey* calls "the way of mortals whenever anyone dies" (11.218). Such is Gilgamesh's journey to the land of Utnapishtim to recover his lost companion, Enkidu; and such are the journeys of Odysseus, Aeneas, and later Dante.

Orpheus' catabasis may originally have been part of a fertility tradition. So it seemed to Diodorus, who associates him with Dionysus, in this respect a vegetation deity who descends to Hades to recover his mother, Semele, herself the survival of an Anatolian earth-goddess. The Orphic religion seems to have developed this aspect of the myth:

Orpheus' descent and return is the model for the soul's successful passage to the Other World. A terra-cotta group from a south Italian tomb, probably of the fourth century B.C., represents Orpheus charming the Sirens with his lyre, perhaps to symbolize his guidance in the soul's successful passage through the trials of Hades to its new life there and eventual rebirth.[9] Virgil, however, assimilates Orpheus' descent to the wisdom tradition, possibly by drawing upon the Orphic religion, but more directly by having Orpheus experience the universality of death in terms that recall Odysseus' descent (*G*.4.475–477 and *Od.* 11.38–41). Yet Virgil has also modified the "wisdom" aspects of Orpheus' descent. Far from returning with a deepened understanding of death and an enlarged perspective on his task in life (as do Gilgamesh, Odysseus, Aeneas, and even the Dionysus of Aristophanes' *Frogs*), Orpheus remains totally immersed in grief, loss, and death. He has not in fact learned anything in Hades. Even Ovid's Orpheus brings back no wisdom. For him the decisive experience is not the visit to Hades but the bitterness of losing Eurydice, which in turns leads him to pederastic love.

Almost as controversial as the question of Virgil's originality in the Fourth *Georgic* is the meaning of the famous Orpheus relief that inspired Rilke's narrative poem *Orpheus. Eurydike. Hermes* and was perhaps important for Virgil as well. This work, extant in several Roman copies, is an Attic relief of 440–420 B.C. It may represent the moment when Hermes hands Eurydice over to a victorious Orpheus after the latter has succeeded in persuading the gods of the underworld to let her return. If so, it would be a positive version of the tale that Plato tells in the *Symposium*.[10] But the relief could also depict the moment of loss and farewell: Hermes, leader of souls (Psychopompos), claims Eurydice for Hades, whether for the first or the second time. In either case, the sculpture already contains the three constituent elements of the myth: love, death, and art (the last embodied in the lyre that Orpheus holds limply at his side, either in exhaustion or in despair). In addition to the vase paintings mentioned above, there are of course numerous other visual representations of Orpheus in antiquity. The largest group are mosaics showing him charming wild beasts with his song. An interesting Hellenistic relief in the Sparta museum shows Orpheus receiving a poet's dedication. The poet, standing on our right, holds out a partially unrolled papyrus scroll. Orpheus is seated on the left, holding his lyre. Several animals, presumably held by the charm of the lyre, are in the background. Here Orpheus is already a divinity of poetic art and a helper of poets.

Whatever the course of the development of the myth from Euripides through Plato and Virgil, there is a fair measure of consensus on its deepest roots. It develops from shamanistic practices to the north, probably among the Thracians, who were still famous for such powers in Herodotus' time. These shamans cross between the living and the dead, have magical power over nature and animals, and are closely associated with music and the ecstatic, trancelike effects of music, possess healing and prophetic powers, and can lead the dead forth from the lower world.[11]

Orpheus' power to bridge the gap between the living and the dead continues after his own death. The severed head of the poet, along with his lyre, floats down the Hebrus River and across the northern Aegean to the island of Lesbos, where the head is consulted for its oracular power. The story is reported in several ancient sources (particularly the Hellenistic poet Phanocles) and is also depicted on a number of vases. In the most popular form of the legend, Apollo, resenting the competition, stands severely over the head and forbids further prophecy. In one scene, however, depicted on an Attic red-figured hydria of the mid-fifth century, the person standing over the head is not Apollo but a bearded man of mature age, crowned with a wreath. He has been plausibly identified as the ancient Lesbian poet Terpander. A female figure stands on the other side of the head and bends toward it, holding a lyre. She may be Orpheus' mother, the Muse Calliope.[12] If this scene does in fact represent the poet Terpander in communion with Orpheus' head, with the Muse standing by, then Orpheus appears not only as a source of prophecy from the realm of the dead but also as a source of poetic inspiration, as he is on the relief from Sparta discussed above.

From time to time the archaic aspect of the myth surfaces with particular clarity in literary texts. The Middle English poem *Sir Orfeo* combines the shamanistic Orpheus of the ancient tradition with the magic of a Celtic fairyland. There the hero's beautiful wife, Queen Heurodis, is mysteriously carried off by the wizard-ruler of the Other World.[13] The poem gradually shifts the issues from knightly combat to a supernatural journey. The beautiful but unearthly inhabitants of the fairy world hold Heurodis in their spell. They enter the human world when she dreams of being carried off from her garden by the fairy king. Orfeo tries to protect her with a guard of a thousand well-armed knights, but to no avail. Desolate at his loss, he entrusts his kingdom to his seneschal, exchanges his regal garb for rags, and lives in the forest for ten years as a wild man. Among the accoutrements of his past identity, he retains only the harp. One day he chances to see the train of the fairy king passing through the woods, Heurodis among them. He follows them through a rock into the Other World and by his singing wins from the king the right to ask for anything he wishes. When he asks for Heurodis, the king refuses. Orfeo chides him with the unchivalric behavior of a false promise, and the king has to yield.

This version connects the magic of music with the magic of love and also with the power of Orpheus to overcome death. It offers a courtly version of the classical Orpheus' persuasion of the gods of the Other World and in fact doubles the persuasion of the harp with the resourceful use of the knightly code of conduct. It also doubles the descent motif. Orfeo makes a symbolical descent by "dying" to his human identity as a king of power, elegance, and art and by living as a hermit in the liminal realm of the wild forest. Only after he passes this stage of trial-by-loss does he gain access to the fairy world that holds Heurodis prisoner. Unlike the classical Orpheus, however, his grief leads him only to the first journey, the forest. The actual descent to the Other World (the second journey) results not from an act of will but from a chance encounter. In this fairyland normal human competence and decisiveness are suspended, as they have been in the knights' initial failure to defend their queen. Only the harp still has its magic.

Though it makes no explicit mention of Orpheus, Milton's early poem *Comus* shares some of *Sir Orfeo*'s shamanistic themes of magic, music, the never-never land of an enchanted, nightlike forest, and a sinister king of the Other World. A lady, separated from her two brothers in the darkness of the "wild wood," is lured into the palace of a licentious spirit, Comus, and held there by his enchantments, with their "soft music." Her purity and the aid of a good spirit save her from temptation and spiritual death and effect her return to her family at Ludlow Castle. In contrast to the classical Orpheus myth, however, both *Sir Orfeo* and *Comus* reintegrate the victim of the Other World into the security of the lost human life. Orfeo wins back his queen, returns to his kingdom, tests the loyalty of the seneschal, and once more takes up his rule. The ancient Orpheus, always a marginal figure, has no such return to a well-defined social identity. To this marginal aspect of the magical singer the modern versions of Tennessee Williams and Jean Anouilh, as we shall see, although reduced in other respects, are perhaps the most faithful.

Milton's famous sonnet "Methought I saw . . . ," like his *Comus*, has close affinities with the Orpheus myth. Though explicitly based on the Alcestis myth, mentioned in the second line, the poem is also a displaced form of the shamanistic Orpheus in its tragic form.

> Methought I saw my late espoused Saint
> Brought to me like Alcestis from the grave,
> Whom Jove's great Son to her glad Husband gave,
> Rescu'd from death by force though pale and faint.
>
> (1–4)

Milton, as speaker, is an Orpheus whose song cannot bring back his lost beloved. When he ascends to the sunlight, figuratively, in awakening from his dream, he is in fact returning to the darkness of his desolation. He is no longer the visionary traveler between worlds but the blind poet who has lost his wife.

> But O as to embrace me she enclin'd
> I wak'd, she fled, and day brought back my night.
>
> (13–14)

The suddenness of her disappearance and the interruption of a hoped-for embrace are perhaps echoes of the Orpheus myth, except that this Orpheus is guiltless. Milton gives the wife's shade the initiative in the embrace, but she too is faultless, "pure as her mind." The dream provides Milton with a powerful equivalent to the ancient mythical motif of the descent to the underworld. The mythical atmosphere is re-inforced by the allusion to Heracles' descent to rescue Alcestis, "Whom Jove's great Son to her glad Husband gave / rescu'd from death by force though pale and faint." But what begins as successful rescue ends, as in the case of Orpheus and Eurydice, as loss.

The interplay of the two myths of descent, the one explicit (Heracles and Alcestis), the other implicit (Orpheus and Eurydice), deepens the emotional resonances of the experience. The night that gave the poet a privileged, Orpheus-like access to the lower world returns at the end as the personal "night" of his life circumstance, marked by the pronominal adjective *my* in the last line: "I wak'd, she fled, and day brought back my night." The multiple associations of blindness and night enable the poet to place his personal pain in the perspective of these mythical encounters with death. Though he does not lose the poignancy of his individual suffering, he establishes his identity as the visionary seer of what is hidden from ordinary mortal sight and as the privileged communicator with the realm of the dead. What a perceptive critic has observed of the myth is particularly apt here: "The unique feature of the Orpheus myth is that in it art enters life as a means of dealing with death."[14]

The journey to the underworld as a means of dealing with intense personal loss remains the focus of the myth in its two best-known film versions, Marcel Camus' Brazilian setting in *Black Orpheus* (*Orfeu Negro*) and Jean Cocteau's surrealistic and self-consciously symbolic *Orphée*. I shall skip over a few centuries and discuss these contemporary versions here.[15]

Black Orpheus develops the hints in Virgil and Ovid that link the protagonist's struggle with life and death to the seasonal cycles. Orfeu is a streetcar conductor in Rio de Janeiro; Eurydice is a young girl running away from home, pursued by a dimly perceived, rejected lover, her "Aristaeus." She and Orfeu meet, are drawn to each other (though he has another girlfriend), and dance together at the Mardi Gras festival, Orfeu as the Sun, Eurydice as Night. A figure disguised as Death (presumably Eurydice's rejected lover) pursues her. Orfeu tries unsuccessfully to fight Death, is defeated, and loses Eurydice. She meanwhile has fled to the trolley car barn at the edge of the city (the urban version of the meadow where the snake bites her in Virgil), and is unintentionally electrocuted by Orfeu as she tries to get away from Death.

Orfeu's journey to the "Other World" to recover her takes the form of a visit to the city morgue. This journey corresponds to the wisdom tradition in mythical descents to the underworld. This Orpheus, like Odysseus, experiences the emptiness of the dead. But instead of embracing an empty shade, he encounters twentieth-century bureaucratic machinery, in which the person becomes only a statistical record. The flesh-and-blood human being becomes an empty cipher amid the great piles of paper that the night watchman sweeps up from the deserted municipal offices.

In despair, Orfeu turns to magic. He visits a seance of drug-smoking Indians. This episode corresponds to the fertility tradition of the descent, wherein magic could actually defeat death and bring the corpse back to life. Orfeu hears Eurydice's voice, makes the fatal turn to look at her, but sees only an ugly hag in her place. Accepting his grief, he recovers her body and carries it up the mountain to his hut. His jealous ex-girlfriend plays the part of the ancient Maenads. She hurls a stone at his head, knocks him off balance, and sends him plunging down the mountainside to his death. After his death a small boy takes up Orfeu's guitar and plays at dawn to make the sun rise.

Many of the correlations with the classical myth are obviously artificial and unsatisfactory, especially the minimal role of song. As in most of the twentieth-century versions, the myth is reduced to a love story. Yet the film tries to recover a mythic dimension through a setting that allows for intense passions, belief in magic, the fertility aspects of the Mardi Gras fesival, and the rather too transparent symmetry between the nocturnal scenes of Eurydice's loss and the sunrise at the end. It also tries to find convincing equivalents for the folkloristic elements in the myth: the nocturnal battle with Death, the lonely journey through the empty public buildings (perhaps the film's most effective scene, juxtaposing myth and the impersonality of death in a contemporary metropolis), and the symmetry between the séance of magical rites to bring back the dead and the quasi-magical singing of the boy at the end.

Cocteau's *Orphée* places the myth in a higher register of mythicality and literariness. Instead of taking the folkloristic direction of Camus, Cocteau uses self-consciously "mythic" symbols and gives Orpheus' artistry its properly prominent place. The visual representation of the passage between worlds, with glass, mirrors, and underground winds, is probably the film's most spectacular contribution. This Orpheus not only journeys between life and death but, in a characteristically modern, psychologizing development, is drawn there by his fascination with the figure of his Death. She is a dark, powerful woman, who is mysteriously connected with his creative powers, perhaps as an anima figure. Her strength, passion, and knowing acceptance of a doomed love contrast with the fair, bland, uninteresting bourgeois Eurydice to whom Orphée is married. It is from this bleak underworld, on the other side of mirrors, that Orphée receives his poetry, in the form of cryptic messages transmitted over a car radio by a younger alter ego, the poet Cégeste (*ses gestes?*) whom Death has carried off to her realm in the dark limousine.

This Orpheus succeeds in rescuing his wife, who has been accidentally killed, from the underworld. The center of the myth, however, is displaced from this happy ending to the tragic love of Death for the poet. This change (doubled by the hopeless love of the Hermes figure,

Heurtebise, for Eurydice) gives Cocteau an opportunity to present some impressive scenes of subterranean landscape and to introduce a modern, bureaucratized version of the judicial machinery of Hades. But it also enables him to recast the myth as a fable of the poet in bourgeois society and to attempt a psychological version of the Romantic association of poetry and Death.

The Orpheus myth deals with death not only through the motifs of loss and descent but also through a poetry of lamentation. A singer who makes his poetry of his passion and his passion of his poetry, Orpheus transforms grief into song. This is a song whose primary character is its intense, personal expressiveness rather than its ritual character as consolation for sorrow. In Greek culture particularly, the ritual lament is the special prerogative of women. The *Iliad* closes with the women in the house of Priam wailing in the mourning rites over the body of Hector. The *Odyssey* transposes this scene to a divine register with the Muses and sea-goddesses lamenting at the funeral of Achilles (*Od.* 24.47–66). Euripides' *Hecuba* and *Trojan Women*, Sophocles' *Electra*, and Aeschylus' *Libation Bearers* are fashioned in large part of female lamentation. Scenes of women in the ritual keening over a dead warrior recur again and again on Greek vases, from the great Dipylon vases of the eighth century B.C. to the end of the classical period.

Uninhibited release of grief in public, though permitted the Homeric warrior, is nevertheless felt as more appropriate to women than to men.[16] Orpheus, however, claims such lamentation for the male voice. His is a voice of total mourning and perpetual lament. The magical sympathy that he establishes with nature through his song becomes the totalizing sympathy of all-absorbing sorrow. In Virgil, Orpheus' grief effaces the order and restraints of art. This Orpheus "weeps to himself" and still "charms tigers and draws oak trees by his song" (*G.* 4.509f.). Yet his song's magical power now belongs more to grief than to art. Song becomes pure feeling, another form of "weeping." Hence Virgil compares Orpheus' weeping not to a work of human artifice but to a cry from nature, the "pitiful song" (*miserabile carmen* [514]) of the nightingale that "mourns" and "laments" its "lost brood" (*maerens . . . amissos queritur fetus* [511f.]).

This overflow of the song-lament into the realm of nature resembles the endless plangency of women who in their grief are metamorphosed into the forms of constant, almost mechanical lamentation, like Ovid's Niobe, Philomela, or Byblis. This confusion of the boundaries between human feeling and nature shows a grief that exceeds any

terms that the human voice could find for it. Such grief is not contain-
able within the normal dimensions of human expression. Virgil's
simile of the nightingale, with the implicit reference to the myth of
Philomela, associates Orpheus with this metamorphic pattern. This
singing, moreover, has turned away from the human world and has
virtually become a part of nature, of a frozen, barren nature that is
itself a mirror of his song's desolation (*G*.4.517f.). Inverting the magical
sympathy that his song establishes between man and nature, Orpheus
transforms the entire world into a "world of lament," *eine Welt aus
Klage,* as Rilke calls it. It permits no clear boundaries from which
normal life could resume.

Whereas the ritualized female lament is a social act and has the
function of reintegrating the loss and the mourners into the community, the lament of Orpheus is starkly individual, isolated, and
asocial. This aspect of the myth has its most powerful form in Virgil;
but of modern writers who have rendered this mood of total loss, perhaps most notable is Anouilh in his *Eurydice,* which I shall discuss
more fully later. The Orpheus of this play refuses to be consoled for the
death of his beloved. He resists being drawn back to the trivia of a life
that no longer contains her; and in the last scene he exits for a rendez-
vous with her, presumably by suicide.

In the softer pastoral inversions of such lamentation, not only does
the poet's grief fill all of nature, but nature also grieves for the poet. In
this "pathetic fallacy" the poet's magical power over nature becomes
nature's sympathy with mankind for his loss. Theocritus' lament for
Adonis in the first *Idyll,* the Hellenistic *Lament for Bion,* Virgil's lament
for Gallus in *Eclogue* 10, and Milton's for "Lycidas" are all versions of
this motif. Ovid adapts this gentler pastoral touch to the Virgilian ending of Orpheus' lament for Eurydice. Nature weeps over the poet in
universal mourning: "Over you [Orpheus] the sad birds wept, over
you the beasts, over you the hard rocks, over you the forests that often
followed your song" (*Met.* 11.44–46). In a later transformation, Dante
replaces Orpheus' triple "Eurydice" in *Georgics* 4.525–527 with a threefold "Virgilio" when the poet loses his guide and model near the top
of Mount Purgatory (*Purg.* 30.49–52).[17] The pathetic fallacy, however, is
essentially an inversion of the Orphic tragedy. It recreates the musical
life of Orpheus in nature, as does the sentimental ending of the film
Black Orpheus, where the boy fancies that he can make the sun rise by
playing Orfeu's guitar. This sublimation of grief into song, with the
triumph of music, implicit or explicit, over sorrow and death, is also

the basis for the operatic versions of the myth (Gluck's *Orfeo ed Euridice* and Monteverdi's *Orfeo*).[18]

There is a feminine version of the Ovidian lament of nature over Orpheus in the myth of Echo, especially as told in Longus' romance, *Daphnis and Chloe* (3.23). Like Orpheus, Echo is the child of a god and a mortal and has a special relation to the Muses, who have taught her to play every kind of music. When she grew up, "she danced with the Nymphs and sang with the Muses." But Pan, jealous of her skill and angry because she scorns him (as she does all men), sends a madness upon the local herdsmen so that they tear her apart "like dogs and wolves, and throw her limbs, still singing, all over the earth. Earth, in kindness to the Nymphs, buries them all and keeps their music." The details of the scorned lover, dismemberment, and still-singing limbs are probably borrowed from the Orpheus myth. The earth's sympathy is a version of the Ovidian pathetic fallacy of the universal lament for the dead poet, with a twist of etiological myth, to explain the origin of echoes. Echo survives over all the earth in her voice that "imitates everything," everywhere. In this tale, to a greater extent than in the motif of the singing head in Virgil and Ovid, the musical afterlife of a dismembered singer provides consolation for the emptiness of loss.

Later developments of the myth also have their happier side. Christian allegorists, from late antiquity to the high Middle Ages, draw on the version that allows Orpheus to succeed in recovering Eurydice and makes him a harbinger of Christ in the Harrowing of Hell.[19] Orpheus' power over beasts here prefigures Christ's power to lead forth the souls of the virtuous.[20] The representation of Orpheus among the animals as an iconographic model for Christ as the Good Shepherd furthered this identification.[21]

This allegorical reading of the myth has proven remarkably tenacious. It reappears, over a millennium later, in the sacramental drama (*auto sacramental*) of Calderón de la Barca, *The Divine Orpheus* (*El Divino Orfeo*), of which he wrote two versions (1634, 1663). The earlier is particularly interesting. The central action is a conflict between Aristeo, symbolizing the Devil, and Orfeo (Christ) over the soul of Eurydice, who symbolizes mankind endowed with free will. Calderón here draws on the late antique fusion of Christ/Orpheus who bears a lyre in the shape of a cross and dies not by dismemberment but on the cross.[22]

Earlier allegorists generally treat the myth in a more critical spirit. The early Christian writers Clement of Alexandria in the second century and Eusebius in the early fourth contrast Orpheus' pagan song with the spiritual music of Christ.[23] This negative meaning was reinforced by Augustine's warnings against the seductive beauty of pagan music and eloquence (long associated with Orpheus), in contrast to the wisdom (*sapientia*) of Christ's teaching.[24]

In retelling the myth in a philosophical perspective in his *Consolation of Philosophy*, the late pagan thinker Boethius (ca. A.D. 480–524) closely follows Virgil and Ovid but stresses the ineffectuality of Orpheus' music to help the singer: "The measures that had subdued all else could not soothe their lord" (*nec, qui cuncta subegerant, / mulcerent dominum modi* [3, metr. 12.16f.]). Boethius then gives a moralizing interpretation to Orpheus' endless lament over his second loss of Eurydice. She embodies the material world and its enticements. Orpheus' backward glance is a backsliding of the unenlightened soul to baser earthly needs and desires.

> Heu noctis prope terminos
> Orpheus Eurydicen suam
> vidit, perdidit, occidit.
> Vos haec fabula respicit,
> quicumque in superum diem
> mentem ducere quaeritis;
> nam qui Tartareum in specus
> victus lumina flexerit,
> quicquid praecipuum trahit,
> perdit, dum videt inferos.

> Alas, near the limits of night Orpheus saw, lost, and destroyed his Eurydice. You who seek to lead your mind toward the bright day above, to you this tale applies [literally, looks back]. For whoever is vanquished and bends his eyes toward the cave of Tartarus loses whatever excellence he draws forth while he gazes on those below. (49–58)[25]

This negative allegorization of the myth has rich development in the numerous commentators on Boethius' popular work, especially from the tenth to the twelfth centuries. With the Christian assimilation of classical learning, Orpheus appears in a more positive light. He symbolizes the union of philosophical wisdom (*sapientia*) and rhetoric (*eloquentia*).[26] Eurydice, however, does not enjoy the same good fortune. She continues to represent the dangers of earthly desire and carnal temptation. This uneven treatment of the two protagonists is due in part to Eurydice's association with Eve tempted by Satan (even though in the classical versions it is in fact Orpheus who yields and breaks divine command) and partly because Eurydice's place is already in Hell and therefore under the sign of the Fall.[27] The pagan underworld, we should recall, is not the Christian Hell but a morally neutral receptacle for the dead, whether good or bad. That the serpent of Virgil and Ovid would be reincarnated as Satan was almost inevitable (the dying serpent in Virgil's Fourth *Eclogue* underwent a similar transformation); but Virgil might have been surprised to find his Aristaeus allegorized as Virtue. Because Eurydice is fleeing Virtue (Aristaeus) for Pleasure, she is fatally bitten by the serpent and condemned to Hell.[28]

The Renaissance recovery of the distinction between mythical and historical time again places Orpheus in a remote, idealized setting. Orpheus the magician or the rescuer of souls once more becomes Orpheus the artist and the civilizer. The classical Orpheus' combination of beautiful music and the power to subdue bestiality by art appealed to the Renaissance humanists. He embodies their cultural ideal of a human figure who combines the discovery of natural and divine mysteries with emotional depth and intensity, intellect, the arts, and love for his fellow men.[29]

This Orpheus, however, is not identical with his classical original. Instead of the marginal, asocial figure of the classical myth, the Renaissance Orpheus is a champion of social life and the bonds that unite men. The Renaissance humanists recover with gusto the ancient tradition of Orpheus the theologian, religious teacher, and natural philosopher. Dante anticipates this movement when he not only joins Orpheus to the mythical Linus but also places him with the moral philosophers Cicero and Seneca and also close to the scientists and mathematicians Dioscorides, Euclid, Ptolemy, Hippocrates, and Galen (*Inferno* 4.140–144).[30] Orpheus the lover had already been revived in the courtly tradition of the late Middle Ages (for example, in *Sir Orfeo*, discussed above),[31] but this Orpheus takes on new meaning, especially among the Italian Neoplatonists. Here the power of love leads the soul to contemplate the highest spiritual good and the secrets of the universe. This development too harks back to late antiquity, where Orpheus' lyre had served as a Neoplatonic symbol of the harmony of the spheres.[32]

The tragic tale of the Virgilian and Ovidian Orpheus reappears in more or less familiar form as part of the recovery of classical literature. Such, for example, is the Orpheus of Politian (Poliziano) and of painters like Giorgione, Titian, and Dosso Dossi.[33] The dominant tone, however, is not so much tragic loss as the celebration of poetry, music, and beauty as the guide to the truly civilized life. Politian, for example, whose *Orfeo* is a dramatized reworking of Virgil and Ovid, pays relatively little attention to the failure of Orpheus. His hero is an idealized artist. Like Ovid, Politian has Eurydice exonerate Orpheus and complain only of "the too great love that has undone us both" (*'l troppo amore n'ha disfatti ambedua*).[34] Virgil's tragic mood was out of keeping with the festive occasion of Politian's poem, and so its darker overtones were muted. Monteverdi, a century later, faced the same problem when he wrote his *Orfeo* to celebrate the marriage of Maria de Medici to Henry IV of France, and he perforce used the version with the happy ending. Even the detail of the severed head ceases to be a mark of defeat, as it was in Virgil and Ovid, and instead symbolizes the triumph of art. Boccaccio uses Ovid's story of Apollo rescuing the head from the threatening serpent as an allegory of the posthumous fame of the artist: his work lives on after his death to defeat all-devouring time.[35]

This predominantly positive interpretation of the myth in Renaissance poetry, painting, and music rests in part on the humanist assumption that language is a source of knowledge and beauty rather than of deception, that intelligent and refined discourse, including the symbolic language of music and the visual arts, unlocks the secrets of nature, and that knowledge and beauty belong together and illuminate each other. Renaissance poets and artists go back to Homer and Hesiod in reasserting that the Muses of poetry and song are inspirers of wisdom as well as of art.

The Renaissance Orpheus, then, draws from the classical tradition the view of Orpheus as a symbol of the cooperation of the arts, sciences, and religion in a still unitary conception of learning. He unites poetry, music, philosophy, theology, and the natural sciences. In Puttenham's *Arte of English Poetry* (1589), the poets are "the first Astronomers, Philosophers and Metaphysicks . . . and Historiographers"; and Orpheus, the "first musitien," stands at their head.[36] Sir Philip Sidney's *Apologie for Poetry* (1595) likewise harks back to the ancient tradition of the philosophic Orpheus in pairing him with Linus "and some others" as among the first writers of poetry and therefore as the ancients' "fathers in learning."[37]

Shakespeare's Orpheus reflects this confident assumption that knowledge is ancient, noble, and poetical. Orpheus becomes a hyperbolic figure for the limitless power of language, conquering not just tigers but whales as well. This Orpheus' lute

> was strung with poet's sinews;
> Whose golden touch could soften steel and stones.
> Make tigers tame and huge leviathans
> Forsake unsounded deeps to dance on sands,
> After your dire lamenting elegies . . .[38]

As a singer whose instrument is made of "poet's sinews," this Orpheus traces his lineage back to Ovid: despite his power to move the creatures at the farthest reaches of wild nature, he makes his song of his own feelings, as his lyre is made of a poet's gut. This feeling quality of Orpheus, a figure whose magic not only moves trees and mountains but also offers a gentle consolation, also marks the song of the accused Queen Katherine in *King Henry VIII*, though in a sadder vein.

> Orpheus with his lute made trees,
> And the mountain-tops that freeze,
> Bow themselves, when he did sing:
> To his music plants and flowers
> Every spring; as sun and showers
> There had made a lasting spring.
>
> Everything that heard him play,
> Even the billows of the sea,
> Hung their heads and then lay by.
> In sweet music is such art:
> Killing care and grief of heart
> Fall asleep, or, hearing, die.
>
> (3.1.4–15)

This music is like the restorative rays and sun of spring; and, like the song of Simonides' ancient Orpheus, it calms the waves and the griefs of the heart.

Only in the seventeenth century, with the development of the empirical scientific method, will poetry and natural philosophy split apart. Yet even for Francis Bacon, at the beginning of this movement, Orpheus still symbolizes the harmonious order of the physical world. In his *De Sapientia Veterum* (*The Wisdom of the Ancients*, 1609) the Orpheus myth is a suitable "representation of universal philosophy," and Orpheus himself may serve as a metaphor for "philosophy personified" through his mastery of "all harmony subdued" by which he "drew all things after him by sweet and gentle measures."[39] But in contrast to this positive view of Orpheus, Bacon also has a darker interpretation. The poet's backward glance signifies the "impatience" of philosophy, and his death shows humanity's failure to heed the wise harmony of his song. The Maenads' "hideous roar" (to use Milton's phrase) is the triumph of unreason, the inability of mankind to rise above its brutishness.[40]

Bacon's combination of a triumphant and defeated Orpheus interestingly resumes the ambivalence of the ancient tradition, although in a different area. Some fifty years later, Thomas Sprat, in his *History of the Royal Society* (1665–66), moves us even farther from the Renaissance optimistic use of the myth to declare the unity of art, music, natural philosophy, and theology. Taking the distancing perspective of rationalistic criticism, Sprat repeats the ancient view in which Orpheus belongs with Musaeus and Homer as a proto-philosopher who "first softened man's natural rudeness." But he emphatically distinguishes between that "fabulous age" of mythical "fictions" and the development of philosophy by "its own strength, without the Assistance of Poetry."[41]

With this sharp divorce between the myth and cultural values, Orpheus (like other figures of classical myth) ceases to be a source of vital images and is largely reduced to the status of a rhetorical topos on the power of music or poetry.[42] Orpheus surrounded by wild animals spellbound by his music is a commonplace in the painting of the sixteenth and seventeenth centuries. Where the myth comes to life again, it tends to be in displaced or indirect form, as in the poems of Milton discussed above.

With the renewed interest in the emotional life of the suffering artist and in the figure of Eurydice in the late nineteenth century, the myth comes into its own as an involving tale with depths to be explored. As I have already noted in the case of the film *Black Orpheus*, dramatic or narrative versions of the myth tend to narrow it to a tale of love and loss. Its full mythic dimension, the magic of art and the power to cross the divide between life and death, becomes secondary. The starkest of the recent versions of the myth, whatever their merits as representations of contemporary life, suffer from this narrowing of focus. These are Jean Anouilh's *Eurydice* and Tennessee Williams' *Orpheus Descending*.

For Anouilh the most interesting aspect of the myth is the impracticality of love and its attraction for death. The marginal status of the Thracian Orpheus is rendered through the youth and precarious economic status of Orphée, an itinerant musician traveling with his equally impecunious father. The setting is a bare railway station buffet and dubious hotel. Eurydice is a somewhat unstable actress in a traveling group and has a compromised past. Against the boredom, triviality, and selfishness of French provincial life, the bond of love between the two young people, brief and implausible as it is, has a surprising beauty.

Orpheus' power lies not in his art (which plays a negligible role in the play), but in the intensity of his love. This wins him the right to meet Eurydice in the "underworld" after she is killed in a railway accident. But he cannot trust her or forgive her for her previous love affairs and so loses her a second time. He is returned to the triviality of his itinerant life with his father, whose chief concern is the comparison of *prix fixe* meals in cheap restaurants. Like his classical predecessor, Orphée never recovers from his loss. Rather than accept the emptiness of "life," he decides to return to the realm of death and to Eurydice. The details are left blurred, but he will presumably kill himself at an appointed hour.

Anouilh strips the myth to the existential situation of two young people who have only their love, and even that is none too sure, at least as far as Eurydice is concerned. There are trains, stations, and towns, but the characters in effect go nowhere. They only circle around love and death. Orphée's art is as trivial as his life: he plays for small change in provincial towns. He rises to a modest lyricism as he falls in love at the end of act 1 but otherwise has little to connect him with the ancient poet-shaman. Yet Anouilh draws on the ancient myth to present the contrast between two irreconcilable attitudes; the complete, desperate commitment to a love that has the status of an absolute, despite and even because of its impossibility, and a practical acceptance of life as it is. Orphée loses Eurydice a second time because he refuses to make concessions: he will not allow her the reality of the impure, inconstant life she has led. But his second loss changes his mind, and he chooses to join her in death rather than reaccept his father's world.

This is a very young Orpheus. His story is, in one sense, a refusal to grow up. To grow into the meaninglessness of his father's adulthood is to lose Eurydice, and himself. Death (not art) offers the only escape. The absolutes of death and love set off the unreality of "life," at least of the only life available in the play. The railway waiting rooms and hotels are more ghostly than the dead. At the same time, it is important that the lover Orpheus also be an artist, even if minimally so, for art serves the function of legitimizing the idealism and emotional intensity of love. Although this artist is only a humble street musician, his true music is of the heart. His art, like his love, protects him against the corrosive dullness and materialism of his surroundings. It helps him retain the childlike quality not so much of innocence as of emotional honesty.

Tennessee Williams' Orpheus is also a young marginal figure whose relation to art is a relatively minor part of his situation. He is a roving guitar player, sensual and attractive to women, who drifts into a small Southern town, full of hatred and violence. In this setting his hedonism, empathetic character, and gentleness are dangerously out of place. Like Anouilh, Williams exploits the Virgilian contrast between a sensitive, vulnerable, artistic figure and a brutal world where his survival is precarious. But the threat of emptiness and routine in Anouilh has a far harsher equivalent in Williams' play. Orpheus renews hope and energy in the most important of the three Eurydice figures, Lady, the wife of a dying merchant. He restores her to life in another way too by making her pregnant after years of a sterile, loveless marriage to a man who has probably killed her father. The suspicious, murderous husband discovers the affair, shoots his wife, and has Orpheus horribly killed.

In this version too art is secondary to love and death. Orpheus is able to rescue a woman from death by a tenderness and sympathy that men in this society lack. But he is too weak to overcome the forces of death and violence everywhere around him. His Orphic artistry consists less in his music than in his capacity to engage with women's hopes, needs, and desires. In this he resembles the Dionysus of the first half of Euripides' *Bacchae* more than he does the classical Orpheus. His countercultural personality also points in this direction. To be sure, Williams gives him a snakeskin jacket and makes his guitar his most precious possession, but these superficial concessions to the externals of the myth are tenuous. This Orpheus remains a rather undeveloped character, far less interesting than Lady, whom he awakens to discover and acknowledge what her husband is and how he has destroyed the love and joy in her world. By giving Orpheus a mysterious past and by making him elusive about it, Williams tries to surround him with a vaguely mythic aura. The vagueness sets off the brutality and prejudice of the town, but it does not create a successful Orpheus.

Both Anouilh's and Williams' works show the difficulties involved in adapting to the psychological and social realism of the modern theater a mythical figure who among the ancients never completely loses the remoteness of a quasi-divinity and never completely enters the world of ordinary humanity. Williams' play, however, anticipates the Orpheus of the sixties, the myth of the emerging hippie counter-culture. Herbert Marcuse, the prophet of this movement, pairs Orpheus with Narcissus as the opponents of the Promethean ethic of guilt and work. They "recall the experience of a world that is not to be mastered and controlled but to be liberated—a freedom that will release the powers of Eros now bound in the repressed and petrified forms of man and nature. These powers are conceived not as destruction but as peace, not as terror but as beauty."[43]

This Orpheus is a countervoice to the postindustrial mentality of enslaving and dominating nature. He releases its beauty so that "the things of nature become free to be what they are." In contrast to modern pragmatism and materialism, Orpheus embodies the lost or neglected aesthetic dimension of life. His language is song rather than statistics; and his attitude is one of playful engagement with the world and with the self in a libidinal and narcissistic freedom.[44]

A Marcusian sociologist, Henry Malcolm, looking back on the hippie movement some twenty years later, uses the myth of Orpheus to describe the release and freedom of the rock singers and the counter cultural hedonism expressed by their music.

> It is no wonder, therefore, that the bard Orpheus should become a culture hero, resembling the endless array of rock musicians. With electric guitar in hand and the primitive beat of the drum, singing the erotic music of the natural realm, the musicians arouse and tame the animal within. As such, they represent in most vivid fashion the post-Promethean world of narcissistic pleasure. Theirs is not the beat of the drum that calls men into lockstep obedience, nor the music of the pied piper leading the blind masses to some unknown destiny, but the music of the body, uniting the physical with the emotional, the soul with the flesh.[45]

Virgil's version had already stamped the myth definitively with its intensely personal tone. Even the classical Orpheus, with the minor exception of his heroic service on the Argonautic expedition, remains apart from the public world. Tennessee Williams' Orpheus has something of the hedonism that Malcolm finds in the narcissistic song culture of the sixties' rock music; but the collectivity of the rock festival is Dionysiac rather than Orphic. Yet here, as other areas, Orpheus and Dionysus bend toward each other.[46] Both are involved in music, emotional responsiveness, and the breakdown of the barriers between self and other. For both the rhythms and beat of music are the means of breaking down those barriers. But, as Malcolm does well to remind us, this music is far removed from the drum or flute that orders an army's ranks and fills the breast with patriotic fervor. It operates in a realm deliberately apart from the civic world and, in the case of both Orpheus and Dionysus, even in deliberate opposition to it. Orpheus' especial hearers are trees and wild animals, not citizens. Yet the Marcusian reading of the myth, though correct to stress its intense individualism, exaggerates the Dionysiac element of libidinal release and neglects Orpheus' commitment to a lost beloved, his journey to bring her back, the fusion of love and death, and the deliberate abandonment of joy and life in perpetual grief.

A more significant renewal of the myth in the twentieth century has come from two different directions: Rilke's profound recovery of the shamanistic Orpheus and the links between art and death in his *Sonnets to Orpheus*, which I have discussed in chapter 6, and a refocusing of the myth on the figure of Eurydice.

Virgil is perhaps the first poet in the tradition to have given Eurydice a voice. Ovid again silenced her. Robert Browning's short poem "Eurydice to Orpheus: A Picture by Leighton" harks back to Virgil, but in a much expanded way. Browning lets us hear Eurydice's voice at the brief, poignant moment of her need for Orpheus. Fully human in her love and her weakness, she feels a reckless, desperate wish to regain her life and her beloved.

> But give them me, the mouth, the eyes, the brow!
> Let them once more absorb me! One look now
> Will lap me round for ever, not to pass
> Out of its light, though darkness lie beyond:
> Hold me but safe again within the bond
> Of one immortal look! All woe that was,
> Forgotten, and all terror that may be
> Defied,—no past is mine, no future: look at me!

This is not the acceptant Eurydice of Ovid or the serenely indifferent Eurydice of Rilke's *Orpheus. Eurydike. Hermes*, or even the reproachful Eurydice of Virgil, but a woman absorbed in the single moment that separates her for eternity from all that she loves. It is a woman who does not want to let go of the physical warmth of life for the unknown aloneness of death. All her fear, need, and love are concentrated in the comfort of the backward glance, which she wants and must have, regardless of the consequences. This last assurance of a world of human ties remains preferable to the dark mystery of death.

A number of twentieth-century women poets have gone beyond Browning and Rilke in "correcting" the ancient tradition and reclaiming the myth for the female voice. Among the most striking of such attempts is the "Eurydice" of H.D. (Hilda Doolittle, 1886–1961).[47] Her poem greatly expands the awareness of the feminine consciousness that enters the myth with Virgil. H.D. takes a sharper, more aggressive tone.

> So for your arrogance
> and your ruthlessness
> I am swept back where dead lichens drip
> dead cinders upon moss of ash;
>
> so for your arrogance
> I am broken at last,
> I who had lived unconscious,
> who was almost forgot;
>
> if you had let me wait
> I had grown from listlessness
> into peace,
> if you had let me rest with the dead,
> I had forgot you
> and the past.
>
>   (6–19)

H.D. crosses the Eurydice myth with that of Persephone and treats Eurydice as a young woman whose completeness in her death has been shattered by the arrogance, confidence, and aggressiveness of Orpheus and, more generally, by the divisive violence of heterosexual relations and male passion.

> So for your arrogance
> and your ruthlessness
> I have lost the earth
> and the flowers of the earth,

and the live souls above the earth,
and you who passed across the light
and reached ruthless;

you who have your own light,
who are to yourself a presence,
who needs no presence;

yet for all your arrogance
and your glance,
I tell you this:

such loss is no loss,
such terror, such coils and strands and pitfalls
of blackness,
such terror
is no loss . . .

(82–100)

This Eurydice has her own journey and her own struggle. She vents her anger and fiercely works through it to a new integrity of personal consciousness. But this is a harshly and painfully won wholeness, very different from the Rilkean Eurydice's peace in death. It is formed of conflict and defiance.

Against the black
I have more fervor
than you in all the splendor of that place
against the blackness
and the stark gray
I have more light . . .

(111–116)

The closing stanza restates the recurrent image of flowers, not to assert a new virginity in death (Rilke's "flowers closed toward evening"), but to reaffirm a strength of self that hangs suspended between sexual and personal integrity and the threat of violence and sexuality.

At least I have the flowers of myself
and my thoughts, no god
can take that;
I have the fervor of myself for a presence
and my own spirit for light;

and my spirit with its loss
knows this;
though small against the black,
small against the formless rocks,
hell must break before I am lost;

before I am lost,
hell must open like a red rose
for the dead to pass.

(124–136)

The spirit of independence momentarily resolves the bitterness at the way that Eurydice has been written out of the literary tradition ("I tell you this: / such loss is no loss; / . . . my hell is no worse than yours" [95f., 108]). But the confidence becomes unstable again at the end, as hell becomes both sexual and feminine, opening "like a red rose." The rhetorical figure of adynaton (hell will sooner release its dead, let them pass, before I am lost) is also ambiguous. It asserts the speaker's certainty of nonloss, but the negative form of assertion restates the loss of all the dead in hell. The myth, then becomes a tale of negated resurrection. At one level Eurydice replies in her own way to the Persephone myth: this is a Persephone who does not require resurrection, who has the strength to come to terms with her death in her own soul. At another level she is stating the hopeless entrapment of the dead even as she asserts that she is not "lost" among them.

Edith Sitwell's "Eurydice" (1942–47) also speaks from the underworld, looking back at the light and warmth of life. There are affinities with H.D.'s poem in the subterranean landscape, the feeling of loss, and the great abyss between the living and the dead. But Sitwell's mood of forgiveness and celebration of love has little of H.D.'s defiant energy of bitterness.

See then! I stand in the centre of my earth
That was my Death, under the zenith of my Sun,
Bringing a word from Darkness
That Death too has compassion for all fallen Nature.

(2.1–4)

Eurydice here becomes an archetypal female figure of the rhythms of birth and death, like Persephone (mentioned in the fourth stanza) and the earth itself. The poem begins with her cry to the life-giving fires in the upper world, a cry that is both nostalgic and celebratory of love.

Fires on the hearth! Fires in the
    heavens! Fires in the hearts of Men!
I who was welded into bright gold in the earth
    by Death
Salute you! All the weight of Death in all the
    world
Yet does not equal Love–the great
    compassion
For the fallen dust and all fallen creatures . . .
            (1.1–5)

This Eurydice feels not disappointment or anger but rather wonder at
the radiance of Orpheus' kiss in a world bound to darkness. Her last
words, and the end of the poem, place her with all mortal beings, moving from one darkness to another; yet it is a darkness illuminated, if
only momentarily, by the joy of love.

I with the other young who were born from darkness,
Returning to darkness, stood at the mouth of the Tomb
With one who had come glittering like the wind
To meet me–Orpheus with the golden mouth,
You–like Adonis born from the young
    myrrh-tree, you, the vine-branch
Broken by the wind of Love . . . I turned to
    greet you–
And when I touched your mouth, it was the Sun.
            (10.1–7)

Sitwell's Orpheus is not only the lover; he is also the life-kindling
force of hope, beauty, and renewal through love. His identification
with Adonis and implicitly also with Dionysus ("the vine-branch") in
the last stanza suggests the male life force in the fertility tradition,
parallel to the knowledge of the cycles of birth and death in Perseph-
one-Eurydice. A middle stanza in fact utilizes the fertility symbolism of
Osiris' resurrection as part of the cycle of Persephone's return as the
grain-goddess: "Osiris . . . who was lying in darkness with the wheat
/ Like a flame springing from his heart." The adaptation of Pindar's
First Olympian Ode in the first stanza already prepares for the notion of
cosmic renewal and also points to the realm of art alongside love.

Love . . . quickening
As is the sun in the void firmament.
It shines like fire. O bright gold of the heat of the Sun
Of love across dark fields—burning away
　　rough husks of Death
Till all is fire, and bringing all to harvest!

(1.4-9)

The poem moves toward the integration of the Pindaric remote, bright sky and the dark, fertile, but also dying earth. It ends with the sunlit kiss between Orpheus and Eurydice, even though she relates this as a past event: "I turned to greet you— / And when I touched your mouth, it was the Sun." The past tense implies subsequent loss. Yet the motifs of union and light place this ending in the tradition of the successful descents of Orpheus.

Muriel Rukeyser's long poem "Orpheus" (1951) resembles Edith Sitwell's "Eurydice" in focusing on regeneration and renewal. Hence it too draws on the fertility tradition of the myth. Rukeyser, however, tells the myth in reverse, beginning with the dismemberment of Orpheus and ending with the renewal of his song. The song celebrates recovery and peace, but (unlike Sitwell) Rukeyser fully recognizes the Maenads' murderous violence with which she began. There is understanding, even forgiveness for the Maenads.

Knowing the enemies, those who, deprived at the root,
flourish in thorny action, having lost the power
to act essentially, they fall into the sin
Of all the powerless. They commit their acts of evil
in order to repent, repent and forgive, murder and begin again.

(3.9.6-10)

The personal emotions of Orpheus and Eurydice play a minor role; and Eurydice is only a dim memory for Orpheus, the inverse of the Rilkean version ("They will say I turned to a face. / That was forbidden. There was a moment of turning, / but not to a face" [2.5.10-12]).

Rukeyser is unusual among recent writers in taking account of the totality of the myth, including Orpheus the religious teacher and even the Orpheus of the Hellenistic Jewish poem, *The Testament of Orpheus*, in which Orpheus has become the disciple of Moses and a teacher of monotheism.

> Arches of music, arches of the brain,
> furrows and harvests plowed by song. Whom song
> could never capture. This it was alive
> led Jason past the sirens, this
> in Egypt and in Hell had heard of Heaven
> and reading Moses found the breath of life,
> looked up and listening felt the breath of death
> at the left ear, finding then every life
> among the men of mud and the men of sunlight
> the women turned to light in the eyes of this head.[48]
>
> (2.6.9–18)

This is again an Orpheus who understands and sings the mysteries of life and death.

Like other recent writers, Rukeyser conflates Orpheus with Dionysus and the Orphic myth of the god's dismemberment and renewal. Orpheus is a god whose passion and return to wholeness signify a victory over chaos.

> His death is the birth of the god.
> He sings the coming things, he sings arrivals,
> the blood reversing from the soaked ground, warmth
> passing over the lands where now the barren resists,
> fertile and wet invite, all in their way receive.
> And all the weapons meld into his song.
>
> (3.5.1–6)

The poet's musical power over nature is expanded to a sympathetic knowledge of the suffering in the cycles of birth and death. He sings not only "the coming things" and "arrivals," but also "all who through the crises of the body pass / to the human life and the music of the source" (3.5.12f). Life and music belong to the same mystery.

Rukeyser's motifs of renewal through death and of reintegration after dispersal also draw on the Orpheus of the wisdom tradition, an Orpheus whose "descent" into death wins back new life and also brings a deeper knowledge of the human condition. Orpheus descends to Hades only after his brutal murder; but as he absorbs the weapons into his song of life,

> He sings the leaves of the trees, the music of
>   immense forests,

the young arriving, the leaf of time and their
     selves
their crying for their needs and their successes.
                    (3.5.8–10)

We may compare the Virgilian Orpheus' encounter with the generality
of death.

matres atque viri, defunctaque corpora vita
magnanimum heroum, pueri innuptaeque puellae,
impositique rogis iuvenes ante ora parentum.

Mothers and husbands and the bodies of great-spirited heroes that
had finished their lives; boys and unmarried girls, and young men
placed on the pyre before the eyes of their parents. (G. 4.475–477)

Rukeyser's Orpheus is not just a lover, but once more a poet of life's
harmonies, though in a more optimistic tone than the ancient
Orpheus, as her last lines show.

Seeming of promise, the shining of new stars,
the stars of the real over the body of love.
The cloud, the mountain, and the cities risen.
Solving the wars of the dead, and offering dream
making and morning. Days and voices, sing
creation not yet come.
                    ("Song," 5–10)

Rukeyser returns to the myth nearly two decades later in "The Poem
as Mask: Orpheus" (1968). This work, deliberately retrospective, expli-
cates the earlier poem as a symbolic expression of inner fragmentation:

When I wrote of the women in their dances and
          wildness, it was a mask,
on their mountain, gold-hunting, singing, in orgy,
it was a mask; when I wrote of the god,
fragmented, exiled from himself, his life, the love
          gone down with song,
it was myself, split open, unable to speak, in
          exile from myself.
                    (1–5)

She returns to the death of Orpheus and identifies herself with the
torn god of the earlier poem, but as a memory of her own giving birth.

There is no mountain, there is no god, there is
    memory
of my torn life, myself split open in sleep, the
    rescued child
beside me among the doctors, and a word
of rescue from the great eyes.

No more masks! No more mythologies!

Now, for the first time, the god lifts his
    hand,
the fragments join in me with their own music.

(6–12)

As she uncovers the personal truth of her earlier identification of herself in childbirth with Orpheus and shifts the setting from the mythical
Thracian mountain to the hospital room, she throws off the mythical
disguise: "No more masks! No more mythologies!" The freedom won
by this confessional gesture clarifies her identity as a woman, with a
woman's experience of birth. But the assertion of truth does not require that she reject the myth. Instead she reaffirms its meaning with
a new clarity and objectivity. She is neither Eurydice nor Orpheus but
the recipient of the blessings of the god's music: "Now, for the first
time, the god lifts his hand, / the fragments join in me with their own
music."

Taking off the mask, the poet discovers Orpheus as if "for the first
time." Simultaneously she recovers his music–the creative energy of
song and of her own poetry–as a restorative power within herself.
Through this rediscovered, demythologized Orpheus, her "fragments" have "their own music." Orpheus' spell works on her to create
a new, interior harmony between the hitherto fragmentary parts of
herself: the woman giving birth to a child, the person seeking spiritual
wholeness, and the poet trying to give musical form to experience.

The phrase "for the first time" reinterprets the myth in the light of
this sense of first beginnings: of birth, of artistic creation, and of personal integration. Her own more truthful recovery of the myth thus
becomes another personal myth of origins. She stands *in illo tempore*,
Mircea Eliade's mythic time when the magic of creation first begins to
work, and we are close to the life-forming energies in nature and in
ourselves.[49] Here Rukeyser experiences the wonder and the newness of
the mythic poet's first gesture. The god "lifting his hand" is both a

sacramental act and the ever-renewed beginning of music, hope, and new life. It is a mood of emergent marveling at the new power coming into the world, similar to what Rilke evokes in the first of his *Sonnets to Orpheus: Da stieg ein Baum. O reine Übersteigung. / O Orpheus singt,* "There rose a tree. O pure transcendency. O Orpheus sings" (1.1.1–2).

Rukeyser frames this archaic magic with her own healthy distance from the myth ("No more mythologies!") and turns the old tale into an intensely personal statement. The promise of "creation not yet come" with which the earlier poem ended now seems completed, but in new, nonmythical terms, as she acknowledges the experience of childbirth that lay behind that poem. At the same time her energetic disavowal of myth is disingenuous, for despite herself she returns, in her last two verses, to a mythologizing of her personal experience. In her own way and in her own personal, feminine terms, she is, after all, celebrating the myth of Orpheus' magic.

Writing at about the same time, Adrienne Rich finds still another personal female voice in the myth. Her "I Dream I'm the Death of Orpheus" (1968) is a response to Cocteau's film version. The speaker identifies neither with the questing hero nor with the sought-after heroine, but with the figure of Death, the strong woman whose life is among the shadows of the underworld.

> I am walking rapidly through striations of light
> and dark thrown under an arcade.
> I am a woman in the prime of life, with certain powers
> and those powers severely limited
> by authorities whose faces I rarely see.
>
> (1–5)

This woman has the bitterness and helplessness of the earlier Eurydices, fighting for her love "on the wrong side of the mirror." But she also has the lucidity of recognizing the conditions that doom this love to impossibility. She combines this passion and clarity with power.

> A woman with the nerves of panther
> a woman with contacts among Hell's Angels
> a woman feeling the fullness of her powers
> at the precise moment when she must not use them.
>
> (11–14)

The very constraints on her power concentrate it. She thus becomes not only a tragic lover but a spectator of her own tragic condition, as if she is watching herself in Cocteau's film.

> driving her dead poet in a black Rolls-Royce
> through a landscape of twilight and thorns.
>
> (7f.)

She sees herself seeing "her dead poet learning to walk backward against the wind / on the wrong side of the mirror" (18f.).

The leitmotif of being a viewer combines understanding and distance. This lover of Orpheus is both "intact" and a helpless onlooker. Her dead poet struggles against the reversal of his world ("learning to walk backward against the wind"), but she can only watch. In this privileged role of both spectator and participant, the speaker seems to be on both sides of the mirror, or (with the intertextual reference to Cocteau's film) on both sides of the screen. As "a woman sworn to lucidity," she may indeed know that Orpheus is looking for another beloved and (in the film version at least) will have a happy reunion with his Eurydice in the upper air. But she withholds this one piece of information that indeed makes her powers "most severely limited."

The latest in this series of women's versions (and inversions) of the Orpheus myth are three recent poems by Margaret Atwood, "Orpheus (1)," "Eurydice," and "Orpheus (2)."[50] Atwood brings together Rilke's device of using Eurydice's point of view and H. D.'s technique of a monologic voice that explores Eurydice's feminine consciousness. In "Orpheus (1)" Eurydice, like the Eurydice of Rilke's *Orpheus. Eurydike. Hermes,* feels herself drawn forcibly back to life after she has already become habituated to the underworld: "Already new skin was forming on me / within the luminous misty shroud / of my other body." Like Rilke too, Atwood contrasts the egotism of Orpheus, caught up in his passion, with Eurydice's detachment in death. Her Eurydice, however, is more compassionate than Rilke's and less angry than H.D.'s. As Orpheus fades back into the distance, Eurydice recognizes the necessity of her withdrawal, but also regrets the hurt to Orpheus. Even so, she has no illusions about him. "You could not believe I was more than your echo" is the closing line. "Echo" here may be an allusion to the echoing name "Eurydice" in the lamentation of the Virgilian Orpheus. If so, it is a comment on the ostantatious, self-absorbed, and possessive male passion, need, and fantasy that have silenced Eurydice over the centuries.

The second poem (in the order of the collection), "Eurydice," develops the tension between the needy, questing poet and his lost beloved, but uses a more removed voice, a companionable female voice that addresses Eurydice. The speaker would protect Eurydice from the emptiness that her death leaves in Orpheus. Eurydice herself prefers the serenity of death, where she "would rather have gone on feeling nothing, / emptiness and silence." Orpheus, however, needs her to confirm his own sense of life, of reality. The speaker sympathetically recognizes both his need and Eurydice's pull to satisfy it, but warns Eurydice of the trap that that role holds for her: "It is not through him / you will get your freedom."

"Orpheus (2)" develops the theme of Rilke's *Sonnets to Orpheus* 1.26 and Rukeyser's "Orpheus." Orpheus is overwhelmed by the murderous rage of his attackers (significantly left unidentified), but he does not abandon his song. Song is a symbol of hope in the face of brutality and despair. The poet knows "what he knows / of the horror of this world," but defies that bitter knowledge by continuing to sing. Atwood goes beyond the mythicized violence of Rilke or Benn, however, in giving a contemporary turn to the tortures and mutilations that the poet witnesses and suffers. These suggest the sufferings of the nameless thousands victimized by mass political repression today, "those with no fingers, those / whose names are forbidden." In the modern world such outrages are impersonal; the executioners and the torturers are as anonymous as the tortured.

This poem seems to glance at Rilke's *Rühmen* ("praising") in *Sonnets* 1.7:

> Praising, that's it! One appointed to praising,
> he came like the ore forth from the stone's
> silence (*Sonnets to Orpheus* 1.7.1–3).

Atwood's Orpheus, like Rilke's, overcomes the horror by singing, which is also praising. But there is a self-consciousness of resistance (in a political as well as moral sense) that is not in Rilke. This gives the closing lines a curt and aggressive thrust: "To sing is either praise / or defiance. Praise is defiance."

As Walter Strauss points out in his valuable discussion of the Orpheus myth in nineteenth- and twentieth-century lyricism, Orpheus becomes the battleground between despairing nihilism and a more optimistic belief in the transfiguring power of the lyric voice.[51] He can be the poet of the broken lyre, of weeping chords, of raucous and furious shrieks (Rilke's and Rukeyser's Maenads), or the poet whose art can redeem the senseless violence and meaningless hyperactivity of modern life. Cocteau's film version of the myth touches on this question in a graphic way, with Orphée listening in rapt attention to a car radio over which he takes down apparently meaningless words and numbers dictated by his dead alter ego, Cégeste.

Rukeyser's earlier poem, as we have seen, works through the murdered to the savior Orpheus, through the Maenadic cries to the restorative music. This affirmative interpretation of the myth, so strong in Rilke, also finds an important and characteristic statement in Paul Valéry's beautiful sonnet "Orphée."[52] This Orpheus does not merely transform nature in accordance with his own inner vision; he clothes the world in its hitherto invisible beauty by touching sympathetically the inner life of matter, the soul of a responsive universe. The soulful obverse of resistant matter is beauty, and Orpheus is its prophet. Valéry here draws on the associations developed in late antiquity and the Renaissance between Orphic song and the harmony of the universe.

The poem begins with a familiar scene: the poet sits under his trees, as in Ovid. His song not only moves the living beings around him on the earth; it transfigures the bare site with celestial radiance.

> Je compose en esprit, sous les myrtes, Orphée
> L'Admirable! . . . Le feu, des cirques purs descend;
> Il change le mont chauve en auguste trophée
> D'où s'exhale d'un dieu l'acte retentissant.

> I compose in my thought, beneath the myrtles, Orpheus the Admirable. The fire descends from pure circus rings. It changes the bald mountain into august trophy, from which the resounding act of a god breathes forth. (1–4)

The life that fills the stones brings a frisson of the uncanny: they feel a "horror," and the process of their transformation is almost painful.

> Si le dieu chante, il rompt le site tout-puissant;
> Le soleil voit l'horreur du mouvement des pierres;
> Une plainte inouïe appelle éblouissants
> Les hauts murs d'or harmonieux d'un sanctuaire.

> If the god sings, he breaks the all-powerful site. The sun beholds the horror of the stones' movement. A lament, unheard of, calls to the high golden walls, harmonious, dazzling, of a sanctuary. (5–8)

As the song proceeds, its site changes from earth to the "splendid heavens."

> Il chante, assis au bord du ciel splendide, Orphée!
> Le roc marche, et trébuche; et chaque pierre fée
> Se sent un poids nouveau qui vers l'azur délire!

> He sings, seated at the edge of the splendid heavens, Orpheus! The rock steps forth and stumbles, and each fairy stone feels a new weight, delirious toward the azure sky. (9–11)

As the stubborn rocks begin to move, they become more than just sentient; they are delirious in their new lightness as "fairy rocks." Now the poet's song accompanies the release of nature's interior radiance. He gives order to the natural world, but he also joins with nature in an all-embracing cosmic rhythm.

> D'un temple à demi nu le soir baigne l'essor,
> Et soi-même il s'assemble et s'ordonne dans l'or
> A l'âme immense du grand hymne sur la lyre.

> The evening bathes the soaring of a temple, half-naked, and by itself gathers and takes order in the gold, for the measureless soul of the great hymn on the lyre. (12–14)

This is a song of gold and glory, a song of praise in the sense of Rilke's *rühmen* in *Sonnets to Orpheus* 1.7 and 1.8 (Rilke was himself deeply influenced by Valéry). This song brings the shining heavens down to the "bald mountain." But it also transforms nature by letting it release matter into spirit in a soaring flight toward the heavens, the soul of Being: "By itself . . . the evening disposes itself into gold, for the measureless soul of the great hymn on the lyre." The poet's lyre becomes virtually the cosmic space on which the world's music is played.

Valéry's Orpheus finds resonances in more recent poetry, for example in a work by the contemporary Swedish poet Hjalmar Gullberg, "Now he plays" (Nun spelar han). Like Rukeyser, Gullberg links artistic creation to the energies of the world's first beginnings. Gullberg, however, follows Virgil and Ovid more closely in connecting Orpheus' victory over death through his song with the creative energy of art, which is also the energy of primordial beginnings. Orpheus' song sets us at the dawn of the world. He is a second Adam, creating the new beauty of life by naming the animals and the birds. This is an

Orpheus who combines the cosmic wisdom of Apollonius' cosmogonic poet with the magical power of the archaic charmer of nature.

Today, as in antiquity, the Orpheus myth has a darker side; and we see this, for example, in the Orpheus poems of two German writers, "Der neue Orpheus" of Yvan Goll (1891–1950) and "Orpheus' Tod" of Gottfried Benn (1886–1950). Goll depicts a world-weary, twentieth-century Orpheus whose sympathy with the earth has become a painful awareness of the exhaustion of "good nature," suffering environmental pollution. Orpheus has forgotten Greece and morning songs of the birds. His music has become the commercialized entertainment of a bourgeois consumerist society. He has little chance of rescuing Eurydice: "Musicless, poor in soul, Eurydice: mankind unredeemed" (*Musiklos / Seelenarm / Eurydike: die unerlöste Menschheit* ["Der neue Orpheus" 22.11–13]). The line almost suggests a move back to the medieval allegorizing of the myth, but on the plane of debased aesthetics rather than endangered salvation. Eurydice here seems to symbolize the contemporary public, with its vulgarized tastes. Goll ends with an image of failure and a prosaic desolation that also recalls Anouilh's play: "Orpheus alone in the waiting room / shoots his heart in two" (*Orpheus allein im Wartesaal / schiesst sich das Herz entzwei!* [stanza 25]).

Gottfried Benn's "Orpheus' Tod," on the other hand, remains entirely within the frame of the ancient myth and sets Orpheus in an Ovidian world of river nymphs and pagan groves. The first third of the poem depicts Orpheus in his barren landscape of mourning, remembering the love he has lost.

> Drei Jahre schon im Nordsturm!
> An Totes zu denken, ist süss,
> so Entfernte,
> man hört die Stimme reiner,
> fühlt die Küsse,
> die flüchtigen und die tiefen—
> doch du irrend bei den Schatten!

> Three years in the northern storm! To think of the dead is sweet, her so far removed. One hears the voices more purely, feels the kisses, the fleeting and the deep—but you, wandering among the shades. (Stanza 2)

Benn also follows Ovid in the sequel, focusing on the erotic aftermath of Eurydice's death. Over against the northern landscape of mourning he sets a sensual landscape of mythicized forests. The woodland nymphs try to attract the widowed Orpheus. He refuses them, and his death follows. The causal connections, however, are not spelled out; instead Benn gives us a few allusive details, ending (like Virgil and Ovid) with the head singing in the stream. The poetical and the gruesome, however, are juxtaposed more sharply than in the classical versions.

Und nun die Steine
nicht mehr der Stimme folgend,
dem Sänger,
mit Moos sich hüllend,
die Äste laubbeschwichtigt,
die Hacken ährenbesänftigt—:
nackte Haune—!

nun wehrlos dem Wurf der Hündinnen,
der wüsten—
nun schon die Wimpern nass,
der Gaumen blutet—
und nun die Leier—
hinab den Fluss
die Ufer tönen—

And now the rocks, no longer following the voice or the singer, who veils himself with moss, the branches leaf-heavy, the mattocks gentled with blades of grass—: naked hoes—! now defenseless against the throwing of the wild she-dogs [Maenads]—now his lashes wet, the palate bleeds—and now the lyre—down along the stream the banks resound. (Stanzas 8–9)

Benn reduces the continuity of the Virgilian and Ovidian narratives to fragments, fragments of verse and fragments of flesh. Like Rilke, he ends with the echoing sound of Orpheus' cry. But in Benn, unlike Rilke, there is nothing triumphant in this sound. We are left with the body of the dismembered singer, wounded even in his voice (*der Gaumen blutet*). Even the lyre seems but another fragment, detached from the poet's body.

In this deliberately disjunctive mode of narration, banks, lyre, and sound no longer relate clearly to one another, as they do in the pathos of the Virgilian ending ("Ah, unhappy Eurydice, he called out as his voice fled; unhappy Eurydice did the banks resound along the whole river" [*G.* 4.526f.]). The harshness is also very different from the consolatory reminder of song's lingering at the end of Rilke's *Sonnets* 1.26: *Während dein Klang noch in Löwen und Felsen verweilte / und in den Bäumen und Vögeln. Dort singst du noch jetzt* ("while your sound still lingered among lions and rocks, and in the trees and birds. There you sing even now"). By breaking down the syntactical structure into discrete, imagistic units, Benn also breaks down the classical coherence of the myth, wherein Orpheus' death has a cause and a purpose that give meaning to his existence even after his body is destroyed. It might be possible to read such a meaning into Benn's closing "the banks resound," but his sharp, isolating focus on the present moment does not encourage the reader to extrapolate to a future music or to a permanent effect of Orphic song.

These two poems adapt the sadness of loss in the classical versions of the myth to a contemporary sense of the loss of creativity. This is the exact opposite of the Renaissance use of the myth (compare Politian and Boccaccio, discussed above), and it also goes counter to the classical feeling for an underlying hope of renewal in the fertility myth of dismemberment (important in the Orphic religion), which Rukeyser also attempts to revivify.

Like Benn's poem, John Ashbery's "Syringa" takes as its point of departure the pain of lost poetic power, implicitly equated with the lost beloved. But Ashbery uses a demythicizing irony to reveal the ease with which the great Orphic themes of love and death may become banal. How does the voice of all-encompassing Orphic grief survive the desiccations and discontinuities of the modern world?

Ashbery's Orpheus starts out squarely in the classical mode. This Orpheus, like Virgil's and Ovid's, is a poet who fashions his art from the deepest strata of his feelings. His is a song of total lament, and his grief for Eurydice creates a universal eclipse of nature's life.

> Orpheus liked the glad personal quality
> Of the things beneath the sky. Of course Eurydice was a part
> Of this. Then one day, everything changed. He rends
> Rocks into fissures with lament. Gullies, hummocks
> Can't withstand it. The sky shudders from one horizon
> To the other, almost ready to give up wholeness.

This Orpheus, like the classical figure, refuses to be consoled or to find in his art sublimation for his loss. As a poet in whom feeling overflows the boundaries between art and life, he refuses the Apollonian voice of aesthetic distance, limit, and control. The poem continues:

> Then Apollo quietly told him: "Leave it all on earth.
> Your lute, what point? Why pick at a dull pavan few care to
> Follow, except a few birds of dusty feather,
> Not vivid performances of the past."

But a poetry that blurs the boundaries between art and life threatens the "quiet" advice of the orderly Olympian god. Orpheus will not accept the lesson of mortality and "get along somehow" with death.

> But it is the nature of things to be seen only once,
> As they happen along, bumping into other things, getting along
> Somehow. That's where Orpheus made his mistake.

In the last stanza, Orpheus raises the question of whether such art can in fact transcend its material. May not all art that moves us emotionally resist being made into "art"? Such a subject is "no longer / Material for a poem. Its subject / Matters too much, and not enough, standing there helplessly". Such intensity risks self-destruction in its own fire. Like a comet, it consumes itself: "its tail afire, a bad / Comet screaming hate and disaster, but so turned inward / That the meaning, god or other, can never / Become known."

Ashbery here reveals an unbridgeable gulf between the two sides of the Orphic voice; like Rilke, he makes Orpheus a figure of contradiction and paradox. The poet is a craftsman, an architect of song: he "thinks constructively" and "builds up his chant in progressive stages / Like a skyscraper." But the intensity of loss that the poem seeks to recover is a self-annihilating darkness, effacing the very world that the poem would create.

> The song is engulfed in an instant in blackness
> Which must in turn flood the whole continent
> With blackness, for it cannot see.

These lines return us to Orpheus' eclipse of sunlight in the opening lines ("The sky shudders from one horizon / to the other").

The poem survives this reaching out toward the universal blackness, but its posthumous fame is irrelevant to the singer ("The singer / Must then pass out of sight, not even relieved / of the evil burthen of the words"). Universality is only a feeble unfreezing of the Orphic work's vital sources; its personal intensity is in some sense lost forever. The anguished lament of one unique individual for another becomes

only the faded notes of "a similar name" in a far-off time and place.
The poem ends:

> Stellification
> Is for the few, and comes about much later
> When all record of these people and their lives
> Has disappeared into libraries, onto microfilm.
> A few are still interested in them. "But what about
> So-and-so?" is still asked on occasion. But they lie
> Frozen and out of touch until an arbitrary chorus
> Speaks of a totally different incident with a similar name
> In whose tale are hidden syllables
> Of what happened so long before that
> In some small time, one indifferent summer.

What was once the piercing song of inconsolable, living grief has
become "hidden syllables" at the edge of recognition, a message to be
decoded among an "arbitrary chorus" of strangers who, in turn, are
enclosed in their own small, quiet prison of space and time.

The myth of Orpheus seems most successful when it is not reduced to
one or two of its elements (for example, love and death only) but
expresses man's attempt to see his life in a twofold perspective, that is,
as part of nature and as unique in its emotional and intellectual consciousness. In this respect the myth brings together man's capacity for
love and his capacity to deal with loss and death through the expressive power of art.

Hardest, perhaps for contemporary writers to recover is the ancient
appreciation of Orpheus as a poet of the world order and of religious
mysteries. A notable exception is Elizabeth Sewell's *Orphic Voice.* For
her, Orpheus is the measure of the distance between science and
poetry. He embodies a poetic discourse that extends beyond the individualism and self-centeredness of Romantic and post-Romantic
poetry to a poetry of man in nature, whether this is the nature
charmed by the magical lyre or rationally ordered by cosmogonic song.
He is the poet both of the unity of the world and of man's power to
grasp and express that unity. He thus approximates the Renaissance
Orpheus, a focal point for the unity of culture, harmony of learning
and lyricism, and a "common search for knowledge about man, mind,
and nature" in many disciplines.[53]

Sewell's reading of Orpheus is almost the diametrical opposite of the narcissistic individualism in the Orpheus of Marcuse, Williams, and Anouilh. She would restore Orpheus to a central place in Western culture, not as a voice of irrational impulse and private emotion, but as a symbol for unifying intuitive and logical modes of thought. This Orpheus harks back to the cosmogonic singer of Apollonius of Rhodes: he is a poet of the correspondences and sympathies between man and nature and of the order of nature that is hidden beneath the shifting surface of the phenomenal world. He reaches back to the philosopher, theologian, cosmogonist, and culture hero of the Hellenistic and Greco-Roman world and forward to the poets whom Sewell sees as his closest modern representatives: Shakespeare, Milton, Goethe, Wordsworth, and Rilke.

Sewell's engagement with the myth exemplifies her own ideal of an Orphic voice. She combines historical study and literary analysis with her own personal commitment and ideals. Thus the analytical portion of the book is followed by a group of "working poems" that aim at a more lyrical and intuitive presentation of her Orphic vision. Not many of these will sustain the kind of scrutiny that one would give to Virgil or Rilke; but two stanzas of the fifth, "Words and Stars," illustrate her conception of Orphic poetry as a language that deciphers, in its way, the order of the world's remotest segments in the "figures" of language.

> If God had spoken stars in the beginning,
> Man's mind no less obeyed its tendencies,
> Astronomers soon busy underpinning
> Grammar and syntax of those sentences;
>
> Astrology could offer only fancy,
> The incantation and the poet's trick;
> Poets divined, in place of necromancy,
> Superlative sidereal rhetoric.

(1-8)

Sewell's Orpheus, understanding science poetically and reconciling learning and art, cosmos and subjectivity, belongs to the religious dimension of the myth as an expression of man's desire for a unifying spiritual center. For modern interpreters, as already for Virgil, Orpheus' creative power does not stand by itself; it is part of a dialectic relation with destructiveness and violence. But in modern readings the threat that Orpheus faces is not so much death per se as the meaninglessness that death symbolizes: chaos in the soul and in the world order.

Martin Buber reads the Orpheus myth along these lines in his dialogue *Daniel*. He makes Orpheus the antithesis to the Dionysus-Zagreus of the "Orphic Mysteries."[54] This Orpheus resists "the demonism of the Unformed." He is the poet of the wisdom tradition, renouncing fusion with death or loss of the self in ecstasy or in the eternal return of cyclical renewal. Instead, he embodies courageous humanity, facing death but not crushed by it, searching for under-standing rather than power, confronting chaos but affirming meaning through the act of singing, through music "as the pure word of the directed soul." The magic of the song is the soul's power of renewal in the face of death, the resilience of the human spirit whose "resolute" sense of direction "makes it inviolable and immortal to all death."[55]

Akin to Buber in focusing on the threat of meaninglessness, but in a darker vein, is the short but intense essay, "The Gaze of Orpheus," by Maurice Blanchot.[56] Blanchot utilizes Orpheus as a myth for under-standing the creative process of the artist who confronts the potential emptiness of literature. He allegorizes Orpheus as the writer who descends into the depths of Being by forgetting himself in the work (not *his* work but *the* work). Eurydice is "the limit of what art can attain," the mysterious, ultimately unnamable infinite that the artist's work must "bring . . . back into the daylight and in the daylight give it form, figure, and reality."[57]

The contradictions between Orpheus' desire for Eurydice, the necessity of keeping his back to her, and his betrayal of her by turning around reflect the paradoxes of the artist. The artistic activity, accord-ing to Blanchot, is essentially paradoxical and essentially transgressive. The Eurydice that Orpheus desires is not the visible Eurydice of day-light but the invisible, mysterious Other, a being that remains in the realm of the infinite and the unattainable. Her primary attraction is "the strangeness of that which excludes all intimacy," "the fullness of death living in her."[58] We may compare Cocteau's Eurydice, beloved and sought after in the underworld but possessing a dark double in Death, a woman of passionate intensity whose hopeless love for Orpheus immeasurably exceeds Eurydice's more domestic affection.

Blanchot's Orpheus is the artist as a figure of absolute desire, whose overreaching impulses toward the infinite coexist with the certainty of his failure. The same energies and yearnings that enable Orpheus to reach Eurydice also lead him to sacrifice her in the necessity of the disobedient backward glance. This backward look is for Blanchot the center of the myth. It holds the paradoxical inseparability of artistic inspiration, desire, and failure. The artist strives to free the work of his personal engagement in it, even though that engagement was indispensable to the work's creation.

Blanchot's suggestive and difficult essay defies facile summary.[59] This is partly because it cultivates an air of mystery, stresses paradox and unnamability, and defines its objects primarily as negative qualities. Blanchot adapts the shamanistic journey of the ancient singer to the contemporary artist's risk in descending into the abyss of his own soul, knowing that imaginative art creates largely *ex nihilo*. As a reader of the myth, Blanchot shares much with Rilke and with Cocteau. Like Rilke, he is interested in the places where opposites cross. But unlike Rilke, he gives little place to the creative and recreative power of song as celebration. Like Cocteau, Blanchot studies the processes of inversion in the love object (in Cocteau, this is the shift from the fair Eurydice of life and daylight to the dark, desperate, powerful lady of Death who lives in the shadows). He is also deeply indebted to the atmosphere of mystery surrounding the hero's descent in Virgil and to the passionate intensity of his desire to recover Eurydice in both Virgil and Ovid.

Where Blanchot differs most radically from Virgil and Rilke is in replacing love, so central to the classical versions, with desire. One result of this change is to narrow the myth by focusing it on the self-absorption of the artist rather than on the Otherness of Eurydice. Blanchot here reverses one of the strong directions in contemporary revisions of the myth, for he transforms Eurydice into a symbol of the (male) artist's search for the infinite. The small bit of individual identity that she had in Virgil and Ovid shrinks to even more minuscule proportions in the negative epithets with which Blanchot surrounds her. She is, for example, "the *profoundly dark* point toward which art, desire, *death, and the night* all seem to lead."[60] This reading of Eurydice in effect returns us to the medieval allegories that make her the materiality that resists the soul's journey to salvation, a dark force against which the soul must strive as it seeks to extend its spiritual domain over the darkness of the unformed. Blanchot's Eurydice has lost not only her voice; she has also lost her concreteness as a living being and her humanity as a woman whom her husband sought after because he loved her and she died.

Like classical antiquity and the Renaissance, the modern age easily slips into treating Orpheus as a cultural symbol. Not only does he embody art's wish for unlimited power to express the unity of man and nature. His myth also conveys the belief that art can reveal to us the mysteries hidden in our mortality, which, if understood, will deepen our vision of existence. Orpheus does not merely know the secrets of life and death. His love for Eurydice is the catalyst for that crossing into the hidden realm of the dead.

Modern writers are drawn to the myth for very different reasons, as we have seen, and make of it very different things. Sometimes the myth yields diametrically opposite messages. Goll, for instance, and to some extent Anouilh and Williams, use it to reflect on the banalization of art and feeling in modern society. Rilke, Valéry, Buber, and contemporaries like Rukeyser, on the other hand, use Orpheus as a voice of hope and renewal amid brutalization and fragmentation.

Though he is often associated with Apollo, Orpheus is not Apollonian in his art. (Aeschylus' lost *Bassaridae*, we may recall, dramatized the disastrous consequences of Orpheus' change from worshiping Dionysus to worshiping Apollo). Nor, though he makes frequent appearances in pastoral, from Virgil through Milton's *Lycidas*, does he belong to the circumscribed frame of pastoral. The feelings that make up his song are not delimited by the safety and artifice of the pastoral conventions. He is (as Blanchot appreciates) a figure of absolutes and extremes, hazarding everything for what he feels and what he loves. Just these features of Orpheus also make him appealing to the modern artist: the closeness to his own emotional life and the risk of isolation and fragmentation that this entails.

The Orphic sensitivity to the otherness of things is not always a positive quality, as is clear from Virgil to Anouilh. The poet's excitability and intensity place his greatest successes at the edge of the abyss of terrible loss. The intersubjective exchange with the life of nature threatens the boundaries of the self. Hence the affinities of Orpheus' end with the Dionysiac death by dismemberment. But, as both the Virgilian and the Rilkean Orpheus show, the poet's closeness to loss is inseparable from his capacity to give the most intense possible expression to beauty in art. This combination is clearest in Rilke's tension between monument and metamorphosis, expression and participation. As a recent critic remarks apropos of Rilke, Orpheus "is that emotion or imagination of estrangement as it returns to the world, moving among things, touching them with the knowledge of death which they acquire when they acquire their names in human language."[61] To this sadder aspect of the myth, however, must be added the spirit of renewal and rebirth in the artist's creative energy, appreciated by its interpreters from Euripides to Rukeyser.

How will this myth continue its life in the poems of generations to come? I can only point to what it has meant over the past twenty-five hundred years of Western civilization that I have so briefly surveyed. It offers the creative artist the power to feel his art as a magic that touches sympathetic chords in all of nature and puts him in touch with the thrill of pure life, pure Being. The myth of Orpheus is the myth of the ultimate seriousness of art.[62] It is the myth of art's total engagement with love, beauty, and the order and harmony of nature — all under the sign of death. It is the myth of the artist's magic, of his courage for the dark, desperate plunge into the depths of the heart and of the world, and of his hope and need to return to tell the rest of us of his journey.

Notes

Abbreviations

Abh.	*Akademie der Wissenschaft und der Literatur, Mainz: Abhandlungen der*
Mainz	*Geistes- und Sozialwissenschaftliche Klasse*
AJP	*American Journal of Philology*
ANRW	*Aufstieg und Niedergang der Römischen Welt*
CF	*Classical Folia*
CJ	*Classical Journal*
C&M	*Classica et Mediaevalia*
CP	*Classical Philology*
CQ	*Classical Quarterly*
CR	*Classical Review*
G&R	*Greece and Rome*
HSCP	*Harvard Studies in Classical Philology*
JHS	*Journal of Hellenic Studies*
MLN	*Modern Language Notes*
RCCM	*Rivista di Cultura Classica e Medioevale*
REL	*Revue des Etudes Latines*
SB	*Sitzungsberichte der Preussischen Akademie der Wissenschaften zu Berlin.*
Berlin	*Philosophisch-historische Klasse*
TAPA	*Transactions of the American Philological Association*
WS	*Wiener Studien*
YCS	*Yale Classical Studies*

Preface

1. The quotations are from Robert Hass, *Twentieth Century Pleasures: Prose on Poetry* (New York, 1984), 233.

2. For a recent scholarly discussion of Orphism and the Orphic theogonies, including the Derveni papyrus, see M. L. West, *The Orphic Poems* (Oxford, 1983), who has an extensive bibliography.

3. John B. Friedman, *Orpheus in the Middle Ages* (Cambridge, Mass., 1970) 210.

Chapter 1. The Magic of Orpheus and the Ambiguities
of Language

1. The most useful discussions are W. K. C. Guthrie, *Orpheus and Greek
Religion* (1952; reprint, New York, 1966); E. R. Dodds, *The Greeks and the Irra-
tional* (Berkeley and Los Angeles, 1957), chap. 5, esp. 147ff.; I. M. Linforth, *The
Arts of Orpheus* (Berkeley and Los Angeles, 1941); M. L. West, *The Orphic Poems*
(Oxford, 1983). Elizabeth Sewell, *The Orphic Voice: Poetry and Natural History*
(New Haven, Conn., 1960) provides a lengthy, if often highly personal, survey
of the Orphic tradition in literature. For the medieval material and especially
the fusion of Orpheus with Dionysus and Christ, see John B. Friedman,
Orpheus in the Middle Ages (Cambridge, Mass., 1970), esp. chap. 3. For briefer
discussions see M. Owen Lee, "Orpheus and Eurydice: Some Modern Versions," *CJ* 56 (1960/61): 307ff.; and his "Orpheus and Eurydice: Myth, Legend,
Folklore," *C&M* 26 (1965): 402–12, with bibliography; Eva Kushner, *Le mythe
d'Orphée dans la littérature française contemporaine* (Paris, 1961), 11–76, with bibliography; Philip Mayerson, *Classical Mythology in Literature, Art, and Music* (Lex-
ington, Mass., 1971) 270–79. For the ancient material see Otto Kern, ed., *Orphicorum Fragmenta* (Berlin, 1922); Giorgio Colli, *La sapienza greca I* (Milan, 1977),
118–289 (with Italian translations); and for the Hymns and theogonic fragments,
Eugenius Abel, *Orphica* (1885; reprint, Hildesheim 1971).

2. Bernat Metge, *Lo Somni*, ed. J. M. de Casacuberta and Ll. Nicolau
d'Olwer (Barcelona, 1925) 85 (bk. 3, and ad init.). *Lo Somni* is thought to have
been composed between 1396 and 1399: see Alison Goddard Elliott, "Orpheus
in Catalonia: A Note on Ovid's Influence," *CF* 32 (1978): 3–15.

3. Text and translations from M. D. Herter Norton, ed. and trans., *Sonnets to
Orpheus by Rainer Maria Rilke* (New York, 1942).

4. See William Berg, *Early Virgil* (London, 1974), 15–22; C. Segal, "Landscape
into Myth: Theocritus' Bucolic Poetry," in A. J. Boyle, ed., *Ancient Pastoral;
Ramus Essays on Greek and Roman Pastoral Poetry* (Berwick, Australia, 1975), 45
with n. 33. I cannot here deal with the full range of Milton's symbolism, on
which see Richard P. Adams, "The Archetypal Pattern of Death and Rebirth in
Milton's *Lycidas*," *Publications of the Modern Language Association of America* 64
(1949): 183–88; and Caroline W. Mayerson, "The Orpheus Image in *Lucidas*,"
ibid., 189–207.

5. *Anthologia Palatina* 7.8 = A. S. F. Gow and D. L. Page, eds., *Hellenistic Epigrams* (Cambridge, 1965), Antipater, X. See also *Anthologia Palatina* 7.10.

6. For Orpheus in the *Eclogues* see in general Marie Desport, *L'Incantation
virgilienne* (Bordeaux, 1952), 154 ff. and 137 on the bucolic realm as "un monde
pastoral soumis à l'enchantement d'Orphée"; Berg, *Early Virgil*, 14; Michael
Putnam, *Virgil's Pastoral Art* (Princeton, N. J., 1970), 200–202 and 256f.; John Van
Sickle, "Studies of Dialectical Methodology in the Virgilian Tradition," *MLN* 85
(1970): 885f., 925–28 (a useful corrective to Desport's enthusiastically positive
view of Orpheus).

7. For this "music of nature" and (pastoral) poetry, Lucretius, *De Rerum
Natura* 5.1379–1398, though taking an ultimately skeptical view, is the *locus clas-
sicus*. See Segal, "Landscape into Myth," 38ff.; Viktor Pöschl, *Die Hirtendich-
tung Virgils* (Heidelberg, 1964), 53ff.

8. See Adam Parry, "Landscape in Greek Poetry," *YCS* 15 (1957): 14, on

bucolic poetry's "incantatory quality" and "magical unreality," which prevail upon us "to believe that rustic life is like this, and that we can share it."

9. See Segal, "Landscape into Myth," 51.

10. Theocritus, *Epigram*, no. 5, in A. S. F. Gow, ed., *Bucolici Graeci* (Oxford, 1952).

11. *Anthologia Planudea* 13 = E. Diehl, ed., *Anthologia Lyrica Graeca*, vol. 1 (Leipzig, 1925), Plato, *Epigram* no. 27; cf. also Plato, *Phaedrus* 230B–C; and for discussion, Segal, "Landscape into Myth," 52f.

12. See Lee, "Myth, Legend, Folklore"; Guthrie, *Orpheus and Greek Religion*, 29ff.; C. M. Bowra, "Orpheus and Eurydice," *CQ*, n.s. 2 (1952): 113–25; Peter Dronke, "The Return of Eurydice," *C&M* 23 (1962): 198–25.

13. See Aristophanes, *Birds* 693–702; Kern, *Fragmenta*, pp. 8off. for other early evidence for the Orphic cosmogonies.

14. See Diodorus Siculus 4.25; Dronke, "Return," 204; Guthrie, *Orpheus and Greek Religion*, 61. I cannot here enter into the early Christian use of this Orphic motif; for discussion see Friedman, *Orpheus*, 57ff., 65ff.

15. Virgil, *G*.4.52of.; Phanocles, frag. 1.7 and 23ff., in J. U. Powell, ed., *Collectanea Alexandrina* (Oxford, 1925), 107.

16. Phanocles, frag. 1.9–10, in Powell, *Collectanea*; see also the works cited above, n. 12, for further discussion.

17. E.g., Kern, *Fragmenta*, Testimonia, nos. 113, 117, 132 (pp. 33ff.); also Guthrie, *Orpheus and Greek Religion*, 44ff.

18. E.g., Kern, *Fragmenta*, Testimonia, nos. 94–101 (pp. 27ff.).

19. E.g., Euripides, *Hypsipyle*, ed. G. W. Bond, (Oxford, 1963), frag. 64.2.93–102; also Alcidamas, *Odysseus* 24; Diodorus 4.25.2–4; Kern, *Fragmenta*, Testimonia, nos. 90–93, 108–112 (pp. 26f., 32f.).

20. Guthrie, *Orpheus and Greek Religion*, 120ff., esp. 125.

21. See Henry Malcolm's Marcusian reading of Orpheus, *The Generation of Narcissus* (Boston, 1971), 37ff., 44, 161ff.

22. For the association of love and magic, see Desport, *Incantation*, 263–70 with the references there cited; C. Segal, "Eros and Incantation: Sappho and Oral Poetry," *Arethusa* 7 (1974): 148–50.

23. See Sophocles, *Trachiniae* 660–62 and also 355; C. Segal, "Sophocles' *Trachiniae*: Myth, Poetry, and Heroic Values," *YCS* 25 (1977): 111f.

24. Bion, frag. 3, in Gow, *Bucolici Graeci*. Cf. also Theocritus, *Idyll* 11.1f., where poetry is a *pharmakon* against love, as opposed to passages like Euripides, *Hippolytus* 509ff., where love is itself the *pharmakon*, the "drug" that causes rather than cures the disease. See in general Desport, *Incantation*, 256ff.; and for some connections with the tragic *logos*, Pietro Pucci, "Euripides: The Monument and the Sacrifice," *Arethusa* 10 (1977): 167–78.

25. For the erotic (and also magical) implications of "Persuasion" (*peitho*) in Gorgias, see Jacqueline de Romilly, "Gorgias et le pouvoir de la poésie," *JHS* 93 (1973): 161 with nn. 35, 36; also her *Magic and Rhetoric in Ancient Greece* (Cambridge, Mass., 1975), 17–22. George Kennedy, *The Art of Persuasion in Greece* (Princeton, 1963), 61ff., esp. 63; C. Segal, "Gorgias and the Psychology of the *Logos*," *HSCP* 66 (1962): 99–155.

26. Cf. the ambiguity of the *pharmakon* in *Phaedrus* 275E, the starting point for Jacques Derrida's well-known discussion, "La pharmacie de Platon," *La Dis-*

sémination (Paris, 1972). Cf. also Plato's comparison of rhetoric with medicine, cookery, and gymnastics in *Gorgias* 464Bff.

27. See Segal, "Eros and Incantation," 148–50.

28. On the incantatory effects of this passage see Paolo Scarpi, *Lettura sulla religione classica: l'inno omerico a Demeter*, Università di Padova, Pubblicazione della Facoltà di Lettere e Filosofia 56 (Florence, 1976), 164ff.

29. Pindar, *Paean* 8, frag. 52 i, in Bruno Snell and Herwig Maehler, eds., *Pindari Carmina cum Fragmentis*, vol. 2, 4th ed. (Leipzig, 1975).

30. Pindar, frag. 94b, lines 13–20, in Snell and Maehler, *Pindari Carmina*, vol. 2 = C. M. Bowra, ed., *Pindari Carmina*, 2d ed. (Oxford, 1947), frag. 85.10–15. Cf. also C. M. Bowra, *Pindar* (Oxford, 1964), 26.

31. Pindar, frag. 140a, in Snell and Maehler, *Pindari Carmina*.

32. See also Pindar, frag. 128c, lines 11–12, in Snell and Maehler, *Pindari Carmina*, vol. 2 (= *Threnoi* 3.11–12), where Orpheus is called "him of the golden sword, the son of Oeagrus," the only other reference to Orpheus in Pindar.

33. The text and meaning of the last sentence are controversial. I have translated it rather freely.

34. Pausanias 6.20.18 (Kern, *Fragmenta*, Testimonia, no. 54). See also Euripides, *Cyclops* 646, Strabo bk. 7. frag. 18; in general Guthrie, *Orpheus and Greek Religion*, 19.

35. Simonides, frag. 567, in D. L. Page, ed., *Poetae Melici Graeci* (Oxford, 1962).

36. Euripides, *Hypsipyle*, frag. 1.3.8–14, and see Bond's note on l. 11 of this passage for *keleusma*, "boatswain's order," as a technical nautical term.

37. Ibid., frag. 64.2.93–102.

38. If "Orpheus" can be restored in a fragmentary papyrus of Alcaeus (frag. 80, line 8, in Diehl, *Anthologia*), this would be the earliest literary reference; but this reading is most uncertain. The next earliest reference would be Ibycus, frag. 306 in Page, *Poetae Melici Graeci* (middle of the sixth century B.C.).

39. Eric A. Havelock, *Preface to Plato* (Cambridge, Mass., 1963), 26 and chaps. 2 and 3 in general.

40. See my "Eros and Incantation," 143f.

41. Gorgias' phrase, *logon echonta metron*, "discourse containing measure," covers both: see my "Gorgias," 127, 133.

42. E.g., Guthrie, *Orpheus and Greek Religion*, 40, pl. 6.

43. For *terpsis* or *hedone* ("pleasure") as the effect of (oral) poetry and song, see Homer, *Od.* 1.347, 8.542; Thucydides 2.65.8 and 3.38.7; Gorgias, *Helen* 14. In connection with Orpheus specifically, see Kern, *Fragmenta*, Testimonia, 54 (Conon); and Plato, *Laws* 8.829D–E.

44. Since the veiled woman won by Heracles is never explicitly identified as Alcestis, as Gerald Fitzgerald of Monash University points out to me, the potential for irony in Heracles' action here has an even wider dimension.

45. For the problem and interpretation of the Orpheus episode, see below, chaps. 3 and 4; also Friedrich Klingner, *Virgil. Bucolica, Georgica, Aeneis* (Zurich, 1967), 326–63; Dorothea Wender, "Resurrection in the Fourth *Georgic*," *AJP* 90 (1969); 424–36; Eva M. Stehle, "Virgil's *Georgics*: The Threat of Sloth," *TAPA* 104 (1974): 347–69, esp. 361ff.; H. J. Tschiedel, "Orpheus und Eurydike: ein Beitrag zum Thema: Rilke und die Antike," *Antike und Abendland* 19 (1973): 61–82, esp. 77–82.

46. For Orpheus as the poetic scientist who understands nature's laws, see Apollonius Rhodius, *Arg.* 1.496–515, cited above, sec. I; also Sewell, *Orphic Voice,* passim.

47. In placing Orpheus in Elysium, Virgil is drawing upon an ancient tradition: see, e.g., Plato, *Apology* 41A and (scornfully) *Republic* 2.363C.

48. For the contrasts between Virgil and Ovid, see below, chaps. 2–4; also William S. Anderson, *Ovid, Metamorphoses, Books 6–10* (Norman, Okla. 1972), 475ff.; Eleanor Winsor Leach, "Ekphrasis and the Theme of Artistic Failure in Ovid's *Metamorphoses,*" *Ramus* 3 (1974):102–42, 119ff.

49. On the significance of shade in the *Eclogues,* see P. L. Smith, "*Lentus in umbra,* A Symbolic Pattern in Virgil's *Eclogues,*" *Phoenix* 19 (1965): 298–304; M. C. J. Putnam, "Virgil's First Eclogue: Poetics of Enclosure," in Boyle, *Ancient Pastoral, Essays in Greek and Roman Pastoral Poetry* (Berwick, Australia, 1975), 81f. Leach "Ekphrasis," who has many stimulating remarks on the Orpheus episode, seems to me to dismiss the motif of shade too lighly: "Retiring to a mountain top, he makes himself quite comfortable by calling up a little grove of trees with his song" (121). The tone of *Met.* 10.88–105 is quite different. Note the solemn and lofty beginning (where no ironic undercutting is easily apparent) in 88–90:

> umbra loco deerat; qua postquam parte resedit
> dis genitus vates et fila sonantia movit,
> umbra loco venit.

> The place lacked shade; but after the inspired singer, born of the gods, sat back in this place and struck his melodious strings, shade came there.

The basic seriousness of the list of trees appears also from the careful study by Viktor Pöschl, "Der Katalog der Bäume in Ovids Metamorphosen" (1960), in Michael von Albrecht and Ernst Zinn, eds., *Ovid,* Wege der Forschung 92 (Darmstadt, 1968, 393–404). Pöschl stresses the trees' mythical associations with suffering and therefore with the theme of Orpheus' grief and the transmutation of suffering to beauty through art; see esp. 394, 400, 403; also G. K. Galinsky, *Ovid's Metamorphoses. An Introduction to the Basic Aspects* (Oxford, 1975), 182f.

50. See Sewell, *Orphic Voice,* 80: "Change and process and transformation become in this poem [Ovid's *Metamorphoses*] a means of relating the inner workings of the mind with the workings of nature. . . . All fixed forms in nature are merely momentary crystallizations of a reality which is in perpetual change, and which, if we are truly to understand it, must be the model for our methods of thought. These have to be as flexible and plastic, *beweglich und bildsam,* as nature is." The last part of these remarks refers to the use Goethe made of Ovidian notions of metamorphosis. See also her discussion of Ovid's poem, ibid., 231ff., esp. 235–36 on its central positioning of Orpheus and "its use of myth as the instrument by which the whole span of natural process is to be understood and interpreted. . . . The reflexive use of that instrument to hold the universe and the mind together. . . ."

51. For the significance and patterning of Orpheus' song, see Robert Coleman, "Structure and Intention in the *Metamorphoses,*" *CQ,* n.s. 21 (1971): 461–77 and also the references cited above, n. 48.

52. Leach, "Ekphrasis," 188–27, while rightly calling attention to ironic and negative elements in the Orpheus episode, seems to me to exaggerate "artistic

failure" (e.g., in her treatment of Orpheus' death [127]). It is however, the merit of her careful and interesting study to have called attention to the often neglected theme of artistic creativity in the *Metamorphoses*. For a very different emphasis, though with some of the same concern for the central importance of the artist, see Simone Viarre, *L'Image et la pensée dans les "Métamorphoses" d'Ovide* (Paris, 1964), 251.

53. On the implicitly happy ending, see Viarre, *L'Image*, 411f., and her "Pygmalion et Orphée chez Ovide (*Met.* X, 243–97)," *REL* 46 (1968): 241f.; see below, chaps. 3–4.

54. In another tradition, probably familiar to Ovid, the presence of Orpheus' head on Lesbos endows that island with special musical qualities: see Kern, *Fragmenta, Testimonia*, nos. 119, 130–35.

55. For the parallels between Orpheus and Pygmalion as representatives of the magic of transformation and artistic creation, see Viarre, *L'Image*, 205; and her "Pygmalion et Orphée," 235–47 passim, esp. 242ff. on the theme of animating lifeless forms; also Hermann Fränkel, *Ovid. A Poet between Two Worlds*, Sather Classical Lectures 18 (Berkeley and Los Angeles, 1945), 93–97. For a more negative view of the relationship between the two myths, see Leach, "Ekphrasis," 123–35.

56. See Leach, "Ekphrasis," 130–32, who calls Midas' power "a travesty of artistic transformation" (131); also Coleman, "Structure and Intention," 470; Otis, *Ovid as an Epic Poet*, 2d ed. (Cambridge, 1970), 192f.

57. Note also the contrast between Midas' favorite, "Pan who lives always in mountain caves" (*Met.* 11.147) and the richly dressed and splendidly accoutred Apollo, described at some length ten lines later (165–170). See also Viarre, *L'Image*, 251.

58. The text and translation are those of J. B. Leishman, ed. and trans., *Rainer Maria Rilke, New Poems* (London, 1964), 142–47. For further discussion see below, chap. 6

59. For this concentration on Eurydice rather than Orpheus, see Sewell, *Orphic Voice*, 330–33; Kushner, *Le Mythe*, 22; H. D.'s "Eurydice" is a good example in recent poetry. See below, chap. 7.

60. See my "Eurydice: Rilke's Transformation of a Classical Myth," *Bucknell Review* 21 (1974): 137–44, esp. 143f.; Tschiedel, "Orpheus und Eurydike," 62–71; Sewell, *Orphic Voice*, 394ff.

61. For this interpenetration of life and death in the *Sonnets to Orpheus*, see Sewell, *Orphic Voice*, 394ff.; Tschiedel, "Orpheus und Eurydike," 72ff.

62. Dronke, "Return," 205f. Citing the end of the *First Duino Elegy*, "Orpheus und Eurydike," Tschiedel, 72f. remarks: "Klar und deutlich ist in diesen Zeilen die Leben und Tod umspannende Einheit des Seins ausgesprochen, und jene gegenseitige Bedingtheit beider Existenzformen, die früher im Bilde von den im Totenreich liegenden Wurzeln des Lebens ihren Ausdruck fand, sie hat sich hier konkretisiert zur Frage nach der Möglichkeit des Lebens ohne die Toten, einer Frage, die die negative Antwort in sich trägt."

Chapter 2. Orpheus and the Fourth *Georgic:* Virgil on Nature and Civilization

1. For these schemes see G. E. Duckworth, "Virgil's *Georgics* and the *Laudes Galli,"* *AJP* 80 (1959): 225-37; Brooks Otis, *Virgil, A Study in Civilized Poetry* (Oxford, 1963) 153-54.

2. Eduard Norden, "Orpheus und Eurydice," *SB Berlin* (1934): 626-83.

3. On the thematic relevance of the Aristaeus-Orpheus episode to the *Georgics* as a whole, see Duckworth, "Virgil's *Georgics"*; S. P. Bovie, "The Imagery of Ascent-Descent in Virgil's *Georgics,"* *AJP* 77 (1956): 337-58; Otis, *Virgil,* 143ff. and esp. 187-90, 213-14, and Appendix 7, 408-13.

4. Otis, *Virgil,* 408-13.

5. Some of these questions are keenly and pointedly phrased by R. Coleman, "Gallus, the Bucolics, and the Ending of the Fourth Georgic," *AJP* 83 (1962): 55ff., esp. "why the *Orpheus and Eurydice,* which forms the central panel of the Epyllion, was permitted by the poet to dominate the ending of the poem and so to cast a melancholy shadow over what is otherwise a joyful and radiant work" (55). But Coleman's answer is inadequate and disappointing, viz. that the episode is Virgil's tribute to Gallus, a poem such as Gallus himself might have written as regards both style and subject matter. One can never ultimately disprove such a hypothesis (any more than one can definitely prove it); but it clashes so violently with all we know of Virgil's sense of poetic unity and structure as to be improbably or at best only a relatively minor contributing factor that might, possibly, have suggested the Egyptian setting of G.4.287ff.

6. On the force of this basic metaphor in book 4 see H. Dahlmann, "Der Bienenstaat in Virgils *Georgika,"* *Abh. Mainz,* no. 10 (1954): 547-62.

7. Otis, *Virgil,* 190-208.

8. Ibid., 214.

9. Ibid., 413. That Virgil might be making a *deliberately* rapid shift from one character to another in *Georgics* 4.527ff. is also suggested by Norden, "Orpheus und Eurydice," 675, although Norden does not explore the reasons for such a shift.

10. Norden, "Orpheus und Eurydice," 652-54.

11. Virgil's emphasis on the "wonderful" (*admiranda,* etc.) in his account of the bees is well brought out by Dahlmann, "Bienenstaat," 555.

12. The role of the birds in this portion of the *Georgics* is noteworthy. A reference to birds occurs at the beginning of the whole episode in connection with the change from winter's barrenness to spring's richness (G.4.306-307). Then a bird simile is used at the beginning of the description of Orpheus' descent to Hades (473-474, the famous comparison of the dead to birds gathering in the leaves); and finally the nightingale simile (511ff.) concludes the account of the descent. With the last passage cf. Sophocles, *Antigone* 425ff.

13. Isak Dinesen, "A Consolatory Tale," in her *Winter's Tales* (1942; reprint, New York, 1961), 308, 311.

14. This contrast between Orpheus and Aristaeus is sensitively developed by Bovie, "Imagery," 355ff. Bovie also suggests (357) some connection between Aeneas and Orpheus but does not elaborate it.

15. The myth of Orpheus—his descent to Hades, his fatal yielding to impatience, uncertainty, passion, his ability to move the natural world by his

song, and the character of his death—makes him an obvious figure to symbolize this two-sided complexity of man's nature. In this role he has continually appealed to poets and has inspired some of the most sensitive of modern poetry on this theme. See Rilke's *Orpheus. Eurydike. Hermes* and esp. his *Sonnets to Orpheus,* discussed below, chap. 6.

16. See Norden, "Orpheus und Eurydice," 631–35; Bovie, "Imagery," 354.

17. On the significance of this passage, see Otis, *Virgil,* 178ff.

18. Coleman, for instance, in the passage quoted in n. 5, speaks of the *Georgics* as "otherwise a joyful and radiant work."

19. Otis, *Virgil,* 151.

20. From a very different critical perspective, Friedrich Klingner, *Virgils Georgica* (Zurich, 1963), 193–239, has strongly argued for the artistic unity of the Fourth *Georgic* and the integral connection of the Aristaeus-Orpheus section with the rest (see his closing chapter, "Das Aristaeus-Finale"). In discussing the relation between Aristaeus and Orpheus themselves (229ff.), he has eloquently called attention to the complementary function of the two narratives in "einer die Gegensätze umspannenden Einheit" (234); and he has put forth an interpretation of their connection that reinforces the approach offered in this chapter: in the Aristaeus narrative, Klingner suggests, we have the restorative aspect of life wherein "verlorenes Leben ist nicht verloren," whereas in the Orpheus story "ist Leben dem Tod unwiderruflich verfallen, Trauer um das Verlorene ewig unstillbar" (236).

Chapter 3. Ovid's Orpheus and Augustan Ideology

1. Franz Bömer, "Ovid und die Sprache Vergils," in Michael von Albrecht and Ernst Zinn, eds. *Ovid,* Wege der Forschung 92 (Darmstadt, 1968), 202. For Ovid's use and transformation of the Virgilian epic style, see also the remarks of Hans Diller, "Die dichterische Eignenart von Ovids Metamorphosen," in ibid., 337–39. The parallels between the Orpheus episodes of Ovid and Virgil are discussed in some detail by Giuseppe Pavano, "La discesa di Orfeo nell' Ade in Vergilio e in Ovidio," *Mondo Classico* 7 (1937): 345–58; and by Rosa Lamacchia, "Ovidio interprete di Virgilio," *Maia* 12 (1960): 310–30.

2. Hermann Fränkel, *Ovid, a Poet between Two Worlds,* Sather Classical Lectures 18 (Berkeley and Los Angeles, 1945), 219, n. 69.

3. Pavano, "Discesa," 358.

4. Ibid., 354–55.

5. Brooks Otis, *Ovid as an Epic Poet,* 2d ed. (Cambridge, 1970), 74 and 184 respectively. W. S. Anderson too stresses Ovid's playfulness and "courtly urbanity": *Ovid, Metamorphoses, Books 6–10* (Norman, Okla., 1972), 475.

6. Bömer, "Ovid," 202: "Durch dieses Spiel gelingt es Ovid, seine Selbständigkeit gegenüber Vergil zu wahren . . . Durch das Spiel . . . geht aber auch das hohe Ethos der vergilischen Sprache verloren."

7. Seneca, *Nat. Quaest.* 3.27.14, a propos of Ovid's description of the flood in *Met.* 1. See also Bömer, "Ovid," 202.

8. Eduard Norden, "Orpheus und Eurydice," *SB Berlin* (1934): 662–71.

9. Ibid., 666: "Es reizte ihn, im Gegensatz zur *maniera grande* des Vorgängers, im Gegensatz auch zu dem *magno ore sonare* . . . , artistisches Können zu zeigen, in dem er jenem überlegen war."

10. Ibid., 665.

11. See W. R. Johnson, "The Problems of the Counter-classical Sensibility and Its Critics," *California Studies in Classical Antiquity* 3 (1970): 123–51, esp. 137ff. See also Robert Coleman's review of the first edition of Otis, *Ovid* in *CR*, n.s. 17 (1967): 46–51, esp. 49–50; and Otis' Conclusion of *Ovid*, 2d ed. 306–74.

12. See Lamacchia, "Ovidio," 329.

13. Leo C. Curran, "Transformation and Anti-Augustanism in Ovid's Metamorphoses," *Arethusa* 5 (1972) 88. Views of Ovid along these lines have become more common in recent years. In addition to the works cited above, n. 11, see also G. K. Galinsky, "The Cipus Episode in Ovid's *Metamorphoses*," *TAPA* 98 (1967): 181–91; and my essay on the Pythagoras episode, "Myth and Philosophy in the *Metamorphoses*," *AJP* 90 (1969): 257–92.

14. On this arbitrary quality in the poem's transformations see my *Landsape in Ovid's Metamorphoses*, Hermes Einzelschriften 23 (Wiesbaden, 1969), chap. 5; also W.-H. Friedrich, "Der Kosmos Ovids," in Albrecht and Zinn, *Ovid*, 368–69, 382–83; W. S. Anderson, "Multiple Change in the *Metamorphoses*," *TAPA* 94 (1963): 23–24.

15. For this contrast between tales of licit and illicit love, see Otis, *Ovid*, chaps. 6–7, passim, e.g., pp. 185–93, 205ff.

16. Ibid., 185 and his chart on 168; Simone Viarre, "Pygmalion et Orphée chez Ovide (*Met.* X, 243–97)," *REL* 46 (1968): 235–47, esp. 237–38.

17. Phanocles, frag.1, lines 7–10, in J. U. Powell, ed., *Collectanea Alexandrina* (Oxford, 1925).

18. Norden, "Orpheus und Eurydice," 658: "Ein schlichtes Motiv, lebensnahe wie manche Grabepigramme, in denen die Antithese von Freud und Leid ergreifenden Ausdruck findet—irgendeine *syntychie* knickt die Blume, die sich eben entfaltet hat."

19. Norden, ibid., 668, relates this *ausus* ("dared") to an earlier source: cf. *paradoxōs etolmese* ("he dared unexpectedly") in Diodorus Siculus 4.25.4.

20. Sophocles, *O.C.* 1606ff.; cf. Norden, "Orpheus und Eurydice," 678–83.

21. See Pavano, "Discesa," 353–54, who considers the lines an infelicitous compromise between the simple and the recherché. Fränkel, *Ovid* too misses the effect when he finds in *Met.* 10.41–76 "the delicate idea [of love's conquest of death] . . . drowned in the din of elaboration."

22. See M. Haupt, O. Korn, R. Ehwald, and M. von Albrecht, eds., *P. Ovidius Naso Metamorphosen*, 5th ed. (Zurich, 1966) ad loc.

23. For the legend see P. Burmann, ed., *Publii Ovidii Nasonis Opera Omnia* (Amsterdam, 1727) ad loc.

24. See Pavano, "Discesa," 354, n. 2, who remarks on *G.*4.487 and *Met.* 10.5off., "Forse in Ovidio la scena è troppo intimamente borghese per giustificare la *lex* che viene dall' alto."

25. Norden, "Orpheus und Eurydice," 668, suggests that Ovid may be closer to the tradition in having Orpheus speak to persuade the dead: cf. Diodorus 4.25.4 and Apollodorus 1.14. For the literary effect of speech versus silence in the two episodes, see also Norden, "Orpheus und Eurydice," 669 with n. 1; Diller, "Dichterische Eignenart," 338.

26. I cannot agree completely with Fränkel, *Ovid*, 219, n. 69, that Ovid "relied less upon the effect on the reader of the speech than upon the force of the plot itself, with Love conquering ([line 26]) even inexorable Death."

27. Ibid.

28. Pavano, "Discesa," 351.

29. Fränkel, *Ovid*, 219, n. 69; W. C. Stephens, "Descent to the Underworld in Ovid's *Metamorphoses*," *CJ* 53 (1957/58): 179 also notes the "simple beauty" in Orpheus' request of l. 31, *Eurydices, oro, properata retexite fata.*

30. See Pavano, "Discesa," 354: "E qui un tratto nuovo ci sorprende e ci dà un senso di trepida attesa: la figura di Euridice aggraziata nella lentezza del suo incedere."

31. C. M. Bowra, "Orpheus and Eurydice," *CQ*, n.s. 2 (1952): 121, speaks also of "the frantic gestures of Orpheus in Ovid."

32. See Pavano, "Discesa," 356, who censures Ovid's handling of this point in *Met.* 10.73–75 – unjustly, in my opinion.

33. Otis, *Ovid*, 277, and see in general 265–77. For qualifications see Coleman, review, 49; and Curran, "Transformation."

34. On this aspect of Virgil's treatment, see chap. 2, sec. III; also Dorothea S. Wender, "Resurrection in the Fourth *Georgic*," *AJP* 90 (1969): 433–36.

35. In Phanocles (frag. 1, in Powell, *Collectanea*) the women are "devisers of evil" (*kakomechanoi* [7]), and the murder is "the savage deeds of women" (*erga gynaikōn agria* [23–24]), which are subsequently punished by the Thracian men.

36. Drawn largely from Moschus, *Epitaph. Bionis*, though there are naturally Theocritean and Virgilian echoes too. Virgil had reserved the pathos of this conceit for Eurydice: *G.*4.461–463.

37. Even here, however, Ovid injects a note of deliberate mock-epic exaggeration that warns us not to take him entirely seriously: the rivers increase with their own tears, which, as E. J. Bernbeck remarks, is "eine Vorstellung, die den Ernst ihrer Trauer bereits wieder in Frage stellt" (*Beobachtungen zur Darstellungsart in Ovids Metamorphosen*, Zetemata 43 [Munich 1967], 109).

38. See Haupt et al., *P. Ovidius Naso on Met.* 11.50ff.

39. See Otis, *Ovid*, 185; Bernbeck, *Beobachtungen*, 98.

40. Norden, "Orpheus und Eurydice," 671. He points out (670) that Ovid repeats his *flebile* three times, just as Virgil does with his *Eurydicen*. Phanocles, frag. 1, line 16, in Powell, *Collectanea*, keeps the motif of the sound more naturalistic and speaks only of the song of the lyre in the sea: "the sound of the clear lyre spread over the sea."

41. See Euripides, *Alc.* 357–359; Hermesianax frag. 2, lines 1–14, in Powell, *Collectanea*. See in general Bowra, "Orpheus and Eurydice," 113–26; also Friedrich Klingner, *Virgil. Bucolica, Georgica, Aeneis* (Zurich, 1967), 351–52.

42. See Viarre, "Pygmalion et Orphée," 241–42: "On dirait une réussite, vengeresse: *tutus, respicit;* ce n'est pas une vraie mort, puisque, comme s'il n'avait pas subi l'influence du Léthé, il reconnaît tout" (242).

43. See Otis, *Ovid*, 185: "[Ovid's] most masterful touch is the description of the reunion in Hades where he tells of how Orpheus deliberately indulged in any number of the glances that had once been so disastrous."

44. See Norden's fine remarks, "Orpheus und Eurydice," 670–71: "Das Tragische dieses Mythus, dessen katastrophenhaften Augenblick ein griechischer Künstler in Marmor, ein römischer Dichter in wehmutvollen Versen festhielt, liess ein anderer Dichter, den die Anmut der hellenischen Sagenwelt mehr anzog als ihr Ernst, in einen befreiend-heiteren Akkord ausklingen:

Eurydicenque suam iam tutus respicit Orpheus lautet die graziöse *koronis.''*

45. See above, n. 33. Curran, ''Transformation,'' 74, points out, correctly, ''The Ceyx-Halcyone story is only a brief glimpse of a better world which elsewhere in the poem Ovid shows cannot exist in this world of real men and women.''

46. See Viarre, ''Pygmalion et Orphée,'' passim, esp. 240–41; also D. F. Bauer, ''The Function of Pygmalion in the *Metamorphoses* of Ovid,'' *TAPA* 93 (1962): 13, who speaks of the connection of the two episodes in terms of ''the art of love . . . the love of art.''

47. Bauer, ''Function,'' 13. See Fränkel, *Ovid,* 93–96, who considers the Pygmalion story ''one of the finest apologues on the marvel of creative imagination'' (96); also Anderson, ''Multiple Change,'' 25–26.

48. See Otis, *Ovid,* 373–74, esp. 374: ''here we can perhaps speak of a symbolically true as opposed to a symbolically false mythology and conclude that the tension between myth and reality is not in this sense ultimate. The 'false' mythology was Ovid's inheritance from epic, from Homer, the Cyclics and Virgil: the 'true' mythology was, basically, Alexandrian and neoteric and in some degree originally Ovidian.''

49. Robert Coleman, ''Structure and Intention in the *Metamorphoses,''* *CQ,* n.s. 212 (1971): 477. See also Norden, ''Orpheus und Eurydice,'' 670–71.

50. This aspect of *amor* in Virgil applies primarily to erotic love. *Amor* in Virgil may also be a creative force: *Ecl.* 10.73; *G.*2.476, 3.117, 4.325; *Aen.* 4.347, 6.889. On this positive side of Virgilian *amor,* see R. R. Dyer, ''Ambition in the *Georgics:* Vergil's Rejection of Arcadia,'' in B. F. Harris, ed., *Auckland Classical Essays Presented to E. M. Blaiklock* (Auckland, N.Z., 1970), 143–64, esp. 153–59.

Chapter 4. Virgil and Ovid on Orpheus: A Second Look

1. It is gratifying to see that the line of interpretation put forth in my essay of 1966 (chap. 2) has continued in more recent studies—Jasper Griffin, ''The Fourth *Georgic,* Virgil and Rome,'' in his *Latin Poets and Roman Life,* (Chapel Hill, N.C., 1985), 163–82; C. G. Perkell, ''A Reading of Virgil's Fourth Georgic,'' *Phoenix* 32 (1978): 211–21; M. C. J. Putnam, *Virgil's Poem of the Earth: Studies in the Georgics* (Princeton, N.J., 1979); and Dorothea Wender, ''Resurrection in the Fourth *Georgic,''* *AJP* 90 (1969): 424–36—with some modifications and refinements that I welcome.

2. See Gary B. Miles, *Virgil's Georgics: A New Interpretation* (Berkeley and Los Angeles, 1980), 258ff.; Putnam, *Virgil's Poem,* 282ff.; Maurizio Bettini, *Antropologia e cultura romana* (Rome, 1976), 236–55 (to be discussed further below).

3. See Anne Pippin Burnett, *The Art of Bacchylides,* Martin Classical Lectures 29 (Cambridge, Mass., 1985), 30–36. For the dive in relation to initiatory motifs and adolescent rites of passage, see also C. Segal, ''The Myth of Bacchylides 17: Heroic Quest and Heroic Identity,'' *Eranos* 77 (1979): 23–37. See also J. Chomarat, ''L'Initiation d'Aristée,'' *REL* 52 (1974): 190ff., Bettini, *Antropologia,* 244ff. Further discussion below.

4. We may also note the contrast between the neoteric periphrasis, ''sweet thefts'' (*dulcia furta* [346]), and Proteus' blunter description of Eurydice as a *coniunx rapta* (456), which could also imply a ravished wife. *Rapta* may simply mean only that Eurydice is ''taken'' from Orpheus, but, given the circumstances

of her death, the harsher meaning is at least a possible implication.

5. For the myth of the watery quest in search of a hidden source of life, cf. the Argonauts' meeting with Triton in Pindar, *Pythian* 4.25ff. and my remarks in *Pindar's Mythmaking: The Fourth Pythian Ode* (Princeton, N.J., 1986), 90ff.

6. On this point see Griffin, "Fourth *Georgic*," 175.

7. William S. Anderson, "The Orpheus of Virgil and Ovid: *flebile nescio quid*," in John Warden, ed., *Orpheus: The Metamorphosis of a Myth* (Toronto, 1982), 32f. In a similar vein, Eva M. Stehle, "Virgil's *Georgics*: The Threat of Sloth," *TAPA* 104 (1974): 363-69, though she also sensitively balances the creative energy of Aristaeus and the barrenness of Orpheus' end and stresses Orpheus' failures, e.g., his inability to "use his poetry to metamorphose his love and subdue his *furor*" (367).

8. See Putnam, *Virgil's Poem*, 310ff.; Perkell, "Reading," 219-21.

9. Griffin, "Fourth *Georgic*," 175.

10. Anderson, "Orpheus," 35f.

11. See Stehle, "Virgil's *Georgics*," 368.

12. The moral judgment against Aristaeus would be even harsher with the reading of P, *ad meritum*, i.e., that the "fates' resistance" to Aristaeus' punishment is not in accordance with what he deserves. The attempt of Will Richter, *Vergil, Georgica* (Munich, 1957), ad loc., to connect the phrase *haudquaquam ob meritum* with *suscitat poenas* rather than with *miserabilis* and make it express criticism of Orpheus is unconvincing. Plato, *Symposium* 179D, which he cites, is irrelevant here. There can be no question of Orpheus' guilt at this stage of the narrative. Cf. also *magna luis commissa* in *G*.4.454.

13. See Gian Biagio Conte, *A Rhetoric of Imitation: Literary Memory in Virgil and Other Latin Poets*, ed. C. Segal (Ithaca, N.Y., 1986), 130-40, esp. 138ff.

14. Howard Jacobson, "Aristaeus, Orpheus, and the *Laudes Galli*," *AJP* 105 (1984): 271-300, passim, esp. 291. The problem of interrupting the narrative at so intense a moment, however, seems to me an obstacle to this theory. See also H. D. Jocelyn, "Servius and the 'second edition' of the *Georgics*," *Atti del Convegno mondiale scientifico di studi su Vergilio* (Rome, 1984), 1:431-48.

15. See Philip R. Hardie, *Virgil's Aeneid: Cosmos and Imperium* (Oxford, 1986), 83f., who suggests that Virgil may also be alluding to the allegorical interpretation of the story of Mars and Venus (Ares and Aphrodite) as a cosmogonic myth.

16. Adam Parry, "The Idea of Art in Virgil's *Georgics*," *Arethusa* 5 (1972): 51f.

17. Ibid., 52.

18. Putnam, *Virgil's Poem*, 315, 322.

19. A. J. Boyle, *The Chaonian Dove: Studies in the Eclogues, Georgics, and Aeneid of Virgil*, Mnemosyne Supplement 94 (Leiden, 1986) 81.

20. See R. R. Dyer, "Ambition in the *Georgics*: Virgil's Rejection of Arcadia," in B. F. Harris, ed., *Aukland Classical Essays Presented to E. M. Blaiklock* (Aukland, N.Z., 1970), 158; in a more positive vein, Miles, *Virgil's Georgics*, 294

21. Putnam, *Virgil's Poem*, 323.

22. Marcel Detienne, "Orphée au miel," *Quaderni Urbinati di Cultura Classica* 12 (1971): 7-23; the quotation is on p. 18 (trans. as "The Myth of the Honeyed Orpheus," in R. L. Gordon, ed., *Myth, Religion and Society* [Cambridge, 1981], 95-109).

23. Chomarat, "L'Initiation," 185-207, esp. 191ff.; J. S. Campbell, "Initiation

and the Role of Aristaeus in *Georgics Four*," *Ramus* 11 (1982): 105–15.

24. Bettini, *Antropologia*, 240.

25. See in general Marcel Detienne and Jean-Pierre Vernant, *Cunning Intelligence in Greek Culture and Society*, trans. J. Lloyd (Atlantic Highlands, N.J., 1978).

26. For recent discussion see Stehle, "Virgil's *Georgics*," 363f.

27. See Adolf Primmer, "Das Lied des Orpheus in Ovids Metamorphosen," *Sprachkunst. Beiträge zur Literaturwissenschaft* 10 (1979): 134.

28. Ibid., 134.

29. Ibid., 135.

30. Anderson, "Orpheus," 40, 41.

31. Primmer, "Das Lied," 129, 130.

32. In addition to *Met.* 10.31, cited above, Eurydice is named only one other time in book 10, when the underworld gods "summon Eurydice" for the upward ascent [48]).

33. Anderson, "Orpheus," 42.

34. E.g., G. K. Galinsky, *Ovid's Metamorphoses. An Introduction to the Basic Aspects* (Oxford, 1975), 245f.

35. Eleanor Winsor Leach, "Ekphrasis and the Theme of Artistic Failure in Ovid's *Metamorphoses*," *Ramus* 3 (1974): 125.

36. Anderson, "Orpheus," 48.

37. Donald Lateiner, "Mythic and Non-Mythic Artists in Ovid's *Metamorphoses*," *Ramus* 13 (1984): 18.

38. Leonard Barkan, *The Gods Made Flesh: Metamorphosis and the Pursuit of Paganism* (New Haven, Conn., 1986), 75, 78.

39. Ibid., 78.

40. See ibid., 75–78, 89.

41. See Anderson, "Orpheus," 45–48.

42. E.g., as in Catullus 64.

43. See Alison Goddard Elliott, "Ovid's *Metamorphoses*: A Bibliography, 1968–78," *Classical World* 73 (1979/80): 390f.

44. See above, chap. 3, sec. III.

45. The passages are Eurydice's speech to Orpheus at the moment of his fatal backward glance (*G.*4.494–498) and the continuing cry, "Eurydice," of the severed head (*G.*4.526f.; cf. *Met.* 10.60–63 and 11.52, *flebile nescio quid*).

46. See *Ecl.* 5.24–28 and 10.9–27, which draw in turn on Theocritus 1.70ff.

47. See chap. 1, sec. V.

Chapter 5. Dissonant Sympathy: Song, Orpheus, and the Golden Age in Seneca's Tragedies

1. For the question of authenticity of *H.O.*, see the bibliography in M. Coffey, "Seneca, Tragedies: Report for the Years 1922–1955," *Lustrum* 2 (1957): 140–43; G. K. Galinsky, *The Herakles Theme* (Oxford, 1972), 167, with n. 3 on p. 183; Ilona Opelt, "Senecas Konzeption des Tragischen," in Eckard Lefèvre, ed., *Senecas Tragödien* (Darmstadt, 1972) 125 n. 87. The question remains unresolved, but there seems to be growing support for authenticity and especially for the notion that the play may be an unrevised work of Seneca. The text of the tragedies is generally quoted from G. C. Giardina, *L. Annaei Senecae Tragoediae* (Bologna, 1966).

2. See G. Solimano, "Il mito di Orfeo-Ippolito in Seneca," *Sandalion* 3 (1980): 151–74, esp. 161, 165. Solimano's article has a focus very different from mine: she is concerned largely with Seneca's specific transmutations of Ovid and Virgil and with the supposed interchangeability of the Hippolytus of the *Phaedra* with Orpheus and Theocritus' Daphnis. I am not convinced by the latter part of her thesis, but the detailed observations of Seneca's use of Virgil and Ovid are useful.

3. For the two sides of Orpheus, see above, chap. 1, sec. I, ad fin., and sec. V. For a recent study of the Virgilian and Ovidian versions of the Orpheus legend, with a bibliography, see William S. Anderson, "The Orpheus of Virgil and Ovid: *flebile nescio quid,*" in John Warden, ed., *Orpheus: The Metamorphosis of a Myth* (Toronto, 1982), 25–50.

4. For the importance of this intellectual and moral "recognition" see Eckard Lefèvre, *"quid ratio possit?* Senecas Phaedra als stoisches Drama," in Lefèvre, *Senecas Tragödien,* 350ff.

5. T. S. Eliot, "Shakespeare and the Stoicism of Seneca" (1927), in his *Selected Essays,* 3d ed. (London, 1951), 132, 139f.

6. See Virgil, *Ecl.* 6.27–30; M. C. J. Putnam, *Virgil's Pastoral Art* (Princeton, N.J., 1970), 200–202, 255–57; C. Segal, *Poetry and Myth in Ancient Pastoral* (Princeton, N. J., 1981), 313–15, 317–21; M. Desport, *L'Incantation virgilienne* (Bordeaux, 1952), 154ff. See above, chap. 1, sec. I.

7. For the theme of man's harmony with nature in the *Metamorphoses,* see Brooks Otis, *Ovid as an Epic Poet,* 2d ed. (Cambridge, 1970), 233 and 256.

8. See Seneca, *Letters* 115.1ff. and *De Beneficiis* 1.3.10; in general P. DeLacy, "Stoic Views of Poetry," *AJP* 69 (1948), esp. 266f.

9. DeLacy, "Stoic Views," 241.

10. See M. Pohlenz, *Die Stoa* (Göttingen, 1948), 1:227f.

11. See Horace, *Ars Poetica* 391–396 with Kiessling-Heinze's commentary on 394; Pausanias 6.20.18 and 9.5.7. For Virgil too Amphion is a mythical forerunner of pastoral song: see *Ecl.* 2.23f.; also Horace, *Odes* 3.11.1f.

12. I have omitted a section on the *Troades* that appeared in the original publication.

13. On this symbolic underworld see Jo-Ann Shelton, *Seneca's Hercules Furens,* Hypomnemata 50 (Göttingen, 1978), chap. 4, esp. 55–57; D. Henry and B. Walker, "The Futility of Action: A Study of Seneca's Hercules Furens,"*CP* 60 (1965): 14f. and 21f.

14. On the danger of physical force see Shelton, *Hercules Furens,* 62ff., 69ff., 73.

15. See above, chap. 1, sec. V, and chap. 3, sec. II, V; also Solimano, "Il mito," 154f.

16. Shelton, *Hercules Furens,* 45.

17. With Orpheus' "loss" (*perdidit* [*H.F.* 589]) of Eurydice cf. Hercules' loss in 1331, *ubique notus perdidi exilio locum,* "known everywhere, I have lost a place by exile." The verb occurs only in these two places in the play.

18. On Hercules' *scelus* see Shelton, *Hercules Furens,* 67–69. For a rather more pessimistic reading of Seneca's Orpheus here, see Seth Lerer, *Boethius and Dialogue* (Princeton, 1985), 160–64, who stresses the legal machinery of the Senecan underworld and therefore the public significance of the Orpheus myth there (p. 162)—an emphasis more in keeping with Virgil's version (which Lerer

does not consider) than Seneca's Cf. Virgil, *Georgics* 4.485–93, and above, chap. 3, sec. I.

19. Note the ambiguity of *inferna* here: it can refer to *mens* as well as to *simulacra*. Hercules' "mind" still retains a quality of "underworld" violence.

20. On the contrast of spiritual and physical endurance in the Stoic tradition, see Galinsky *Herakles Theme*, 130f. and 174, citing *De Constantia sapientis* 2.2. On the antiheroic elements in *H.F.*, see also Henry and Walker, "Futility of Action," 15–19, who, however, seem to me to exaggerate the element of the ludicrous and mock-heroic in their interpretation.

21. Hercules' descent to the underworld: *H.O.* 1141ff., 1161ff., 1197ff., 1208ff., 1293ff., 1369ff., 1525ff., 1550ff.; his ascent to the stars: 1705ff., 1765ff., 1916ff., 1940ff., 1947ff., 1963ff., 1978, 1983ff.

22. There is perhaps an allusion to the shady beech tree of Virgilian pastoral, *Ecl.* 1.1–5.

23. Aside from the motif of the descent to Hades, there are perhaps other points of comparison with Orpheus in Hercules' giving laws to the Getae (*H.O.* 1964; cf. 1092) and his wish that Athos might topple on him (1382f.: cf. 1048–1051).

24. A. Traina, "Due note a Seneca Tragico," *Maia* 31 (1979): 273, pointing out the alliteration in 362f., calls Medea "il simbolo della femminilità selvaggia e passionale." He suggests (273–75) that Seneca uses an alliterative pattern of *m*-sounds to associate Medea with "evil" and "monstrosity" (*malum, monstrum*). But the alliteration also conveys the tension with Medea's other side, *Medea-mater*, "Medea-mother": see *Med.* 171, 288f., 933f., 947f., 950f. See also C. Segal, "*Nomen Sacrum:* Medea and Other Names in Senecan Tragedy," *Maia* 34 (1982): 241–46.

25. See O. Regenbogen, "Schmerz und Tod in den Tragödien Senecas," in Fritz Saxl, ed., *Vorträge der Bibliothek Warburg, 1927–28* (Leipzig, 1927–28), 7:197f. As frequently in Seneca, geographical hyperbole expresses the movement beyond the safe limits of action and feeling. In addition to the passages cited, see also *Med.* 211ff., 438ff., 720ff.

26. For Medea and the sea, cf. *Med.* 121–125 and 131f. In 452f., however, she speaks of her brother's blood as "poured forth over fields" (*quaeque fraternus cruor/perfudit arva*). For Phaedra's passion and the sea, cf. *Phd.* 88, 181–83, 241, 273, 661, etc.

27. N. Costa, *Seneca, Medea* (Oxford, 1973) ad loc., quotes T. S. Eliot's remark on this scene, "I can think of no other play which reserves such a shock for the last word." Note too the parallel between the serpents that draw Medea's chariot in 1023 and the serpents she calls up by her spells in 684f.: around her there crystallizes gradually a world of monsters and, in the last lines, a monstrous world.

28. With the "narrow waves" of Pelias' cauldron in *Med.* 667 cf. also Medea's complaint about the "too narrow number" of victims in 1011 (*nimium . . . numerus angustus*). The fact that the latter passage is followed by Medea's wish to probe her womb to tear out any further traces of her bond with Jason (1012f.) supports the association of the cauldron with the powers of female creation, and destruction, in 667.

29. For a somewhat different view of the themes of the exploration and conquest of nature, see Gilbert Lawall, "Seneca's *Medea:* The Elusive Triumph of

Civilization," in G. Bowersock, W. Burkert, and M. Putnam, eds., *Arktouros. Hellenic Studies Presented to B. M. W. Knox* (Berlin, 1979), 421–23.

30. See F. Ferrucci, *The Poetics of Disguise: The Autobiography of the Work in Homer, Dante and Shakespeare,* trans. A. Dunnigan (Ithaca, N.Y., 1980), 30–33, 34–36, 63f. 78–84.

31. The repossession of the scepter, symbol of male political power and male phallic power, parallels Medea's refusal of sexual domination by the male. Cf. the scepter's association with the rights of the old patriarchal king, Laius, in *Oed.* 241, 513, 634f., 642f., and cf. 670. Note too Phaedra's entreaty to Theseus "by the scepter of your power" (*Phd.* 868) when she is about to accuse Hippolytus. At this point in the play, Medea takes on not only the power of the *monstra* that she calls forth but also some of the power of the androgyne.

32. See Lawall, "Seneca's *Medea,*" 426: "The Chorus's dream of unlimited progress and harmony between man and nature (364–79)—one of the most profound visions in pagan Latin literature—vanishes before the raw, untamed fury of Medea and the sea."

33. For this theme of the "distorted heavens," see W. H. Owen, "Commonplace and Dramatic Symbol in Seneca's Tragedies," *TAPA* 99 (1968): 310.

34. E.g., Tacitus, *Annals* 13.57–58.

35. Cf. Horace, *Epodes* 2.61–64: *has inter epulas ut iuvat pastas oves / videre properantis domum, / videre fessos vomerem inversum boves / collo trahentis languido,* "What joy it is amid such meals to see the well-fed sheep hastening homeward, to see the weary oxen 'with tired neck' dragging the upturned plow". Cf. also Virgil, *Ecl.* 2.66f.

36. Cf. Thyestes' *me dulcis saturet quies,* "let sweet tranquillity satisfy me" (393). Contrast Atreus' gloating *satur est,* "he is full" (913), and his expressions of malcontent satiety in 889–891: *bene est, abunde est, iam sat est etiam mihi, / sed cur satis sit? pergam et implebo patrem / funere suorum,* "It is well, it is abundant, it is enough even for me. But why should it be enough? I shall go on and fill the father with the death of his own sons."

37. For the sinister past of Phaedra and of Crete, see Lefèvre, "*Quid ratio possit?*" 365; G. Runchina, "Sulla *Phaedra* di Seneca," *RCCM* 8: 32 with n. 68; A. J. Boyle, "In Nature's Bonds: A Study of Seneca's *Phaedra,*" in H. Temporini and W. Haase, eds. *ANRW* 2.32.2 (Berlin, 1985), 1293 with n. 29. (I thank the author for allowing me to see this in advance of publication). For the motif of sea and land in Euripides' *Hippolytus,* see C. Segal, "The Tragedy of the *Hippolytus:* The Waters of Ocean and the Untouched Meadow," *HSCP* 70 (1965): 117–69.

38. With *Phd.* 1093, cf. Virgil, *G.*4.522, *discerptum latos iuvenem sparsere,* "they scattered the youth, torn apart, over the broad fields," Hippolytus' death, however, does not have the sacral associations of the Virgilian Orpheus' (cf. *G.*4.521, *inter sacra deum,* "among the holy rites of the gods"). I cannot agree with Solimano, "Il mito," 170–74, that Seneca has separated out the positive elements of the bucolic ideal and attached them to Orpheus, while the negative side of Orpheus remains associated with Hippolytus. L. Herrmann, *Le Théâtre de Sénèque* (Paris, 1924), 441, takes a misguidedly positive view of Hippolytus, "un héros sans tache, dont la misogynie même semble approuvée par l'auteur"; see Lefèvre, "*Quid ratio possit?*" 349–53; and Boyle, "In Nature's Bonds," pt. 2, passim.

39. Analyzing Hippolytus' opening song, Boyle "In Nature's Bonds," 1292,

concludes: "Diana, the goddess to whom Hippolytus prays, seems a divinity not of life but of death."

40. On the hunter's ambiguous relation to civilization, see Marcel Detienne, *Dionysus Slain*, trans. M. and L. Muellner (Baltimore, 1979), 20–52; J.-P. Vernant and P. Vidal-Naquet, *Mythe et Tragédie*, (Paris, 1972), 135–84; C. Segal, *Tragedy and Civilization: An Interpretation of Sophocles* (Cambridge, Mass., 1981), 31 and 300–303.

41. Cf. the image of the Amazon as an uncivilized and monstrous creature in *Tro.* 243 and *H.F.* 242ff. Hercules' victory over them, like Theseus', has a suggestion of sexual violation (*H.F.* 542ff.). On the Amazon's marginal relation to civilization, see Segal, *Tragedy and Civilization*, 30; Page duBois, *Centaurs and Amazons* (Ann Arbor, Mich., 1982), 34ff., 53ff., 67ff.

42. E. Burck, *Vom Römischen Manierismus* (Darmstadt, 1971], 13ff., 36–38, 45ff. See also Shelton, "Hercules Furens," 30 with n. 15; A. D. Leeman, "Seneca's *Phaedra* as a Stoic Tragedy," in J. M. Bremer, S. L. Radt, and C. J. Ruijgh, eds., *Miscellanea Tragica in Honorem J. C. Kamerbeek* (Amsterdam, 1976), 212.

43. See Henry and Walker, "Futility of Action," 223–39.

44. Images of fulness: *Thy.* 899f., 912, 974; heaviness: 909f., 1000, 1006, 1020; spatial interiority and enclosure: 902, 1007, 1021; interior of body: 999–1001, 1041–1051.

45. See, e.g., R. F. Newbold, "Boundaries and Bodies in Late Antiquity," *Arethusa* 12 (1979): 93–114, with bibliography; Leo Curran, "Transformation and Anti-Augustanism in Ovid's *Metamorphoses*," *Arethusa* 5 (1972): 71–91, esp. 78–82; C. Segal, "Boundary Violations and the Landscape of the Self in Senecan Tragedy," *Antike und Abendland* 29 (1983): 172–87.

46. The prophecy of Seneca's Apollo is characterized by the related imagery of sinuosity and concealment (*Oed.* 214f.): *ambage flexa Delphico mos est deo / arcana tegere*, "In twisting curves the Delphic god is wont to hide his secret things". Cf. also 92f.

Chapter 6. Orpheus in Rilke: The Hidden Roots of Being

1. Translations of the *Sonnets* are from M. D. Herter Norton, ed. and trans., *Sonnets to Orpheus by Rainer Maria Rilke* (New York, 1942), sometimes slightly modified. For this kind of rhythmic effect, cf. also the late poem, *Wann wird, wann wird, wann wird es genügen / das Klagen und Sagen? Waren nicht Meister im Fügen / menschlicher Worte gekommen? Warum die neuen Versuche?* "When will it, when will it, when will it suffice, the lament and the saying? Had masters in the joinings of human words not come? Why the new attempts?" Rainer Maria Rilke, *Sämtliche Werke* (Wiesbaden, 1956) 2:134f. On this aspect of Rilke's "Orphism," see Walter A. Strauss, *Descent and Return: The Orphic Theme in Modern Literature* (Cambridge, Mass., 1971), 153.

2. Rilke to von Hulewicz, 13 Nov. 1925, cited in Norton, *Sonnets*, 131–32. For a powerful discussion see Martin Heidegger, *Holzwege*, 6th ed. (Frankfurt am Main), 285f.

3. Translation from J. B. Leishman and Stephen Spender, eds. and trans., *Rainer Maria Rilke, Duino Elegies* (New York, 1939). For discussion see Strauss, *Descent and Return* 165f.

4. See Heidegger, *Holzwege*, 302f., 312–16.

5. Paul de Man, *Allegories of Reading* (New Haven, Conn., 1979), 46f.

6. R. M. Rilke, *Die Aufzeichnungen des Malte Laurids Brigge*, in *Ausgewählte Werke* (Leipzig, 1942), 2:171–72; Letter no. 21 (23 Jan. 1912) in Jane Bannard Greene and M. D. Herter Norton, eds. and trans., *Letters of Rainer Maria Rilke, 1910–26* (1948; reprint, New York, 1969), 46–48.

7. On this passage see G. H. Hartman, *The Unmediated Vision* (1954; reprint, New York, 1966), 81.

8. See Elizabeth Sewell, *The Orphic Voice: Poetry and Natural History* (New Haven, Conn., 1960), 331.

9. Rilke to von Moos, 20 Apr. 1923, cited in Norton, *Sonnets*, 7.

10. See, for example, Rilke's important letter to Witold von Hulewicz, 13 Nov. 1925, cited in Norton, *Sonnets*, 131–32: "*Affirmation of life and death appears as one in the 'Elegies.'* To admit the one without the other is, as is here learned and celebrated, a limitation that in the end excludes all infinity. Death is the *side of life* that is turned away from us: we must try to achieve the fullest consciousness of our existence, which is at home in *the two unseparated realms, inexhaustibly nourished by both.* . . . The true figure of life extends through *both* domains, the blood of the mightiest circulation drives through *both: there is neither a here nor a beyond, but the great unity,* in which those creatures that surpass us, the 'angels,' are at home" (Rilke's emphasis). See H. J. Tschiedel, "Orpheus und Eurydike: ein Beitrag zum Thema: Rilke und die Antike," *Antike und Abendland* 19 (1973): 72ff.; Sewell, *Orphic Voice*, 394ff.

11. Rilke to von Hulewicz, 13 Nov. 1925, cited in Norton, *Sonnets*, 133. Rilke's emphasis.

12. See Beda Allemann, *Zeit und Figure beim Spätem Rilke* (Pfullingen, 1961), 114.

13. On this poem in relation in Rilke's notion of "figure," see Allemann, *Zeit und Figur,* 61; de Man, *Allegories,* 44.

14. For this negative view of the process of figuration, see de Man, *Allegories,* 52; see also Sewell, *Orphic Voice,* 395f., 403.

15. My emphasis.

16. For the "cosmic tree" see, e.g., Mircea Eliade, *Patterns in Comparative Religion,* trans. R. Sheed (1958; reprint, New York, 1963), 265f.

17. For Orpheus as a founder of temples, see Otto Kern, ed., *Orphicorum Fragmenta,* Testimonia, nos. 108–109; for Orpheus as a culture hero in general see ibid., nos. 82–112, 123. For Orpheus and Amphion see Pausanias 6.20.18 = Kern, *Fragmenta,* Testimonia, no. 54.

18. Translation from J. B. Leishman, *Rainer Maria Rilke, New Poems* (London, 1964), 145.

19. See C. Segal, "Eurydice: Rilke's Transformation of a Classical Myth," *Bucknell Review* 21 (1974): 143f.; also Hartman, *Unmediated Vision,* 81ff.

20. Good examples are Virgil, *Ecl.* 6.27–30; Ovid, *Met.* 10.86–105.

21. See Tschiedel, "Orpheus und Eurydike," 72f.; Peter Dronke, "The Return of Eurydice," *C&M* 23 (1962): 205f.

22. On this passage see Allemann, *Zeit und Figur,* 71.

23. Note also the importance of "the hesitant hour" (*die zögernde Stunde*), 1.10.13.

24. For the motif of flowing water, streams, fountains, cf. *Sonnets* 1.10, 2.7, 2.12, and 2.15. See also Hartman, *Unmediated Vision,* 93f. with n. 40, p. 191.

Chapter 7. Orpheus from Antiquity to Today: Retrospect and Prospect

1. The complex of Orpheus' three attributes of song, magic, and a descent to Hades to restore the dead to life is present in part or whole, e.g., in Euripides, *Alc.* 962–971; Virgil, *Aen.* 6.119; Horace, *Odes* 1.24.

2. Aeschylus, frags. 23–25, in Stefan Radt, ed., *Tragicorum Graecorum Fragmenta* (Göttingen, 1985) = frag. 83, in H. J. Mette, ed., *Die Fragmente der Tragödien Aischylos* (Berlin, 1959) = Pseudo-Eratosthenes, *Catasterismi*, no. 24, in A. Olivieri, ed., *Mythographi Graeci*, vol. 3, pt. 1 (Leipzig, 1897); see M. L. West, *The Orphic Poems* (Oxford, 1983), 12f. with n. 33.

3. Hermesianax, in J. U. Powell, ed., *Collectanea Alexandrina* (Oxford, 1925), 98.

4. Cf. ἔτλη, "endured," l. 7; ὑπέμεινε, "withstood," l. 10.

5. Augustus Nauck, ed., *Tragicorum Graecorum Fragmenta*, 2d ed. (Leipzig, 1889), frag. 563.

6. Conon, *Narrationes* 45. For a good survey see Raymond J. Clark, *Catabasis: Virgil and the Wisdom Tradition* (Amsterdam, 1979), 120–24.

7. E.g., Euripides (?), *Rhesus* 943–947; Alcidamas, *Odysseus* 24; Ps.-Demosthenes, *Against Aristogeiton* 11; Diodorus Siculus 1.23.2, 1.96.4, 5.64.4; Strabo 7, frag. 18; Pausanias 2.30.2 and 3.14.5; Plutarch, *De Pythiae Oraculis* 18, 402E; Athenagoras, *Pro Christianis* 18.3–6.

8. Clark, *Catabasis*, 15ff.; on Orpheus' catabasis see ibid., 99.

9. Illustrated in West, *Orphic Poems*, p. 4; and see ibid., 24f. The group is in the Getty Museum in Malibu, Calif.

10. For this view of the relief, see David Sansone, "Orpheus and Eurydice in the Fifth Century," *C&M* 36 (1985): 53–64; Fritz Graf, "Orpheus: A Poet among Men," in Jan Bremmer, ed., *Interpretations of Greek Mythology* (London, 1987), 80–106.

11. See most recently Emmet Robbins, "Famous Orpheus," in John Warden, ed., *Orpheus: The Metamorphosis of a Myth* (Toronto, 1982), 3–23; Graf "Orpheus"; also West, *Orphic Poems*, 4–6. On the passage between upper and lower worlds, see Robert Böhme, *Orpheus: Der Sänger und seine Zeit* (Bern, 1970), 192ff.

12. For the legend of Orpheus' oracular head in both literary and visual sources, see W. K. C. Guthrie, *Orpheus and Greek Religion* (1952; reprint, New York, 1966), 35–39. The Terpander vase is in a private collection in Basel. It is reproduced and discussed in Margot Schmidt, "Ein neue Zeugnis zum Mythos vom Orpheushaupt," *Antike Kunst* 15 (1972): 128–37. See also Emily Vermeule, *Aspects of Death in Early Greek Art and Poetry* (Berkeley and Los Angeles, 1979), p. 197 with fig. 21; Graf, "Orpheus," in Bremmer, *Interpretations of Greek Mythology*, 93f.

13. Text in Brian Stone, ed. and trans., *Medieval English Verse* (Harmondsworth, England, 1964), 213–29. For discussion see John B. Friedman, *Orpheus in the Middle Ages* (Cambridge, Mass., 1970), 207; Patricia Vicari, "Sparagmos: Orpheus among the Christians," in Warden, *Orpheus*, 73.

14. Vicari, "Sparagmos," 227.

15. For helpful brief discussions of the film versions, along with the versions of Williams and Anouilh, see Lee, "Orpheus and Eurydice: Some Modern Versions," *CJ* 56 (1960/61): 307–13.

16. See, for example, Margaret Alexiou, *The Ritual Lament in Greek Tradition*

(Cambridge, 1974); Loring Danforth, *The Death Rituals of Rural Greece* (Princeton, 1982).

17. See Gilbert Highet, *The Classical Tradition* (1949; reprint, Oxford, 1957), 586; Charles Singleton, *Dante Alighieri, The Divine Comedy, Purgatorio*, 2, *Commentary* (Princeton, 1980), ad loc.

18. See Timothy J. McGee, "*Orfeo* and *Eurydice*, the First Two Operas," in Warden, *Orpheus*, 163–81, and, most recently, Peter Conrad, *A Song of Love and Death: The Meaning of Opera* (New York, 1987), 19–29.

19. See Friedman, *Orpheus*, 173–75.

20. See Eleanor Irwin, "The Songs of Orpheus and the New Song of Christ," in Warden, *Orpheus*, 57.

21. See Friedman, *Orpheus*, 40ff.

22. See Pedro León, "Orpheus and the Devil in Calderón's *El Divino Orfeo*," in Warden, *Orpheus*, 184–206. The lyre in the shape of the cross occurs as early as the third century: see the third-century fresco from the catacomb of St. Calixtus in Rome in Friedman, *Orpheus*, p. 47, fig. 4.

23. Clement, *Protrepticus* 1.8; Eusebius, *Praise of Constantine*, c. 14. See Friedman, *Orpheus*, 54ff.; Irwin, "Songs," 54–57.

24. See Friedman, *Orpheus*, 100–102.

25. On Boethius' use of the myth, see Friedman, *Orpheus*, 92ff. For further discussion of Boethius' Orpheus, with additional bibliography, see Seth Lerer, *Boethius and Dialogue* (Princeton, 1985), 154–65 and 124, nn. 1, 3. It is significant that Seneca, in his more favorable view of Orpheus (and also under the influence of Ovid), allows Orpheus "true love" (*verus amor* [H.F. 582]), whereas Boethius, perhaps deliberately correcting the Senecan myth, stresses love's insistence on being a law unto itself (*maior lex amor est sibi*, "love is a greater law to itself" [3, metr. 12, 48]). See Lerer, *Boethius*, 161; see also above, chap. 5, sec. III, with n. 18.

26. See Friedman, *Orpheus*, 101ff.

27. For the identification of Eurydice with Eve in the thirteenth-century *Ovide Moralisé*, see Vicari, "*Sparagmos*," 70. Cf. the discussion of Calderón above.

28. See Friedman, *Orpheus*, 104ff.; and Vicari, "*Sparagmos*," 69 on William of Conches.

29. For these aspects of the Renaissance Orpheus, see Giuseppe Scavizzi, "The Myth of Orpheus in Italian Renaissance Art," in Warden, *Orpheus*, 90ff.

30. Dante is here using the ancient tradition of Orpheus the theologian, drawing on St. Augustine's *City of God* 18.14 and 37, who classes Orpheus with Musaeus and Linus as the "theological poets," (*theologi poetae*). See Charles Singleton, *Dante Alighieri, The Divine Comedy, Inferno*, 2, *Commentary* (Princeton, 1980), ad loc. For further implications of the passage, see Robert Hollander, "A Note on Dante's Missing Musaeus (*Inferno* IV.140–141)," *Quaderni d'italianistica* 5 (1984): 217–21.

31. See Friedman, *Orpheus*, 167ff.

32. See ibid., 76; also West, *Orphic Poems*, 30–32.

33. See Scavizzi, "Myth," 136f.

34. Angelo Poliziano, *Fabula di Orfeo*, ll. 306ff.

35. Giovanni Boccaccio, *Genealogia Deorum Gentilium*, 2.2.5. See Vicari, "*Sparagmos*," 212; Friedman, *Orpheus*, 141.

36. See Elizabeth Sewell, *The Orphic Voice: Poetry and Natural History* (New Haven, Conn., 1960), 76.

37. Ibid., 72.

38. William Shakespeare, *Two Gentlemen of Verona* 3.1., ad fin. See Sewell, *Orphic Voice*, 59.

39. Quoted in Sewell, *Orphic Voice*, 58.

40. I am indebted here to Vicari's discussion of Bacon, "*Sparagmos*," 225f.

41. Quoted in Sewell, *Orphic Voice*, 72f.; see her comments, 73ff.

42. See Scavizzi, "Myth," 148f.; Douglas Bush, *Mythology and the Renaissance Tradition in English Poetry*, rev. ed. (New York, 1963), 134; also 265, 296–98; Bush, *Pagan Myth and the Christian Tradition* (Philadelphia, 1968), 24f. A notable exception in the visual arts is Poussin's suggestive "Death of Eurydice" in the Louvre. On the other hand, Rubens' "Orpheus and Eurydice" comes close to reducing the myth to bathos.

43. Herbert Marcuse, *Eros and Civilization*, 2d ed. (Boston, 1966), 164. See also Walter A. Strauss, *Descent and Return: The Orphic Theme in Modern Literature* (Cambridge, Mass., 1971), 11f.

44. See Marcuse, *Eros*, 166, 167–71.

45. Henry Malcolm, *The Generation of Narcissus* (Boston, 1987), 45.

46. See above, chap. 1, sec. I, ad fin., apropos of the chorus in Euripides, *Bacchae*, 560ff.

47. In Louis Martz, ed., *H.D.: Collected Poems, 1912–1944* (New York, 1983).

48. For the Hellenistic *Testament of Orpheus*, see Friedman, *Orpheus* 20–28; West, *Orphic Poems*, 34ff.

49. Mircea Eliade, *Cosmos and History: The Myth of the Eternal Return*, trans. W. Trask (Princeton, 1954), 34ff., 77ff.

50. Margaret Atwood, *Selected Poems II: Poems Selected and New 1976–1986* (Boston, 1987), 106–115.

51. See Strauss, *Descent and Return* 218–72, esp. 270, on the modern tendency to stress "the plunge into darkness, inwardness, death." See also his remarks on Pierre-Jean Jouve, 239f. See also Eva Kushner, *Le Mythe d'Orphée dans la littérature française contemporaine* (Paris, 1961), 264–346.

52. See the brief remarks on this poem in Strauss, *Descent and Return*, 235f.

53. Sewell, *Orphic Voice*, 335.

54. Martin Buber, *Daniel*, trans. Maurice Friedman (New York, 1964), 55ff. The passage is well discussed by Strauss, *Descent and Return*, 271f.

55. Buber, *Daniel*, 56.

56. Maurice Blanchot, *The Gaze of Orpheus and Other Literary Essays*, trans. Lydia Davis (Barrytown, N.Y., 1981), 99–104. For discussion see Strauss, *Descent and Return*, 251–57.

57. Blanchot, *Gaze*, 99.

58. Ibid., 100.

59. Dorothy Z. Baker, *Mythic Masks in Self-Reflexive Poetry* (Chapel Hill, N.C., 1986), 18f., e.g., devotes three paragraphs to Blanchot's essay, and these consist primarily of extended quotations from it.

60. Blanchot, *Gaze*, 99, my emphasis.

61. Robert Hass, *Twentieth Century Pleasures: Prose on Poetry* (New York, 1984), 261.

62. This is the implication of Blanchot's dark essay, and it is a correct perception and one of the strengths of Blanchot's reading.

Select Bibliography

Allemann, Beda. 1961. *Zeit und Figur beim Spätem Rilke.* Pfullingen.

Anderson, William S. 1982. "The Orpheus of Virgil and Ovid: *flebile nescio quid.*" In Warden, *Orpheus,* 25–50.

———. 1972. *Ovid, Metamorphoses, Books 6–10.* Norman, Okla.

Barkan, Leonard. 1986. *The Gods Made Flesh: Metamorphosis and the Pursuit of Paganism.* New Haven, Conn.

Bauer, D. F. 1962. "The Function of Pygmalion in the *Metamorphoses* of Ovid." *TAPA* 93:1–21.

Bettini, Maurizio. 1976. *Antropologia e cultura romana.* Rome.

Blanchot, Maurice. 1981. *The Gaze of Orpheus and Other Literary Essays.* Trans. Lydia Davis. Barrytown, N.Y.

Bloom, Harold. 1973. *The Anxiety of Influence. A Theory of Poetry.* Oxford.

Bowra, C. M. 1952. "Orpheus and Eurydice," *CQ,* n.s. 2:113–24.

Boyle, A. J. 1985. "In Nature's Bonds: A Study of Seneca's *Phaedra.*" In W. Haase and H. Temporini, eds., *ANRW* 2.32.2: 1284–1347. Berlin.

———. 1986. *The Chaonian Dove: Studies in the Eclogues, Georgics, and Aeneid of Virgil. Mnemosyne* Supplement 94. Leiden.

Brower, R. A. 1971. *Hero and Saint: Shakespeare and the Graeco-Roman Heroic Tradition.* Oxford.

Burck, E. 1971. *Vom Römischen Manierismus.* Darmstadt.

Bush, Douglas. 1963. *Mythology and the Renaissance Tradition in English Poetry.* rev. ed. New York.

———. 1968. *Pagan Myth and the Christian Tradition.* Philadelphia.

Campbell, J. S. 1982. "Initiation and the Role of Aristaeus in *Georgics* Four." *Ramus* 11:105–15.

Chomarat, J. 1974. "L'Initiation d'Aristée." *REL* 52:185–207.

Clark, Raymond J. 1979. *Catabasis: Virgil and the Wisdom Tradition.* Amsterdam.

Coffey, M. 1957. "Seneca, Tragedies: Report for the Years 1922–1955." *Lustrum* 2:113–86.

Coleman, Robert. 1971. "Structure and Intention in the *Metamorphoses*." *CQ*, n.s. 21:461–77.

Curran, Leo. 1972. "Transformation and Anti-Augustanism in Ovid's *Metamorphoses*." *Arethusa* 5:71–91.

Dahlmann, H. 1954. "Der Bienenstaat in Vergils *Georgika*." *Abh. Mainz*, no. 10:547–62.

de Man, Paul. 1979. *Allegories of Reading*. New Haven, Conn.

Desport, M. 1952. *L'Incantation virgilienne*. Bordeaux.

Detienne, Marcel. 1972. *Les Jardins d'Adonis*. Paris.

——. 1979. *Dionysus Slain*. Trans. M. and L. Muellner. Baltimore.

Dodds, E. R. 1957. *The Greeks and the Irrational*, Berkeley and Los Angeles.

Dronke, Peter. 1962. "The Return of Eurydice." *C&M* 23:198–215.

duBois, Page. 1982. *Centaurs and Amazons*. Ann Arbor, Mich.

Dyer, R. R. 1970. "Ambition in the *Georgics*: Virgil's Rejection of Arcadia." In B. F. Harris, ed., *Auckland Classical Essays Presented to E. M. Blaiklock*, 143–64. Auckland, N.Z.

Eliot, T. S. 1951. "Seneca in Elizabethan Translation." *Selected Essays*. 3d ed. London.

Elliott, Alison Goddard. 1979/80. "Ovid's *Metamorphoses*: A Bibliography, 1968–78." *Classical World* 73:385–412.

Ferrucci, F. 1980. *The Poetics of Disguise: The Autobiography of the Work in Homer, Dante and Shakespeare*. Trans. A. Dunnigan. Ithaca, N.Y.

Fränkel, Hermann. 1945. *Ovid. A Poet between Two Worlds*. Sather Classical Lectures 18. Berkeley and Los Angeles.

Friedman, John B. 1970. *Orpheus in the Middle Ages*. Cambridge, Mass.

Galinsky, G. K. 1972. *The Herakles Theme*. Oxford.

——. 1975. *Ovid's Metamorphoses. An Introduction to the Basic Aspects*. Oxford.

Giardina, G. C. 1966. *L. Annaei Senecae Tragoediae*. Bologna.

Graf, Fritz. 1987. "Orpheus: A Poet among Men." In Jan Bremmer, ed., *Interpretations of Greek Mythology*, 80–106. London.

Griffin, Jasper. 1985. "The Fourth *Georgic*, Virgil and Rome." In his *Latin Poets and Roman Life*, 163–82. Chapel Hill, N.C.

Guthrie, W. K. C. 1952; reprint, 1966). *Orpheus and Greek Religion*. New York.

Hardie, Philip R. 1986. *Virgil's Aeneid: Cosmos and Imperium*. Oxford.

Hartman, Geoffrey H. 1954; reprint, 1966. *The Unmediated Vision*. New York.

Haupt, M., O. Korn, R. Ehwald, and M. von Albrecht, eds. 1966. *P. Ovidius Naso Metamorphosen*. 5th ed. Zurich.

Heidegger, Martin. 1980. *Holzwege*. 6th ed. Frankfurt am Main.

Henry, D., and B. Walker. 1965. "The Futility of Action: A Study of Seneca's Hercules Furens." *CP* 60:11–22.

——. 1966. "Phantasmagoria and Idyll: An Element of Seneca's "*Phaedra*." *G&R*, n.s. 13:223–39.

Herrmann, L. 1924. *Le Théâtre de Sénèque*. Paris.

Irwin, Eleanor. 1982. "The Songs of Orpheus and the New Song of Christ." In Warden, *Orpheus*, 51–62.

Jacobson, Howard. 1984. "Aristaeus, Orpheus, and the *Laudes Galli.*" *AJP* 105:271–300.

Kern, Otto. 1922 ed., *Orphicorum Fragmenta.* Berlin.

Klingner, Friedrich. 1967. *Virgil. Bucolica, Georgica, Aeneis.* Zurich.

Kushner, Eva. 1961. *Le Mythe d'Orphée dans la littérature française contemporaine.* Paris.

Lateiner, Donald. 1984. "Mythic and Non-Mythic Artists in Ovid's *Metamorphoses.*" *Ramus* 13:1–30.

Lawall, Gilbert. 1979. "Seneca's *Medea:* The Elusive Triumph of Civilization." In G. Bowersock, W. Burkert, and M. Putnam, eds., *Arktouros. Hellenic Studies Presented to B. M. W. Knox,* 419–26. Berlin.

Leach, Eleanor Winsor. 1974. "Ekphrasis and the Theme of Artistic Failure in Ovid's *Metamorphoses.*" *Ramus* 3:102–42.

Lee, M. Owen. 1960/61. "Orpheus and Eurydice: Some Modern Versions." *CJ* 56:307–13.

——. 1965. "Orpheus and Eurydice: Myth, Legend, Folklore." *C&M* 26: 402–12.

Leeman, A. D. 1976. "Seneca's *Phaedra* as a Stoic Tragedy." In J. M. Bremer, S. L. Radt, and C. J. Ruijgh, eds., *Miscellanea Tragica in Honorem J. C. Kamerbeek,* 199–212. Amsterdam.

Lefèvre, Eckard, ed. 1972. *Senecas Tragödien.* Wege der Forschung 310. Darmstadt.

——. 1972. "*Quid ratio possit?* Senecas Phaedra als stoisches Drama." In Lefèvre, *Senecas Tragödien,* 343–75. Originally published in *WS* N.F. 3 (1969): 131–60.

Leishman, J. B., ed. and trans. 1964. *Rainer Maria Rilke, New Poems.* London.

Leishman, J. B., and Stephen Spender, eds. and trans. 1939. *Rainer Maria Rilke, Duino Elegies.* New York.

León, Pedro. 1982. "Orpheus and the Devil in Calderón's *El Divino Orfeo.*" In Warden, *Orpheus,* 183–216.

Linforth, I. M. 1941. *The Arts of Orpheus.* Berkeley and Los Angeles.

Malcolm, Henry. 1971. *The Generation of Narcissus.* Boston.

Marcuse, Herbert. 1966. *Eros and Civilization.* 2d ed. Boston.

Miles, Gary B. 1980. *Virgil's Georgics: A New Interpretation.* Berkeley and Los Angeles.

Newbold, R. F. 1979. "Boundaries and Bodies in Late Antiquity." *Arethusa* 12:93–114.

Norden, Eduard. 1934. "Orpheus und Eurydice," *SB Berlin* 626–83.

Norton, M. D. Herter, ed. and trans. 1942. *Sonnets to Orpheus by Rainer Maria Rilke.* New York.

Otis, Brooks. 1970. *Ovid as an Epic Poet.* 2d ed. Cambridge.

——. 1963. *Virgil, A Study in Civilized Poetry.* Oxford.

Owen, W. H. 1968. "Commonplace and Dramatic Symbol in Seneca's Tragedies." *TAPA* 99:291–313.

Parry, Adam. 1972. "The Idea of Art in Virgil's *Georgics.*" *Arethusa* 5:35–52.

Perkell, C. G. 1978. "A Reading of Virgil's Fourth *Georgic.*" *Phoenix* 32:211–21.

Primmer, Adolf. 1979. "Das Lied des Orpheus in Ovids Metamorphosen." *Sprachkunst. Beiträge zur Literaturwissenschaft* 10:123–37.

Putnam, M. C. J. 1970. *Virgil's Pastoral Art.* Princeton, N.J.

———. 1979. *Virgil's Poem of the Earth: Studies in the Georgics.* Princeton, N.J.

Regenbogen, O. 1927/28. "Schmerz und Tod in den Tragödien Senecas." In Fritz Saxl, ed., *Vorträge der Bibliothek Warburg, 1927–28,* 7:167–218. Leipzig.

Robbins, Emmet. 1982. "Famous Orpheus." In Warden, *Orpheus,* 3–23.

Ross, David O. 1987. *Virgil's Elements: Physics and Poetry in the Georgics.* Princeton, N.J.

Runchina, G. 1966. "Sulla *Phaedra* di Seneca." *RCCM* 8:12–37.

Sansone, David. 1985. "Orpheus and Eurydice in the Fifth Century." *C&M* 36:53–64.

Scavizzi, Giuseppe. 1982. "The Myth of Orpheus in Italian Renaissance Art." In Warden, *Orpheus,* 111–62.

Segal, C. 1965. "The Tragedy of the *Hippolytus:* The Waters of Ocean and the Untouched Meadow." *HSCP* 70:117–69.

———. 1969. *Landscape in Ovid's Metamorphoses.* Hermes Einzelschriften 23. Wiesbaden.

———. 1972. "Ovid's Orpheus and Augustan Ideology." *TAPA* 103:473–94.

———. 1974. "Eurydice: Rilke's Transformation of a Classical Myth." *Bucknell Review* 21:137–44.

———. 1977. "Euripides' *Bacchae:* Conflict and Mediation." *Ramus* 6:103–20.

———. 1978. "The Magic of Orpheus and the Ambiguities of Language." *Ramus* 7:106–42.

———. 1981. *Poetry and Myth in Ancient Pastoral.* Princeton, N.J.

———. 1981. *Tragedy and Civilization: An Interpretation of Sophocles.* Cambridge, Mass.

———. 1982. "*Nomen Sacrum:* Medea and Other Names in Senecan Tragedy." *Maia* 34:241–46.

———. 1983. "Boundary Violations and the Landscape of the Self in Senecan Tragedy." *Antike und Abendland* 29:172–87.

Sewell, Elizabeth. 1960. *The Orphic Voice: Poetry and Natural History.* New Haven, Conn.

Solimano, G. 1980. "Il mito di Orfeo-Ippolito in Seneca." *Sandalion* 3:151–74.

Stehle, Eva M. 1974. "Virgil's *Georgics:* The Threat of Sloth." *TAPA* 104:347–69.

Strauss, Walter A. 1971. *Descent and Return: The Orphic Theme in Modern Literature.* Cambridge, Mass.

Tschiedel, H. J. 1973. "Orpheus und Eurydike: ein Beitrag zum Thema: Rilke und die Antike." *Antike und Abendland* 19:61–82.

Vernant, J.-P., and P. Vidal-Naquet. 1972. *Mythe et tragédie.* Paris.

Viarre, Simone. 1964. *L'Image et la pensée dans les "Métamorphoses" d'Ovide.* Paris.

———. 1968. "Pygmalion et Orphée chez Ovide (*Met.* X, 243–97)," *REL* 46:235–47.

Vicari, Patricia. 1982. *"Sparagmos:* Orpheus among the Christians." In Warden, *Orpheus,* 63–82.

———. 1982. "The Triumph of Art, the Triumph of Death: Orpheus in Spenser and Milton." In Warden, *Orpheus,* 207–30.

von Albrecht, Michael, and Ernst Zinn, eds. 1968. *Ovid. Wege der Forschung* 92. Darmstadt.

Warden, John, ed. 1982. *Orpheus: The Metamorphosis of a Myth.* Toronto.

Wender, Dorothea. 1969. "Resurrection in the Fourth *Georgic.*" *AJP* 90:424–36.

West, M. L. 1983. *The Orphic Poems.* Oxford.

Index

Orpheus

Designed by Ann Walston.

Composed by A. W. Bennett, Inc.
in Palatino.

Printed by BookCrafters